Trekking and Climbing
in the Himalaya

Dedicated to
Faye Kerr, Stafford Morse, Nick Reeves and
Richard Schmidt
who never made it home from Annapurna III.

Trekking and Climbing in the Himalaya

by Jonathan Chester

CLOUDCAP
SEATTLE

AUTHOR'S NOTE: There is no standardisation of English spellings for places and names in the Himalayan region. Throughout this book I have tried to use the most commonly accepted western spellings, with occasional alternatives given where the word first occurs. Historical, cultural and national political considerations have led to some features having several names. There are also differences in accepted heights of many mountains.

Every attempt has been made to make this book as up to date as possible at the time of going to press. However, readers planning a trip should obtain the most recent information from trekking experts and recently returned travellers. Maps are included only for planning purposes and should not be used to walk by or as a substitute for a guide or local knowledge.

Any changes to the information contained in this book would be appreciated and should be addressed:
C/- Simon & Schuster Australia,
P.O. Box 263, Gladesville NSW 2111 Australia

TREKKING AND CLIMBING IN THE HIMALAYA
First published in North America in 1989 by
CLOUDCAP
Box 27344
Seattle — Washington 98125
Published simultaneously in Australasia in 1989 by
Simon & Schuster Australia

Chester, Jonathan
Trekking and Climbing in the Himalaya

Bibliography.
Includes index.
ISBN 0-938567-17-9

Designed by Maree Cunnington
Maps by Alistair Barnard
Typeset in Australia by Excel Imaging Pty Ltd
Produced by Mandarin Offset
Printed and bound in Hong Kong

FRONT AND BACK COVERS
The Himalaya has many attractions for trekkers and climbers — the highest mountains, the largest glaciers (outside the polar regions) and some of the toughest, most friendly mountain people in the world.
PAGE 1
Since the construction of bridges such as this over the Trisuli River in Nepal, many remote areas and villages in the Himalaya are now open to safe travel.
PAGES 2–3
The rugged glaciers and towering peaks of the Karakoram offer some of the most challenging climbing and trekking in the Himalaya.
PAGES 10–11
Seen from the south face of Annapurna III, following a heavy storm, Machupuchare and the Annapurna Sanctuary are veiled in white. Climbers face dangerous avalanche conditions, when heavy falls of very dry snow occur in a matter of hours.

CONTENTS

FOREWORD

One of my greatest passions began when I saw my first Himalayan peaks towering to an unaccustomed height above the thunder clouds that billowed up from the valley of the Ganges in Garhwal. Coming to grips with the vast extent of the world's greatest mountain range is something that I am still grappling with, more than a decade later. Had there been a single volume such as this, that encompassed the Himalaya in its entirety, I would certainly have had a more rapid overview of this most fascinating place in the world.

Jonathan Chester has taken a refreshingly broad, holistic perspective which encompasses the geographical, historical, political, cultural and religious factors of the whole region. It is the complex mosaic created by these factors which makes the Himalaya so very interesting and so hard to fully comprehend. Rare is the person, however, who having been exposed to the complexity and raw grandeur of the Himalaya, is not profoundly moved in some positive and fundamental way and who does not come away with a lingering addiction to be back there. This book is as much for these people as for those who have never been but only dreamed of going. The 'old Himalayan Hands' whose essays are included are clearly well addicted and their contributions are windows to the magic and diversity of the Himalaya.

The days when trekkers and climbers travelled through the Himalaya without regard to what impact they may have had on the surroundings they so admired, are now hopefully on the wane. Those lucky enough to journey there now must take the responsibility of fully exploring ways in which to minimise their impact. If the Himalayan experience is to remain as worthwhile, we must be strong in doing our bit to help protect it. Part of this is realising that hot showers, not being self-sufficient in fuel and staying in local lodges, is indeed leading to deforestation in popularly trekked areas, and that the indigenous people have still to come to terms with the concept of non-biodegradable rubbish. Tin cans, plastic wrappers and film containers do not break down and blend into the undergrowth like bamboo containers nor are there council rubbish tips with twice weekly garbage pickups. The answer is to be as self-sufficient in fuel as possible and to reduce the demand for heavily packaged goods. Despite these problems, I believe that the Himalaya can withstand the modern influx of visitors — but only if they care enough.

Jonathan's book with its stunning photographs is testament enough that the Himalaya is worth caring for. I hope that the thousands that this book will help get to the Himalaya, will accept the challenge of not damaging the culture and environment which they travel through.

Tim Macartney-Snape

6

INTRODUCTION

Jonathan Chester

In ten years of climbing, trekking and photographing around the world, my visits to the Himalaya have been among the most formative experiences of my life. The awesome sight of towering snowcapped peaks, the joy of reeling around a campfire with Sherpa companions and the anguish of burying mountaineering companions killed in an avalanche will remain with me forever. My camera has been a constant companion on these journeys. The images and introductions to the fascinating countries detailed in *The Himalayan Experience* will, hopefully, enable others to appreciate these exotic places from afar and serve as a stimulus for those wishing to go themselves.

To encompass the full scope of who goes to the Himalaya and why, where to go and what to do when you get there, I have included a number of first-hand accounts of trekking, climbing and rafting adventures from a select group of contributors. All these individuals have a longstanding involvement with the Himalaya and have visited one or more areas many times. Several are among the most experienced adventure travel company operators in the world: Warwick Deacock; Christine Gee; Bob Ashford and Garry Weare. Others are very experienced trekkers, mountaineers and/or guides: Doug Scott, Lincoln Hall, Greg Child, Mick Chapman and Sorrel Wilby. Their accounts illustrate the diversity of the region.

The book is divided into four parts. The first part looks at the history of the Himalayan region and describes the main adventure activities available — trekking, climbing, rafting and skiing. Part Two details the basics you need to know to prepare for your own Himalayan adventure, while in Part Three, the Himalayan region is examined. In the final part, the five main countries that span the Himalaya are considered. For each country a summary of useful information is provided, as well as brief descriptions of some of its places and features and, of course, the activities available.

Visiting any of the countries that span the Himalaya is an experience you are bound to treasure, providing you go with an open and enquiring mind. Western preconceptions may sometimes cause you to find fault with living conditions, sanitation, corruption, bureaucracy and at times even the weather. In spite of such shortcomings the mountains and the people of the region can be the source of re-evaluation, enlightenment, challenge and great pleasure when approached in a humble and understanding way. I hope you too can find such rewards from this book and from your own journeys to the mightiest mountains on earth.

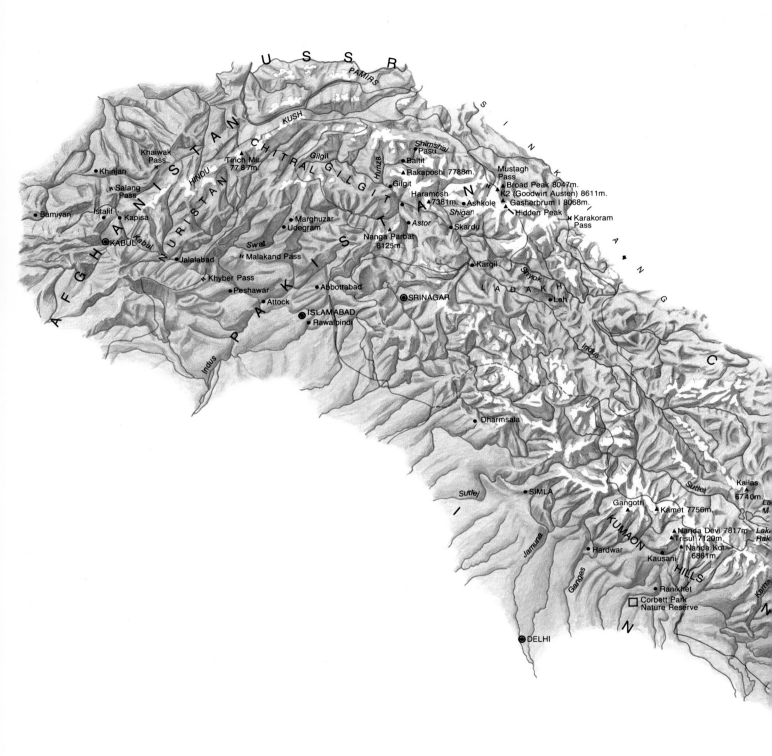

U S S R

PAMIRS

KUSH

HINDU

CHITRAL

GILGIT

GILGIT

NURISTAN

AFGHANISTAN

PAKISTAN

SINKIANG

LADAKH

KUMAON
HILLS

• Khaiwak
Pass

• Khinjan

✕ Salang
Pass

• Bamiyan

Istalif
•

Kapisa
•

◎KABUL

Kabul

▲ Tirich Mir
77 8 7m.

Gilgit

Hunza

Shimshal
• Pasu

• Baltit

▲ Rakaposhi 7788m.

Gilgit
•

Haramosh
▲
7381m.

Shigan

Mustagh
Pass

• Broad Peak 8047m.
✕ K2 (Goodwin Austen) 8611m.
▲ Gasherbrum I 8068m.
✕ Hidden Peak

Karakoram
Pass

• Marghuzar

• Udegram

Swat

Astor

Nanga Parbat
8125m.

• Ashkole

• Skardu

Shyok

▼

• Leh

Indus

• Jalalabad

✕ Malakand Pass

• Kargil

✕ Khyber Pass

• Peshawar

• Abbottabad

Attock
•

◎ SRINAGAR

Indus

◉ ISLAMABAD
◉ Rawalpindi

Indus

• Dharmsala

Sutlej

• SIMLA

Sutlej

Kailas
6740m.

La
M

Gangotri
▲

▲ Kamet 7756m.

Lak
Rak

Jamuna

▲ Nanda Devi 7817m
▲ Trisul 7120m.

• Hardwar

Kausani
•

▲ Nanda Kot
6861m.

Ganges

• Ranikhet

Karnia

□ Corbett Park
Nature Reserve

◎ DELHI

I N D I A

N

C

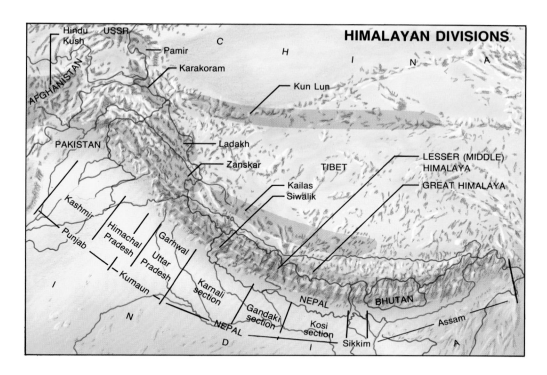

HIMALAYAN DIVISIONS

Hindu Kush
USSR
Pamir
Karakoram
Kun Lun
C H I N A
AFGHANISTAN
PAKISTAN
Ladakh
Zanskar
Kailas
Siwalik
TIBET
LESSER (MIDDLE) HIMALAYA
GREAT HIMALAYA
Kashmir
Punjab
Himachal Pradesh
Garhwal
Uttar Pradesh
Kumaun
Karnali section
Gandaki section
Kosi section
NEPAL
BHUTAN
Sikkim
Assam
I N D I A
NEPAL

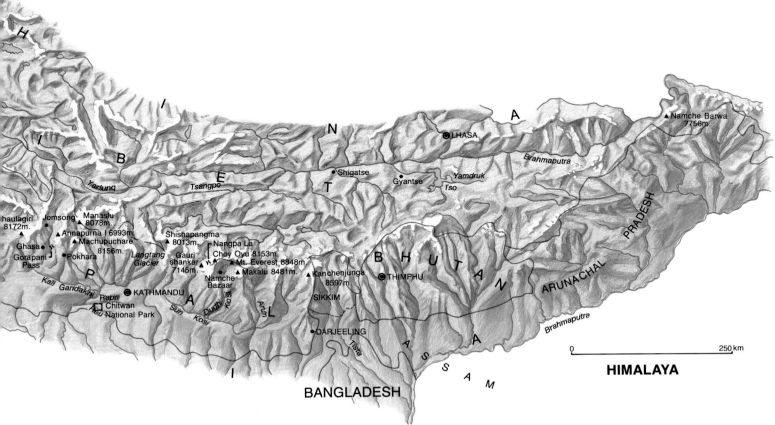

H
I
I
B
E
T
N
A
Namche Barwa 7756m.
LHASA
Yarlung
Tsangpo
Brahmaputra
Shigatse
Gyantse
Yamdruk Tso
haulagiri 8172m.
Jomsong
Manaslu 8078m.
Annapurna I 6993m
Machupuchare 8156m.
Ghasa
Gorapani Pass
Pokhara
Shishapangma 8013m.
Nangpa La
Choy Oyu 8153m.
Langtang Glacier
Gauri shankar 7145m.
Namche Bazaar
Mt. Everest 8848m.
Makalu 8481m.
Kanchenjunga 8597m.
B H U T A N
THIMPHU
PRADESH
ARUNACHAL
Kali Gandakhi
P
Raptii
Chitwan National Park
KATHMANDU
Sun Kosi
Dudh
Arun
Kosi
SIKKIM
DARJEELING
Tista
A
S
S
A
M
Brahmaputra
BANGLADESH

| 0 | 250 km |

HIMALAYA

PART ONE

Avenues for Adventure

E ach year the Himalaya is the focus for many thousands of Western trekkers, travellers and climbers. Some seek spiritual awakening, many aim for new physical and mental heights, others look for a rewarding holiday or cultural experience. This section outlines the main avenues for adventure in the Himalaya, their history, what's involved and how you might take part in trekking, climbing or rafting.

TREKKING

'Beware, trekking is addictive,' warns Warwick Deacock, the founder of Ausventure, in his notes to prospective visitors to the Himalaya. With some of his clients taking their fourth or fifth trekking holiday in as many years, he is well-placed to judge. To many, trekking is the most rewarding experience imaginable. The world's most spectacular mountain scenery, combined with first-hand contact with age-old customs and culture in remote villages are just some of the reasons why they find themselves becoming Himalayan addicts.

What's in a Name?

The word '*trek*' was borrowed in the 19th century from an Afrikaans word meaning 'a long migration by ox cart'. The name originally came from the Middle Dutch, *trekken*, meaning to travel. Dictionaries

> When we walk into the Himalaya and away from the web of roads and electricity, we are reaching for a unique experience, not a . . . predictable vacation . . . Most of us move at a pace entirely different from the Himalayan farmers or merchants and it takes some time to accomplish the shifting of gears. Gradually the terrain imposes a tempo . . . The days of foot pace allow you to absorb awesome mountain scenery. The immediacy of such an experience imparts a perspective on home life that cannot be gained from long weekends at the state park.
>
> **HUGH SWIFT**
> *The Trekker's Guide to the Himalaya and Karakoram, 1982*

today variously define trekking as 'to travel arduously' and 'to walk over long distances especially for recreation'.

To trek in the Himalaya is to take an extended walk along recognised paths with the bonus of dramatic scenery and traditional village life on the roof of the world. Put in these simple terms it sounds within everyone's grasp but no trekking trip should be undertaken lightly.

Trekking at its best is usually found in areas where there are no other practical forms of ground transportation and this is mostly because the terrain is too rugged and remote. For most of the time therefore, trekking in such regions involves going up and down hills, crossing passes,

(Above) Backpacking all your gear is unnecessary and in many instances impossible when trekking or going on expedition in remote areas of the Himalaya — particularly up the Baltoro Glacier. Porters, however, have to be sheltered, fed, insured and often provided with equipment.

(Right) The deep valleys and snowcapped peaks of Nepal's Khumbu region have been a magnet for trekkers and climbers for twenty-five years. The 10,000 visitors a year who now enter the Sagamatha National Park place severe demands on the environment, particularly the dwindling forests.

coping with high altitude and extremely variable weather.

Today, the term trekking is synonymous with all levels of recreational walking. It applies equally to individuals and to groups but more recently the name has become associated with packaged treks.

A Far Cry from Wilderness

Trekking is rarely a wilderness experience. Many popular trekking trails, such as the route to Jomsong (Jomosom) up the Kali Gandakhi Valley in Nepal, are also ancient trading routes with a busy traffic of local people and porters, mules or yaks bearing supplies in addition to visiting trekkers. Most routes also connect villages and pass through intensely culti-

vated valleys and hillsides. It is not until you reach higher altitudes and remote valleys that signs of settlement recede, but even then there may be grazing.

Trekking in the Himalaya usually does not involve climbing. Even so, trekking may involve going to altitudes higher than you would go if climbing serious mountains on many other continents. At times, it may also involve being above the snowline. Trekking does not normally require technical climbing equipment such as ropes, ice-axes or crampons.

Before you go trekking you need to understand what it's really like. No matter what glowing descriptions, beautiful photos or persuasive sales pitch you are exposed to, in reality trekking is sometimes frustrating, physically hard work and at times potentially dangerous.

Experiencing traditional culture in remote villages of the Himalaya can be most rewarding. Accessible only by foot, the Warvan Valley of Kashmir is little changed by the outside world.

Being a third world region in Asia, the Himalaya has to be appreciated differently. As a traveller there you will find that Western values and notions of organisation, time, justice and health care often do not apply.

Be Forewarned!

Though they rarely show photos of bad weather or exhausted trekkers, adventure travel companies are well aware of the limitations of adventure travel and their brochures always carry a 'conditions of contract' or some form of 'fine print' disclaimer which they assume you have read and comprehended before signing up.

The rugged nature of the Himalaya means that sometimes when trekking, even though you are physically and mentally exhausted, you will still have to push on to reach the haven of a campsite or village. A sudden snowstorm may mean that you are trapped in one place for days and even then you might have to abandon the rest of the trek just to have a chance of getting out on time. If a flight to or from a remote airstrip is part of your itinerary, you should allow for delays and bad weather which regularly occur.

In most remote areas of the Himalaya there are no doctors, pharmacies or hospitals. Accidents or illnesses that elsewhere might be quickly attended to by a doctor can be debilitating in the mountains. A simple cut that gets infected, for example, and is not treated with antibiotics may become septic and make it impossible for you to walk. In most places you would then face the discomfort of having to be carried, perhaps for days. Alternatively, you may risk staying where you are and try sending word to be evacuated by a helicopter, which may or may not come.

Forewarned is forearmed. If you do have realistic expectations and are well prepared you are less likely to be disappointed. You will also be more able to accept a change of plans or bad weather as part of the adventure.

Why go Trekking?

I grow into these mountains like a moss. I am bewitched. The blinding snow peaks and the clarion air, the sound of earth and heaven in silence, the requiem birds, the mythic beasts, the flags, great horns and old carved stones . . . the silver ice in the black river . . . Also, I love the common miracles — the murmur of my friends at evening, the clay fires of smudgy juniper, the coarse dull food, the hardship and simplicity . . . Though we talk little here, I am never lonely; I am returned into myself.

PETER MATTHIESSEN
The Snow Leopard, 1979

Spiritual quest, adventure, and the fascination with the turbulent history and culture of the mountain people are reasons why travellers are drawn to the Himalaya. These are far more diverse than the machismo of conquest, as the vast body of mountaineering literature would have one believe. The books of Bonington and Messner, for example, chronicle the cutting edge of contemporary Himalayan climbing. Insights from modern travel writers such as Peter Matthiessen, Geoffrey Moorhouse and Eric Newby, however, attest to the rewards of the journey rather than the destination.

A Western fascination with Buddhism, particularly the Tibetan way, has also led many people to the Himalaya. The *gompas* of Ladakh, the home of the exiled Dali Lama in India, Lumbini (Lhumbini), Buddha's birthplace in Nepal, and what is left of Tibetan culture in Lhasa — all such aspects are drawcards for Western travellers. The Hindu religion, while less appealing to many westerners, is no less colourful or mysterious. Great festivals such as Duserra (Dussehra) in the Kulu region and Kumbha Mela at Allahabad are spectacular sights.

Unlike most climbers who walk just to get to the base of their mountain, most trekkers walk for the journey itself. Some like to extend themselves by trekking as high as 6000 m (19,680 ft) and to such prized destinations as Kala Pattar (Kala Pathar) in the shadow of Everest or Concordia near the Baltoro Glacier.

For those experienced in outdoor pursuits, the Himalaya is but another place to practise their favourite form of recreation in spectacular physical and cultural settings. These individuals are more likely to 'do their own thing' but can waste time finding their way around in an unfamiliar culture and country. So they, too, often join an organised group.

With the rise in disposable income and leisure-time over recent years, and the increased publicity for trekking, a new breed of trekker has emerged. People who would never think of walking around the block now go trekking because it's fashionable. Others are looking for a holiday with a difference — Bali one year, the Himalaya the next.

Some people are drawn to the Himalaya for one particular reason or ambition, like climbing to Everest Base Camp, but come away having enjoyed the trip for totally different reasons. No matter what the motivation, few regret the experience.

Who can Go?

There are no real age barriers to trekking: all that really matters is your level of fitness, experience, motivation and ability to pay. Some children can manage easier treks and occasionally you will come across a fit seventy-year-old on a trail. Most trekkers, however, are aged between twenty and fifty-five.

With the support of professional leaders and staff, lack of experience in outdoor living need not be a problem. If you have never camped before, trying to sleep on a thin foam mat in a sleeping bag night after night could be a shock to your system. Better to go on some weekend camp-

> Trekking is not an activity exclusive to youth — age is no barrier. In fact, people of more mature years often do better than the younger generations. It is essential to approach the Himalaya with a sound and tolerant attitude.
>
> **GARRY WEARE**
> *Trekking in the Indian Himalaya*, 1986

ing trips at home to see if you can cope with the day-to-day aspects of trekking before you take on the potential stresses of Asia, altitude and remoteness.

Trekking for the first time is probably a far more demanding form of holiday than you may ever have embarked on before. If you strike bad weather you may find yourself wishing you had never come. You need to be emotionally able to cope with strange situations and be able to tough out the hard times if you are really to enjoy trekking. If you are looking for a relaxing, 'do nothing' holiday, you may be wise to stick to the Maldives.

As far as the cost is concerned, there is a trek for most budgets. Some cost little more than a few dollars a day. Others can run to several hundred dollars a day for one person. You should shop around to find an affordable trek that fits your experience and interest.

Trekking gives you the opportunity to meet individuals from all over the world. The most likely nationalities you will meet on the trail are American, British, Japanese, French, German and Australian, for most recreational travellers are westerners.

Just fifteen years ago trekking was normally restricted to individuals who were experienced mountain travellers. Today, thanks to cheap airfares, advertising and word of mouth, people from all walks of life are enticed to spend their annual holidays in the Himalaya. The advantages and disadvantages of all the different forms of trekking are dealt with in detail in the section on trekking styles.

History of Trekking

Sometimes the baron rode, more often he was carried in a sedan chair by twelve bearers; he walked only to stretch his legs. His principal tent had poles twenty-five feet high and the roof alone weighed quarter of a ton ... Sixty porters and seven mules carried his luggage while thirty-seven servants ministered to his every need. There was a secretary, an interpreter, a torch-bearer, a butler, three cooks, a water-carrier, a tailor and a man for lighting his pipe. There were plant gatherers, huntsmen and butterfly catchers and, out in front, a herald and two messengers with the baron's initials emblazoned on their breast-plates.

JOHN KEAY
Where Men and Mountains Meet, 1977

The days of being able to travel like Baron Carl von Hugel are long past. Even in 1836 such an entourage was quite the exception for a westerner. His style was more in keeping with the wealthy mogul emperors of the day.

For centuries walking has been the main means of travelling in the Himalaya. Altitudes, rugged terrain and high costs have even limited the use of horses, mules and yaks.

Soldiers, traders and explorers, pushing further into the far-flung valleys were similarly constrained to foot travel by the often tortuous landscape. Walking was the main means of movement and human load carriers, bearers, porters or coolies, as they are variously known, were (and in many regions still are) the only economical means of transporting supplies.

The birth of trekking as we know it today occurred in India at the time of the Raj. Then the English set out from the summer hill-stations like Darjeeling, Simla (Shimla) and Mussoorie on excursions for hunting and to admire the mountain scenery from the ridgetops. In 1833 W. W. Graham became the first recorded mountain tourist when he travelled from England to the Himalaya 'more for the sport and adventure than for the advancement of scientific knowledge'.

Commercial trekking companies

The first professional trekking company, Mountain Travel, was begun in 1964, by Colonel Jimmy Roberts, a leading British mountaineer and Himalayan expert of the 1950s and 1960s. He had joined the then British Indian Army in 1936 with the ambition of spending a lifetime mountaineering and exploring in the Himalaya. He was able to combine his army career with this personal goal by spending his two or three months of leave not 'poodle-faking' (as lying around on houseboats was known) but on hunting or climbing trips. For a number of years he also served in a Gurkha regiment at Dharamsala within striking distance of the Pir Panjal Range in what is now known as the state of Himachal Pradesh. World War II circumvented Roberts's desire to be a part of early attempts on Everest but he did participate in a number of other notable pioneering expeditions.

In 1958 Jimmy Roberts was appointed as the first military attaché of the British Embassy in Kathmandu, Nepal. After retiring from the army in the early 1960s he became completely embroiled in Himalayan mountain exploration. In 1963 he took charge of transportation for the highly successful American Everest Expedition which made the first traverse of the mountain. Following on from this experience, Roberts decided to set up his own business providing the same sort of logistic support to adventurous tourists as he had given to expeditions. He was well-equipped with detailed knowledge of the country, the people and their language but, most importantly, he also had the ear of senior government officials.

Jimmy Roberts acknowledges that he borrowed the scheme of providing tents, camping gear and organising porters for an agreed daily sum from local agents, who provided a similar but limited service on his earlier hunting forays in Kashmir. In those days the agents' methods were old-fashioned and the gear heavy and antiquated. This style was developed for the British Raj. They used china cups and plates, sheets and blankets, army tents and camp cots. As well as using modern lightweight tents, sleeping bags, cane chairs and plywood table tops, he offered the services of trained and experienced guides who could take charge of trekking parties.

In response to his first advertisement in *Holiday Magazine* he had five replies. One, from a woman, read 'Mount Everest! . . . here we go again, get out the Entero . . . Vioform . . . rush me details'. (Colonel Jimmy Roberts, lecture transcript, 'How it all began'.)

The very first commercial Everest trek in the spring of 1965 was comprised of three American matrons whom Roberts later commended: 'A more sporting trio of enthusiastic and appreciative ladies I have never since handled.'

In 1967 Leo Le Bon, the manager of Thomas Cook in San Francisco, brought several American parties to trek with Jimmy Roberts's Mountain Travel company. As a result, late in 1968 he founded Mountain Travel USA with mountaineers Barry Bishop and Allan Steck.

In 1967 Australia's Warwick Deacock also became associated with Jimmy Roberts. The pair had been mountaineering companions in the army and through his company, Ausventure, Deacock began sending and often accompanying groups that were looked after while in Nepal by Mountain Travel.

Trekking and Mountain Travel grew quickly and within five years other agents had begun to set up in competition. However, Roberts was able to establish very high standards from the outset because of his well-trained and loyal sherpa staff whom he held in very high regard.

Teahouse trekking

Paralleling this rapid growth of organised trekking was the development of what is called 'teahouse trekking'. When rock singers sang about Kathmandu in the 1960s, they sang for a generation of travellers who thought Asia was paradise. Hippies from all over the world came to Nepal in search of the exotic, the mystic and the simple life. Their hangout was Freak Street, a lane right in the heart of Kathmandu. There they would find cheap hotels, the heavy beat and blare of acid rock, the aroma of incense and freely available hashish.

Often these hippies, decked in homespun fabrics, were passing through, en route to and from Europe; but sometimes they stayed for years, haunting dingy pie shops, temples, and street stalls. Some hippies took to the hills. Because they had few possessions and were trying to travel as cheaply as possible, they stayed at the inns and teahouses traditionally used by the local travellers. As some trails became popular at idyllic places such as Tatopani, the hippies would linger and the locals gradually learned to cater to their whims. Menus began appearing on the walls listing misspelt Western dishes. In a few years teahouses and very basic hotels catering solely to westerners began to develop in many of the villages along selected routes in the Annapurna and Everest regions of Nepal. It then became possible to trek very cheaply by eating and sleeping in these establishments along the way. Teahouses and lodges are still being built and now there is competition amongst them to provide greater levels of comfort and sophistication. Today for example, Namche Bazaar and Thyangboche (Tangboche) in the Everest region of Nepal have electric light. Hot showers are not uncommon and it is also possible to buy beer and soft drinks at most teahouses on the main trails. The social aspects of teahouses can be rewarding, such as exchanging experiences and learning about conditions of the trail.

As lodges have been built to meet the demands of 'teahouse trekkers', sizeable villages have grown up on the more popular routes in the Annapurna foothills north-west of Pokhara.

The new breed

The types of people who go trekking have become more diverse over the years. In the 1950s and 1960s there were, apart from hippies who did not venture very far from the main routes, the pioneering climbers who were pushing into seldom visited regions chasing unclimbed peaks.

With the advent of commercial trekking the early participants were hardened bushwalkers and backpackers. They set out on month-long treks aware of the potential hazards involved. They were fully prepared, emotionally and practically, for the rigours of mountain travel. They knew and accepted that the Himalaya was a dangerous place, that conditions could be unpleasant and sometimes unbearable, that they could get sick, break a limb or, at worst, die. They had a commitment to trekking which meant an understanding of the demands as well as the rewards of their adventure.

Today the face of trekking has changed considerably. In addition to freelance guides, there are now hundreds of companies catering to trekkers throughout the Himalaya. In Nepal alone there are over seventy government accredited agencies and many more smaller organisations providing guides and Sherpas.

Thus, in the twenty-five years since Jimmy Roberts's commercial outfit first put up a tent, there has been a boom in organised trekking, not only in Nepal but in all other countries that lie abreast of the Himalaya. Teahouse trekking has not expanded to quite the same degree, especially outside Nepal, but there are various ways of trekking other than going from teahouse to teahouse or with a commercial group.

I REMEMBER THE DAYS OF COMPLETE EUPHORIA

WARWICK DEACOCK

The father of commercial trekking 'down under', Warwick Deacock, reflects on the variety of events that led him to spend his business life enabling others to experience the joys of the Himalaya.

It is nice to know that twenty-five years after I unleashed the first Australian party to enjoy walking in the Himalaya the enthusiasm remains undimmed. It has been a long trail.

My first trek in the greater mountains of the Himalaya is chiefly memorable for the recollections of pain! Slogging through the desert-like Lower Karakoram of the Himalaya in Pakistan, bombarded with insufferable 40°C (104°F) heat coming off the bare red rocks, carrying a 27-kg (60-lb) load. This was only justified by the aim — the first ascent of 7788 m (25,545 ft) Rakaposhi, or the poor man's Everest, for our expedition could not afford oxygen.

That was in 1958 and as we reached our summit sooner than planned, two of us turned our thoughts to our wives who had arranged their own expedition, planning to be the first across India's 'Inner Line' into Ladakh.

We caught a lift on a Pakistan Air Force plane to Lahaul then hitched across the border into India. Rickety buses deposited us in Dalhousie only to find that our wives' party had diverted to Manali in the Kulu Valley. We chugged on and found their vehicle parked at Manali but they had long since headed off across the Rhotang La (Pass of Bones).

We eventually caught up with them at the Dak Bungalow in Keylong (Keylang), the district headquarters.

They were not all that delighted to see us, sensing male interference in their strictly female endeavour. However, we observed complete efficiency and bought our way in with a large salami left over from Rakaposhi. [It was] wrapped in plastic [and] we had to shave off the green of age before reaching the garlic-protected interior which proved a popular change to the diet.

There followed four days of swinging along the tracks together at about 3049 m (10,000 ft). The weather was fine, the peaks invigorating. The passing Tibetans, Ladakhi traders and Dogras were immensely interesting. Antonia (my wife) and I were young, not long married, in love, and as we walked and talked [we] re-organised the world as young people will do.

I remember days of complete euphoria. I also remember that good outfitting, food, cooking gear and a civilised walking pace provided a vastly different memory to that horror walk to Rakaposhi. Trekking could be fun!

My steps brought me to Australia where, after three years of setting up an Outward Bound School, I decided to undertake an Australia-wide survey studying attitudes to leisure and recreation. I worked my way around with the family and saw the vast potential of Australia for outdoor activities.

I registered myself at the Company Registrations office as Warwick Deacock Enterprises. The clerk asked if I had a trading name in mind and I invented Ausventure, explaining that Aus meant in German 'to get out'. He was concerned that I might be perverting the good name of Orstrylier! My aim was to encourage participative recreational outings. Much of the leisure that I had observed had been either purely competitive or placid consumerism.

During this time I had also been looking for ways to offer trips to the Himalaya for Australians. I eventually discovered the Himalayan Mountaineering Institute in Darjeeling, where Tenzing Norgay was chief instructor and an old friend, Colonel Jimmy Roberts, a retired army officer, ... had just started to arrange walking holidays through his company Mountain Travel. I sent fifteen schoolboys to the Institute for a three-week adventure and six people (four women and two men) to Everest Base Camp with Mountain Travel.

The next year I invited Paddy Pallin and, later, John Bechervaise to lead Everest groups. Gradually I broadened the scope of the trips and moved into the Annapurna area of Nepal and then into Kashmir.

The next ten years for me were indeed euphoric as I gradually opened up new trek routes. Slowly the stories circulated and the colour slides spread. So too did the sophistication of the trips increase. I recognised that the better the administrative backup, the greater the enjoyment of the experience. Although such things as hygiene and cooking, sensible unrushed itineraries, trained trek staff, and good equipment watered down the rawness of the experience, they also enhanced the enjoyment for many travellers.

In 1977 trekking began to take off and companies began to proliferate. Now more and more adventurous people have the opportunity to experience the magic of the high places and the delights of meeting those peoples and their cultures.

My only regret is that not all who go to the Himalaya do so with a sense of awe and privilege. Some are consumers from more affluent societies who can only be called arrogant users. Hopefully, as countries like Nepal, India and Pakistan develop, so too will the need for National Parks be seen and a caring attitude to help preserve these places and educate visitors will grow.

In 1960 my wife Antonia published the book of her expedition. Her final paragraph reads: 'Our appetite for this type of experience had been whetted, and I have no doubt that the other two share my secret aim to go again. I prefer to regard this as the end of a chapter rather than the end of a story'.

Oh to be euphoric again!

Leader of over 100 treks in the Himalaya, Warwick Deacock was for many years Honorary Consul General for Nepal. Through Ausventure he has pioneered adventure holidays in Australia and overseas. Never happier than when he is trekking, Warwick and Antonia walked through Nepal from 1988 to 1989 for a holiday!

The Rhotang Pass crosses the Pir Panjal Range at the head of the Kulu Valley.

Trekking Styles

We had been on the march for a month. We were all rather jaded; the horses were galled because the drivers were careless of them and their ribs stood out because they had been in places only fit for mules and forded innumerable torrents filled with slippery rocks as big as footballs; there was no more sugar to put in the tea, no more jam, no more cigarettes, and I was reading *The Hound of the Baskervilles* for the third time; all of us suffered from a persistent dysentery. The ecstatic sensations we had experienced at a higher altitude were beginning to wear off. It was not a particularly gay party.

ERIC NEWBY
A Short Walk in the Hindu Kush, 1972

There are various ways of trekking. Each one has its own level of security and degree of comfort. The style you choose should be dictated by where you want to go, how much time you have available, your level of experience in outdoor survival, your knowledge of local customs and languages, how much adventure you are after and what you can afford. Local regulations and weather conditions must also be taken into account. The first consideration is whether to organise your own programme or to go as part of a pre-arranged group.

Do it yourself

Even if organising your own details there are several options. These include: backpacking, either by yourself or with someone else; hiring one or more porters to relieve you of your load; or hiring a guide. When a guide is taken on he usually assumes the responsibility for hiring porters, language translation and route-finding.

On do-it-yourself treks you have the option of living off the land, staying in lodges or teahouses, or with local families, or being self-sufficient and camping. Camping requires more equipment, which means heavier loads or more porters, but you have more flexibility and safety this way.

A day in the life of a teahouse trekker

You wake up at 6 a.m. but do not feel very rested. There was so much noise from the six other people sleeping in the dormitory. The previous evening you had paid extra for a single room but there were none left by the time you arrived last night. You relieve yourself at the toilet perched on the cliff at the back of the lodge then order a bowl of hot washing water from the kitchen. For breakfast you have a pancake with sugar and a glass of sweet milky tea.

You are anxious to be on your way and to get to the top of the long hill before the heat of the day. Your rucksack is packed in ten minutes. It's heavier than you are used to but already you're glad you hired a warm sleeping bag and down jacket in Kathmandu. You have no tent and stove as you're not planning to venture off the main route, but occasionally you would like a little privacy.

The lack of roads in Nepal means villagers have to carry heavy loads from a very early age. Working as porters on treks or expeditions is a lucrative way for locals to supplement their income, but some westerners still prefer the independence of backpacking.

You have plenty of time to think about the world and especially the local countryside as you walk on your own but there are other westerners on the trail with whom you can pass the time in the evenings.

You stop at several villages during the morning and take some photos and a cup of sweet milky tea the locals call *chi* (chiya), but by one o'clock you're hungry and a small inn that is under construction seems like a good place to rest and have lunch. The climb wasn't so bad but you have a slight headache from the altitude gain and perhaps you're also dehydrated.

You have done some bushwalking at home but have never been to any altitude before and you're not too sure just how far to push on, feeling as you do.

Lunch is of baked potatoes straight out of the fire with chilli sauce, and some hot orange cordial as you are sick of milky tea and there are no lemons for lemon tea.

After lunch you have been walking for an hour when the sky clouds over and it starts to snow lightly. Rather than push on and be caught out you decide to stay at the next inn. This turns out to be a ramshackle timber-sided hut, but at least it is a roof over your head. You share the dormitory with a lone Japanese trekker and a French couple, neither of whom speaks English very well. This gives you an excuse to read and write your journal. Inside the inn is dark and smoky. There is just room to huddle by the fire where you try to dry your socks. It's now snowing heavily and you're glad you stayed put, especially because you still have a headache.

The evening meal is rice and lentils again — *dal bhat*, as it is known to the locals. You practise some of your Nepali on the owner's children who bring out their school books to read you some of their English lessons by the light of a kerosene pressure lantern. This is what you have been enjoying even more than the villages and mountains: getting to know something of the Nepali way of life.

On your own or with others

While it is still possible for experienced individuals to trek on their own without problems, it is becoming increasingly less advisable. This is mostly due to the rising incidence of attacks upon lone trekkers. Theft is occurring more often and in several instances people have disappeared altogether. Altitude sickness, getting lost trying to cross a high pass in a snowstorm, avalanches, being set upon by terrorists or overly zealous officials, are just some of the dangers that may befall the solo traveller regardless of his or her level of preparation and experience. It is especially not advisable for women to travel on their own in Muslim countries such as Pakistan. Despite these hazards, with proper precautions the chances of seriously coming to grief are still very low for most trekkers.

One of the main problems of being on your own is the possibilility of falling ill or having an accident. If you are with others then there is some chance of being looked after, but on your own you cannot expect any help from the locals (if there are any around). Finding a suitable travelling companion in Kathmandu, Leh or Srinagar at the right time of year is relatively easy, but it is far better to have a friend from home who can be trusted. When on trek, trying situations are not uncommon and it is in your interests to have a companion who will not desert you in times of stress. In most other countries apart from Nepal it is less likely that you will be able to meet up with a suitable companion by chance.

There are rewards in being completely independent but there is safety in numbers. Three is an ideal size for a group but beyond this, unless there is a common understanding about aspirations and abilities, decision-making can become a problem. If you are set on being master of your own destiny yet do not want to travel alone it is possible to hire a guide or a porter who may give you the degree of security and companionship you are looking

for. This is not always foolproof. Check an individual's references carefully but, better still, try to find someone who comes personally recommended.

Given the potential pitfalls of travelling on one's own it is hardly surprising that travelling with organised groups has become so popular.

Organised groups

We are trying to show you the mountains of Nepal, its valleys and villages and people under the best possible conditions, but without shielding you from reality . . . The final total experience remains yours to create, and to enjoy to the full without the organisational worries or distractions.

COLONEL JIMMY ROBERTS
founder of Mountain Travel,
lecture transcript, 'How it all began'.

There are various levels of organisation and roles in the trekking business and knowing where a particular company or person fits into the hierarchy helps you to know what you can expect in the way of service and support.

On an organised group trek in the Himalaya you will be looked after by guides, cooks and sherpas who work for a trekking agent, a locally-based company. In Nepal these agencies might be Mountain Travel, Himalayan Journeys or Ama Dablam Trekking. There are now over seventy such businesses affiliated with the Trekking Agents Association of Nepal and many more smaller operators who may be nothing more than one individual in Thamel. In India and Pakistan there are also agencies but not as many as in Nepal.

It is possible to turn up on the doorstep of local agents in any one of these countries and book the same trip you might have signed up for back home, perhaps even for some saving in cost. There is always the risk that one element of the trip may not be included, however. If an internal flight is part of the itinerary, for example, there may not be space on the aircraft. This type of thing frequently happens in India. On the other hand, there is a much greater choice of companies and itineraries in the local country. If you have limited time, you would be advised to join an organised trek, as days and sometimes weeks can be wasted taking care of details or trying to find a suitable trek.

Sirdars, sherpas, yaks and zopkioks

The growth of the business of trekking has led to various names and roles of the support staff becoming more clearly defined but their unfamiliar names can make it hard to choose a trek and understand what it's all about.

Porters, as the name suggests, are load carriers and nothing more. They may be subsistence farmers who supplement their living working for expeditions or trekking groups. Some porters do no other work but carry loads. These professionals will transport virtually anything on their backs: firewood, building materials, food, even pilgrims or the sick. Working for their own kind, porters are often paid much less than they can earn carrying for trekking groups.

Porters carry very heavy loads on their backs, taking the weight on their foreheads with straps known as *tump* lines. On trek the loads typically weigh 30 kg. They are often carried in a conical cane basket called a *doko*. In some situations strong porters will carry a double load, 60 kg (132 lb), for double pay. Males and females carry dokos from a very early age and they regularly go barefooted through mud, over rough rocky paths and sometimes on snow.

In some areas pack animals are used instead of porters. In Nepal's Khumbu region the famous *yak* or the less well-known female, the *nak*, are sometimes used. Various domesticated crossbreeds called *zums* (cows) or *zopkioks* (bulls), are more commonly used for load-carrying as they produce more milk, live longer and

(Previous pages) Namche Bazaar has become the hub of the Khumbu for trekkers and climbers as well as the Sherpas. Electricity for lighting comes from a small-scale hydro-electricity plant nearby, but timber still has to be cut for cooking and heating.

can carry loads down to lower altitudes.

In Kashmir mules are mostly used while in other parts of Nepal and Ladakh it may be either mules or people. A team of *ponymen*, as they are known, look after a string of twenty to thirty animals, loading and unloading them at the beginning and end of the day and keeping an eye on them overnight. Each ponyman is usually the owner of several animals. At night the beasts are tethered or hobbled and allowed to graze. Each also wears a distinctive bell around its neck. Pitching your tent next to a grazing herd of mules or yaks does not make for a very restful night's sleep!

When on the trail, beware of passing animals, especially in mountainous country. If possible give them a wide berth or get off the trail on the uphill side. Otherwise you might be brushed over a steep drop by an animal's wide load or horns.

The person in charge of the porters or ponymen and other local staff in an organised trekking party is known as the *sirdar* (sardar) or *head sherpa*. The sirdar has a good deal of responsibility. On big mountaineering expeditions he may well be in charge of hundreds and occasionally thousands of porters. In such instances there is an extra expedition member known as a *niki* who is a kind of foreman or shop steward. There is usually one niki per twenty or thirty porters.

Sherpa, which comes from *shar* (meaning east) and *pa* (meaning people), has two different meanings in the context of trekking. It applies to the distinct race of people who come from the Khumbu region of Nepal and it also applies to the position of a guide in a climbing or trekking party. There are usually two or three sherpas per group of ten or twelve trekkers and they lead the way on the trail or bring up the rear and assist anyone who is ill or unsure of himself on steep terrain. These sherpas usually carry their own gear and a first-aid kit. If you are ill or having trouble keeping up with the rest of the group they will invariably walk with you and carry your day-pack as well.

Sherpa guides may or may not be of the Sherpa people. They may also be Chettris, Tamangs or Gurungs, for example. They usually speak some English. Most sherpa guides are male but in recent times some women have begun to guide trekking groups too.

On a packaged trek there will also be an experienced *cook* and one or more *cook's assistants*. They will serve meals, wash up and carry the cooking and kitchen equipment during the day.

The sirdar or head sherpa is responsible to the *leader* who may be a local or a westerner, depending on the policy of the particular trekking company. The leader is ultimately responsible for the entire group, including trekkers, local staff and porters.

In the early days of commercial trekking it was common for leaders to be westerners experienced in the outdoors in their own country who, in return for being in charge, received a free trip. In this capacity they escorted a party to and from Asia, looked after the travel and accommodation arrangements and also led the trek. For individuals who had never travelled before, it was reassuring to be fully escorted. These days, as more and more companies use local leaders, the practice is declining.

Today a leader is usually a trained local or westerner who can speak the local language, knows the culture of the region, has experience in medical matters, has communication skills and has trekked the route before. Such a leader, however, is unlikely to be leading for the love of it.

Local leaders are not normally paid at the same rate as Western leaders, but local leaders are ethically more acceptable to some trekkers as their wages stay in the country and contribute more to the well-being of the local community.

Local leaders are usually better able to deal with staff problems and have a greater knowledge of local terrain and culture. A western leader, on the other

hand, is more likely to understand the problems of western clients and to be more approachable about delicate medical or social matters.

If signing up for an organised trek you should ask about the types of leaders you will encounter. This may help you to decide on one company or another.

A day in the life of an organised trek

On a normal trekking day you are woken around 6 a.m. with a cup of 'bed tea' delivered by a sherpa or cook's assistant. A little later you are brought a small bowl of warm washing water. You then dress for walking and pack away your sleeping bag and gear into your kitbag. It is usually still very chilly so you wear a hat, gloves, jacket and long trousers. After a quick dash to the toilet tent about 20 m (66 ft)

downwind from the line of six sleeping tents, you run to the mess tent and again wash your hands in a bowl of hot water. Breakfast of porridge or muesli, an omelette and toast and a hot drink is served around 7 a.m. While you are eating the sherpas strike the tents and make up the porters' loads with your kitbags and tents. This may be the last you will see of your kitbag until the evening so you make sure you have all you need for the rest of the day in your day-pack.

Over breakfast the leader, who also eats with you, will describe the day's programme. He explains where the lunch-stop will be, where you are camping that evening and what the track will be like. You then have half an hour to wait while the kitchen is dismantled and the rest of the porters' loads are made up before set-

In Kashmir, mules (instead of porters) are used to carry loads. Each ponyman looks after several beasts, loading and unloading them at the beginning and end of the day. At night the mules are hobbled and allowed to graze.

ting off. At last the sun is creeping down the distant mountain face but you won't feel any of its warming rays for another hour at least. A sherpa leads off and another brings up the rear as you take up your place in the file of trekkers. After an hour's walking you are in sunshine and it is time to stop and shed the jacket, gloves and woolly hat, and place them in your day-pack. It is now time for the sunhat, sunglasses, lipsalve and sunblock. For the rest of the morning you pass along a rocky path that takes you through villages, across rivers, past fields. The party is now spread out but the leading sherpa stops regularly to let the stragglers catch up. The cook and his assistants, carrying dokos filled with stoves, food and pots, race past you singing: 'mid-morning!' As you come down the hill at midday, you see them preparing lunch. At last you reach the other side.

For lunch you may have curried potatoes, chappatis and spinach with rice. After the second helping and black tea with lemon and sugar you doze for half an hour in the sun before it's time to go.

The afternoon's walking is through forest and along the side of a steep valley before you finally have a long steady climb uphill. You are beginning to feel the effects of the altitude. It's now 3500 m (11,480 ft) so you take it slowly and even with regular rests you are still not the last one into camp at 4.30 p.m. The cooks have already been there for over an hour so there is a welcome mug of orange cordial waiting for you. After resting for a while, tea and biscuits are served in the mess tent and by this stage the tents and kitbags have begun to arrive. Unfortunately yours is being carried by one of the porters with a double load so it will probably be the last into camp.

You feel tired though satisfied, having managed the 12 km (7.45 miles) without too much of a struggle. It is getting chilly now that the sun is behind the range and the clouds are rolling up the valley so out come all the warm clothes once again.

Dinner is at 6.30 p.m. More rice and vegetables with tinned fruit for dessert. You are beginning to savour the hot chocolate, last thing before turning in, something you would never drink at home. You are in bed by 8 p.m. and after a few minutes of reading by torchlight, you begin to nod off. Tomorrow is an early start – 5.30 a.m. bed tea – as there is a pass to cross and the weather looks threatening.

Choosing a trekking company
In all places, local companies or trekking agents act on behalf of overseas principals undertaking the actual business of running the trek.

These local businesses may cater to the needs of adventure travel companies from a number of different western countries, or they may work exclusively for (or be a branch of) the foreign principal. This local outfitter and the foreign specialist company, or wholesaler, work together to produce a series of standard itineraries with one or more departure per season. These itineraries are published in a brochure or guide which is then distributed to retail travel businesses or direct to the public. Many of the specialist companies retail their own programmes.

These specialist organisations are the best placed to provide information and guidance, as most of their staff usually have first-hand experience of the regions and various programmes. Such specialisation and service is costly to provide but the chances of having your own specific needs catered to are much greater than if you turn up at a general travel agent and book a trip just on the basis of a brochure.

Many general travel agents are sufficiently experienced to give competent advice. However, it is wise not to sign up on the basis of one persuasive sales pitch without studying the brochures in detail and talking with others who may have already done the same or a similar trip. Shop around as well and don't be afraid to ask questions. It is important to find a trip that suits you.

Brochures

Glossy brochures have become the major selling tool of adventure travel companies and, as well as itineraries and departure dates, they usually contain a good deal of important background information. The quality of the trek, however, does not necessarily relate to the sumptuousness of the catalogue.

Treks are graded in most catalogues according to difficulty but it is vital to note that with the change of seasons the degree of difficulty or seriousness will also vary. These grades, usually expressed as either numbers 1, 2, 3, 4, 5, or adjectives such as easy, gentle, moderate, hard, strenuous, should be taken as only a rough approximation of the usual conditions. Adverse weather such as an unseasonable snowfall can make a moderate trek into a hard one overnight. These gradings usually mention or take into account the problem of altitude. More information can be found in the section on fitness and medical matters on page 58.

Before signing up for a package trek, study all the literature you can lay your hands on and do not overestimate your capabilities, experience or fitness. There is nothing worse than always being the last in a group and holding everyone else up because you lied about or overestimated your experience or fitness. If you are exhausted all the time you will not have a very enjoyable holiday and you could be a danger to yourself and others.

When you have paid a deposit or the full amount for a packaged trek you will usually receive detailed instructions about how to join and what equipment to take, and you will be required to have a medical test. More details can be found in Part 2, Preparing to Go, on page 48.

Within the sphere of trekking companies, quality and levels of service vary. At the most professional level, full travel agent services are available where airline tickets and visas are obtained on your behalf and staff can advise on health, itinerary and equipment matters. Slide evenings and the loan of videos that explain about the region you plan to visit are now part of such companies' sales promotion.

Convenience is one good reason to go with an organised group. Much time and needless frustration can be avoided by making use of local experts. Many travellers with plenty of time at their disposal still regularly use such specialist travel companies as a stepping-stone to visiting parts of the Himalaya they would otherwise not have the experience or skill to safely explore by themselves.

Drawbacks of organised treks

High cost is one of the main drawbacks of packaged treks. The land content for a three-week trek typically costs between US $2000 and $3000 and there are still airfares and spending money to be found. If you have limited vacation time, however, it may be money well spent.

Having to follow the set itinerary and daily timetable of a packaged trek may be irksome. Even though the pace is usually moderate everyone has a tempo they feel comfortable with. This can vary from day to day and whether you are going uphill or downhill. If you are fit, you may find the group's pace frustratingly slow. Alternatively, you may be feeling unwell and would like to take it easy. Or you may come across an interesting village, bird species or beautiful scene over which you would like to linger. The need, however, to keep up with the group forces you to continue on.

Having little say over one's travelling companions can sometimes also be a problem. Packaged treks are usually costed on the basis of two people per tent. If you are not travelling with a friend or partner, you could end up having to share with someone who is not your type. They may seem OK on day one but after a week of being kept awake by snoring you might feel less charitable. A good leader will attempt to match individuals from

Providing you are reasonably fit and choose an appropriate objective, age need not be a barrier to trekking in the Himalaya. Medical evidence suggests that older people may have less problems acclimatising to the altitude.

the outset and should be amenable to catering to your needs if circumstances change along the way.

The larger the group the more likely you are to find someone you have something in common with. Being stuck with a group, whatever the nationality, might, however, not be much fun if you do not have anything in common, and large groups also quickly become unwieldy.

There is also little privacy on a packaged trek. During the day you may happily wander along on your own but at meal times or when you retire there is often the pressure to be sociable. Burying your face in a book or listening (or pretending to listen) to music on a Walkman can sometimes take care of garrulous party members, but sometimes they're hard to escape. There are ways around some of these drawbacks.

Private charter groups

By organising your own group of friends together and having a trek itinerary tailored to suit your needs, you can have the advantages of an organised trek yet avoid the problem of being landed with undesirable companions. Most adventure travel companies offer this service and, providing the numbers are right, a private trek may even be cheaper than a regular package deal.

Another option is to join a special interest trek that focuses on a particular aspect of a country or activity that you are keen on. It may be art, photography or birdwatching led by an artist, photographer or wildlife specialist. In these cases the itinerary is usually specially prepared for you to have time to paint, photograph or immerse yourself in a particular aspect of the region through which you are travelling.

CLIMBING

> . . . the sight which awaited us at the top of the hill far exceeded anything we had imagined. At the first glance we could see nothing but filmy mist; but looking more closely we could make out, far away in the distance, a terrific wall of ice rising above the mist to an unbelievable height, and blocking the horizon to the north for hundreds and hundreds of miles. This shining wall looked colossal, without fault or defect, with seven-thousand-metre (22,960 ft) peaks leading up to the eight-thousanders, and we were quite overwhelmed by the magnificence and grandeur of the sight. This was the Himalaya, our promised land, and from now onwards we would carry this vision with us wherever we went.
>
> **MAURICE HERZOG**
> *Annapurna,* 1952

Mountaineering in the Himalaya is no longer just for experts with years of experience and numerous ascents of lesser peaks. While the competition for permits to climb Mount Everest and the other 8000 m peaks is intense, there are hundreds of smaller challenging mountains available to be climbed. (See page 218 for available details.)

With the opening of many areas in Tibet, Pakistan, India and Nepal previously forbidden to westerners, there are many peaks awaiting a first ascent. Finding new, more difficult routes up very high peaks, climbing in better style and traversing 8000 m peaks, are current preoccupations of the leading climbers from all over the world who flock to the region.

In the course of 130 years of Himalayan mountaineering there have been many significant achievements and advances in technique and style.

Brief History of Himalayan Mountaineering

Climbing mountains for pleasure has been part of the human experience for less than 300 years. The development of this pursuit also parallels the growth of Western interest in the Himalaya. So it is hardly surprising that the earliest notable ascents of the region were by explorers and mapmakers.

The surveyors

By 1850 the Great Trigonometrical Survey of India, an ambitious scheme to map the Indian subcontinent, had pushed into the foothills of the Himalaya. This survey enabled the heights and position of mountains to be accurately determined without actually setting foot on them.

In the course of this work, armed with plane-tables and theodolites, dedicated surveyors established observation posts and spent days atop remote peaks taking measurements. According to Kenneth Mason in his history of Himalayan climbing, *Abode of the Snow*, the height record belongs to a local surveyor who in 1860 reputedly climbed Shilla, at 7030 m (23,058 ft), to erect a survey pole.

In 1852 the highest mountain in the world was determined by and later named after Sir George Everest. As the previous Surveyor-General of India, he had been behind the mapping project that has been described as 'perhaps the greatest geographical achievement on any continent in any age'.

As the surveyors were pushing into the Himalaya they were in many instances following in the footsteps of trophy hunters on leave from the British and Indian armies.

On the heels of the explorers and surveyors came scientists, seeking knowledge about the formation and nature of mountains and those who were interested in conquering unclimbed peaks.

(Above) Australian, George Ingle Finch was the first mountaineer to use oxygen apparatus. As a member of General Bruce's 1922 expedition, he reached the record height of 8250 m (27,060 ft) on the north face of Mount Everest.

(Right) Mount Everest, or Sagamatha as it is known to the Nepalese, was first successfully climbed via the treacherous Khumbu icefall snaking up the right of the mountain and the Western cwm. The border between Nepal and China lies along the west ridge of Everest running towards the camera.

Combining these interests of science and sport established a pattern of dual expedition objectives that was to continue for many decades.

For sport and adventure

W. W. Graham arrived in Kathmandu in 1883 'purely to climb and purely for sport and adventure' to quote his own words. Accompanied by a Swiss guide, he succeeded in ascending a 6100 m (20,008 ft) unnamed peak in the vicinity of Kanchenjunga. This led to other ascents including attempts on Nanda Devi and Dunagiri. Graham's reports were examined in England with great interest by alpinists and scientists, particularly the Royal Geographical Society.

The Society went on to sponsor a major scientific and mountaineering expedition to the Karakoram led by an experienced alpinist, Martin Conway. Among the party was Lt Bruce of the 5th Gurkhas who, over the next forty years, did more to promote mountaineering in the Himalaya than any other individual.

Next on the scene was a rich middle-aged American couple. Fanny Bullock Workman and her husband spent fifteen years in the Himalaya. During eight expeditions, Fanny became the first woman to be seriously involved in Himalayan climbing.

Following the British incursion into Tibet concessions were agreed upon that gave mountaineers permission to climb specific Tibetan peaks. In 1907 an Englishman, Tom Longstaff, climbed Trisuli, at 7215 m (23,665 ft), and this was to remain the highest peak climbed for the next twenty years. Two years later the Duke of Abruzzi, Prince Luigi Amedo of Savoy, a seasoned mountaineer and traveller, arrived in the Karakoram to attempt K2, the second highest mountain in the world. His hope of attempting Everest had been thwarted by the closure of Tibet and Nepal. His team included Filippo de Filppi a doctor, and naturalist Federico Negrotto, as topographer, Vittorio Sella, a highly reputed photographer, seven Italian guides and over 300 local porters.

Though the Duke and his party did not reach a summit, they explored, mapped and documented their activities in the Baltoro Glacier. They laid the foundations for the siege style of Himalayan ascent where a series of camps are established with the aid of local porters.

Between the wars all the major peaks

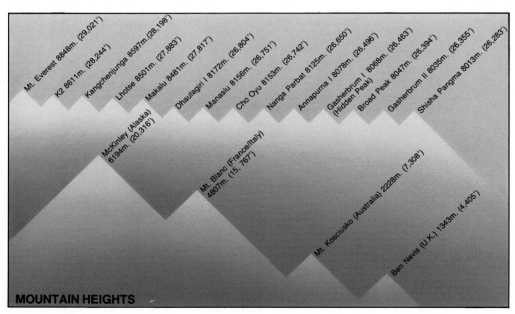

MOUNTAIN HEIGHTS

K2, in Pakistan, at 8611 m (28,244 ft), was first climbed by an Italian team in 1954 via what is now known as the Abruzzi Ridge. It is considered by mountaineers as being much harder to climb than Mount Everest because of the ferocious weather and steep terrain.

were attempted, but prior to 1950 only two major summits had been attained: Kamet, at 7761 m (25,456 ft) in 1931 by Holdsworth, Shipton, Lewa and Smythe; and Nanda Devi, at 7822 m (25,656 ft) in 1936 by Tilman and Odell.

The 8000 m peaks

The breakthrough came when the French climbed Annapurna I in 1950, the first 8000 m peak to be conquered. A powerful team eventually succeeded after an epic ascent and descent in which the summiteers Maurice Herzog and Louis Lachenal were seriously frostbitten. Herzog's vivid account *Annapurna*, is a classic of mountaineering literature.

Within five years of the French success, nearly all the highest peaks were climbed. K2 fell, fittingly enough — as the

Italians had explored the region — to an Italian team in 1954, after it had repulsed several strong American attempts. Compagnoni and Lacedelli ascended the Abruzzi Ridge and, like the French, had an epic descent. The Germans eventually succeeded on Nanga Parbat through the efforts of a mountaineering legend, Herman Bhul, who made a solo summit push and miraculously survived a night balancing in the middle of a rockface at 7930 m (26,010 ft) without any bivouac equipment.

The British conquest of Mount Everest by Hillary and Tenzing in 1953 came as the culmination of over thirty years of ef-fort by the Mount Everest committee, a joint venture between the Alpine Club and the Royal Geographical Society. The first attempt sponsored by this committee

35

CLIMBING JITCHU DRAKE

DOUG SCOTT

In May 1988 Doug Scott, Sharu Prabhu and Victor Saunders climbed a new route on Jitchu Drake 6790 m (22,271 ft) a peak 8 km (5 miles) north-east from Chomalhari. Jitchu Drake is currently the only peak in Bhutan open to climbing expeditions. Here Doug Scott recounts the final days of his ascent.

On 30 May, I woke Victor for a time check at 12.30 a.m. Both tents were creaking under the weight of spindrift. He came down to my tent at 1 a.m., the other two were not very well he said and definitely did not want to go up that day. He himself had not slept so well in the storm because of the angle of their platform. We had brews and noodles and eventually Sharu and myself set off at 6 a.m. to fix two ropes. It was a glorious morning with a sprinkling of light snow like icing sugar on all the lower hills. Rivers were shining silver threads, small lakes glinted in the sun, not a bad place to be! May as well be here as anywhere.

Eventually Victor arrived with a third rope. After fixing that we descended back to the camp, which we re-arranged, hoping to provide for a better night's sleep. Lindsey was flat out in his tent, a 6 ft 5 incher [1.95 m] trying to fit in a 6 ft [1.85 m] tent hadn't helped, and he was very groggy. He said he had no other symptoms, than sleeplessness, but why sleeplessness? I think that it was probably due to the

Doug Scott and Sharu Prabhu weather a storm on Jitchu Drake, Bhutan.

fact that he had suffered a severe accident the year before when his partner had pulled him off a pitch in the Alps and he had damaged again the side he had injured ten years before. Perhaps his body was still recovering from that.

We sat by the tents in the calm afternoon, such a pity that we were not able to make the best of this weather. A huge black and yellow butterfly fluttered around Sharu's yellow javlin salopette — I wonder if that meant anything. The next day at 12.30 a.m. Sharu and Victor set about making breakfast. It was miserable up there, with the wind shaking the tent and blowing powder snow over frosty gear every time we opened the entrance. After three brews and a pan full of noodles, we were off by 2.30 a.m., pulling the hanging ropes as we went on up the ridge, in the bitter cold. Gradually the dawn colours appeared

on the eastern horizon, but it was still very, very cold. We moved fast as if there were only two, with the second and third climbers climbing together as the leader took in both ropes. By the time the sun was up it was time to stop. Occasionally our ice-axes poked through the actual cornice and we could look right down the east face. Beyond the east face between that and Chung Kang, we could look across and down onto the Tibetan plateau in complete contrast, brown and mauve, stretching north as far as the eye could see. From time to time we came across Japanese rope. It would have been churlish to ignore it and occasionally we clipped on for protection or as an additional belay to our ice-axes and deadmen. There was very little chance of getting ice-screws in as the snow and ice were of a lacy texture, with two-thirds of a metre (two feet) down to more solid ice.

Victor's lead took us to the south summit and right on the summit we found the end of the Japanese rope. It was good to be there, to sit on our sacks and look around on that wonderful morning. Victor had done well to lead half the climb, considering he had damaged his ankle on the walk in. So had Sharu, and she had pulled out all the stops and had moved as fast as any of us. In our discussion with David, who was covering the story for our sponsor the *Guardian* newspaper, we had agreed that if Sharu had been tired she would have waited here at the south summit whilst Victor and I made the crossing down and up to the higher north summit about 305 m (1000 ft) away, but there was no question of her waiting, she was raring to go and off we went down 1000 ft along the intervening cornice ridge and up the steep but easy snow slopes west of Jitchu Drake's main summit.

By midday we were on the summit. We stayed there an hour, just below the actual crest, not wanting to completely upset the gods that may reside up there. There can be few pastimes more satisfying than climbing mountains and seeing it through to the end. The summit not only marks the end of the route and the effort in getting there but is also the place for immense satisfaction and elation. We all know it's the journey and not arriving that matters, but from the summit of Jitchu Drake we had that 360-degree panorama which I always look forward to.

We could see all the Tibetan plateau in this part of the world, a high altitude desert stretching out northwards from the main Himalaya Divide. What a dramatic division of countries it is here. The whole of the Tibetan plateau is higher than the forests of Bhutan. Below us we could see the remarkable triangular peak of Chung Kang and the even more remarkable south face and beyond that Kang Cheda, Massang Kang, Tsendakang, Table Mountain, Kankar Punzum and Kunlar Kangri and even the mountains of Arunachal Pradesh, about 322 km (200 miles) away.

In the opposite direction we could clearly see Kanchenjunga (Kangchenjunga), Jannu and Kabru on the borders of Nepal and Sikkim. We could see Pauhunri and many smaller peaks To the south - west, below us was Chomalhari II and Chomalhari itself. We could make out the long, easy-angled south-west ridge which Spen-

cer Chapman and Pasang had taken in 1937 — easy-angled, but a long way and taking them to a point about 500 m (1640 ft) higher than ourselves — what an effort that must have been . . .

Not all the mountains of Bhutan lie on the edges. There are considerable peaks to the south and in the central part of Bhutan, poking up into the clouds which were now gathering. These clouds never looked threatening, they didn't strike fear into our hearts and so we were in no rush to leave the summit. Time for a panorama of photographs and photographs of ourselves and then off back down to share the good news with the others, but we knew we had to take care for this is when most accidents seem to happen. We had to concentrate all our thoughts on this tricky descent.

The next day after down climbing two pitches and abseiling twelve full rope lengths, we were back on the glacier to pack up our tent and supplies left there and then to carry our huge sacks down through the ice to the grass and flowers. The climb was over and we had survived it.

In my tent at Advance Base Camp, there was a message from Karma, which told us that he had come up on the day of the storm. The message read "I pray for the victory I want to see in your smiling faces. May God be victorious. Love and regards. Karma".

After another beautiful morning the winds rose with a vengeance and from then on there was always a mist and snow plume blowing off our mountain as we walked out via Lingchi Dzong. We had climbed the mountain on the only day there was not snow and cloud hanging over it. That is not to say any of us seem deterred from making another visit to the mountain and people of Bhutan. Whether or not we ever get that chance again, we are grateful to have been there in 1988.

Doug Scott is one of the world's foremost mountaineers. His insatiable appetite for high mountains and first ascents has taken him on more than twenty expeditions to the Himalaya. In 1975 he climbed Mount Everest, surviving in a bivouac without oxygen or sleeping-bag just below the summit.

was in 1921. The second full-scale attempt in 1924 from the north side led by Colonel Norton almost met with success, but when Mallory and Irving disappeared on the upper slopes of the North Col at a height of about 8525 m (27,962 ft) another mountaineering legend came into being.

Harder and better style

Following the so-called golden age of Himalayan climbing in the 1950s and 1960s, when all the highest peaks were climbed by the easiest routes, there came an era when more difficult ways were sought up the same mountains. Apart from the brief closure of Nepal to climbers from 1966 to 1968, due to problems with the border security, climbing developed at a steady pace.

The ascent of the south-west face of Annapurna I in 1970 by a British expedition led by Chris Bonington heralded a new direction in Himalayan climbing. Using technical skills that had been honed in the European Alps almost every year teams attempted Everest and many of the other 8000 m peaks by the original or new routes.

Further breakthroughs came in 1975 when the first female, a Japanese mountaineer, Juiko Tabei, climbed Everest by the South Col Route, and Bonington led a British party that climbed Everest by the difficult south-west face.

The major milestones of Himalayan climbing are advances in levels of difficulty. Since 1975 the trend has been towards trying to climb the highest peaks in better style. This means using less equipment and fewer, or perhaps no sherpas above base camp. This means attempting more challenging lines (steeper, more technical ways up faces instead of ascending the long easy ridges) and climbing in alpine style (without the backup of fixed ropes and safety of a string of permanent camps).

The most recent advances have been climbing very high mountains without the aid of supplementary oxygen (Reinhold Messner and Peter Habler, Everest 1980); climbing solo (Messner, Everest 1980); and climbing in the winter season (Polish Expedition, Everest 1980).

Today there are numerous expeditions on the 8000 m peaks every season and there are three climbing seasons each year — pre-monsoon, post-monsoon and winter. Some mountains now have several teams on different routes at the same time. Base camps in these areas are becoming tent cities. Many of the slightly lower mountains, however, see no more than one or two parties each year.

There are some 122 peaks in Nepal alone now open to foreign expeditions and as many again in the Indian Himalaya, the Karakoram of Pakistan, Bhutan and Tibet. Climbers continue to seek out first ascents of unclimbed peaks or new and more difficult routes up popular mountains. There are, however, many smaller expeditions and climbing teams attempting more modest climbs but with the growth in numbers on the major peaks rubbish and overcrowding have become significant problems.

White wilderness

Just as trekkers are becoming conscious of the environmental damage in the Himalaya as a result of mountain tourism, so climbers are beginning to develop a sense of the diminishing areas of true mountain wilderness. Reinhold Messner has proposed the concept of 'white wilderness', areas where human beings have not yet changed anything and where people can explore but have to depart leaving no trace of their presence. These areas should not be studied and should be left unmapped so that anyone venturing there would have to explore the unchartered areas step by step.

Himalayan climbing is destined to focus on small expeditions making very technical alpine-style ascents of big faces, traversing 8000 m (26,240 ft) peaks, or making first ascents of unclimbed 7000 m (22,960 ft) peaks.

Climbing Styles

I realised that my main interest did not consist in trying to test my strength; nor was it essential for me to achieve some victory. The mountains had taught me about life. The mountains had already given me physical fitness and friends, a deeper appreciation of the planet in which we live, a clearer perception of values, distinguishing the stable and the essential from the petty and ephemeral.

TREVOR BRAHAM
Himalayan Odyssey, 1974

There are now several styles of climbing in the Himalaya. You can climb a high peak with a large siege-style expedition; or the same peak with a smaller group in semi-alpine style. In Nepal, where there is an additional system of classification called trekking peaks, you can organise and climb one of these on your own, or with friends; or you can climb a trekking peak with a guide or trekking agency.

In Pakistan, permits are only needed for peaks above a certain altitude (6000 m), in areas that are freely accessible to trekkers. More details can be found in the sections for the respective countries on pages 116 to 213.

Royalty peaks

The traditional way of climbing in the Himalaya was to join a large, often nationally sponsored siege-style expedition. Many of these team efforts still occur but they are very expensive and usually involve a high level of sponsorship and commercialisation.There are also a growing number of smaller alpine-style teams attempting the highest peaks. For the experienced mountaineer this is the most satisfying form of climbing with a small team of friends attempting an unclimbed peak or new route off the beaten track.

Regardless of the type of expedition, however, for the very high mountains the cost is substantial and there is a great deal of bureaucracy to deal with. Applications, including the payment of a substantial royalty or fee, must be sent at least six months (but more often one or more years) in advance to the national government, to gain permission. Most Himalayan governments see mountaineers, like trekkers, as a lucrative source of foreign income. The peaks of each country are graded according to height and popularity and the price of the permit varies according to the category and the height. The fee for Everest for example, in July 1988, was approx. US$6000. As well as a means of raising revenue, these permits serve as an attempt to ration the number of expeditions on a particular mountain or route in a given season. The more popular mountains, especially those with summits over 8000 m are often booked up years in advance, and may have several teams attempting them at any one time.

To gain a permit, expeditions must be endorsed by the government or national alpine club of the country organising the expedition. This can involve more paperwork and delays. Detailed rules and regulations which are enforced by a liaison officer (appointed by the government) who must be paid and outfitted by the expedition. Any local porters and staff must also be equipped, paid and insured according to strict government guidelines.

Such climbs commonly take over a year to organise and much of this time can be spent dealing with the government bureaucracy and raising the sizeable amount of money needed.

Expeditions to the Himalaya, large or small, are usually required to work through a local agency for the provision of services within that country. Trekking companies have considerable experience in outfitting climbing teams. On bigger expeditions trekking agencies may also supply high-altitude sherpas and base camp staff.

The climbing of any peak where a royalty has to be paid is a serious undertaking. By the time you can contemplate being a member of this scale of venture, or think about organising an expedition yourself, you will no doubt have climbed many lesser peaks. It is now possible, however, to experience your first taste of mountaineering or build on other experience in the Himalaya through the ascent of a trekking peak.

Trekking peaks

In line with the 'small is beautiful' trend in Himalayan mountaineering, the Nepalese government in 1978 introduced a category of trekking peaks to capitalise on the demand and interest by climbers in less complicated arrangements. In Pakistan the procedure for climbing smaller peaks has been streamlined somewhat but so far full permits are still required for all available peaks in the Indian Himalaya, Bhutan and Tibet.

Trekking peaks in Nepal are usually the stamping-ground for guided parties and less experienced teams, but such climbs can be equally challenging and rewarding. Under no circumstances should trekking peaks ever be taken lightly.

The term 'trekking peak' denotes a small mountain that may be attempted with few formalities instead of an expensive expedition permit, liaison officer and complex regulations.

Self-organised climbs

Organising to climb a trekking peak in Nepal is not much more complicated than organising a trek. You will need more gear and food to be self-sufficient and a trekking peak permit as well as an ordinary trekking permit.

The Nepal Mountaineering Association issues the trekking peak permits which range in cost from US$200 for peaks above 6100 m (20,008 ft) to US$100 for peaks less than 6100 m. The permits are readily obtained, and extend to a group of up to ten people – an extra levy is charged for additional people. They are valid for one month. A sirdar who is registered with the Nepal Mountaineering Association must also be employed. Any Nepalese staff that climb above base camp must be insured and supplied with climbing equipment.

Apart from the technical problems associated with the climb, a full-scale trek has to be made just to reach the base of the mountain. Supply lines are stretched and rescue possibilities very limited.

Climbing on trekking peaks usually commences at high altitudes and the summits are on or near the danger zone, above 6000 m (19,680 ft), even for relatively modest peaks. Acclimatisation therefore becomes another very serious consideration for self-organised expeditions where there is little previous experience of altitude or Acute Mountain Sickness (AMS). The rate of acclimatisation varies greatly from one individual to the next and is not related to fitness. A measured rate of ascent is best.

Spending weeks, sometimes months, in areas with poor sanitation can also lead to debilitating health problems. Many a climb has failed through sickness before the mountain was even reached. See page 67 for more details on acclimatisation and health and page 66 for AMS. It is important to be as fit as possible to ward off infection and to take every precaution as far as hygiene is concerned.

Guided ascents

Today the distinction between trekking and climbing is becoming increasingly blurred. Trekking companies now offer high-altitude treks that involve the option of limited climbing or guided ascents of more modest peaks as part of their advertised programme. This is an ideal way for inexperienced climbers to have a relatively safe introduction to the snow-capped heights.

Guided ascents of higher peaks are also becoming more common. Nun, in the Indian Himalaya, receives about twenty guided ascents each year.

(Previous pages) Small, alpine-style expeditions to the highest peaks of the Himalaya, such as Annapurna III in Nepal, are now commonplace, but even the most lightweight parties sometimes find it necessary to fix climbing ropes on ice cliffs and vertical sections to enable rapid ascent and descent while acclimatising.

OTHER ACTIVITIES

During those years Boris spent much of his free time 'up country' shooting ... He missed the beauty of the jungle with its teeming life of countless animals treading mysteriously the rusty carpet of leaves in the undergrowth, the vision of fleeing bucks lit by the pale-hued sunlight filtered by the great branches of majestic trees. Confined to the city, Boris would dream of the open spaces of the elephant-grass swamps, their endless, undulating surface cut only by sandy rivers, and the dark blue outline of the lazy, distant Himalayan foothills. There alone, close to nature, was Boris able to become oblivious of the tumultuous world of his city life.

MICHAEL PEISSEL
Tiger for Breakfast, 1966

One of the gentler ways of enjoying the Himalaya is a visit to a wildlife lodge or camp. These lodges are predominantly found in India and Nepal and are associated with wildlife sanctuaries and National Parks such as Chitwan and Karnali in Nepal, and Corbett and Dachigam in India.

For the more active there are several other adventure activities that have been introduced to the Himalaya by individuals and expeditions. These include: ballooning, hang-gliding, para-gliding, ski-mountaineering, heli-skiing, mountain running, mountain biking, jetboating, kayaking and rafting. Of these, only rafting and skiing have so far become commercially significant, but mountain biking is gaining in popularity. There is great potential for the development of cross-country skiing in many places, but so far rafting is the most successful additional activity.

Rafting

Given the right river conditions and managed by experienced boatmen, rafting can be one of the most exciting and adventurous pastimes available to the visitor. It can also be one of the least demanding and leisurely ways of experiencing remote areas of the Himalaya.

Early days of rafting

River running in the Himalaya first came to public notice in 1968 when Edmund Hillary attempted to ascend the Sun Kosi river by jetboat. Since then various kayak expeditions have made descents of many of the major rivers. In 1976 Al Read, a former American consul in Kathmandu, systematically began exploring the Trisuli and upper Sun Kosi Rivers by more conventional means. He subsequently went on to form the first local river running company, Himalayan River Exploration. In 1977 Hillary took to the water again, this time with three jetboats on the Ocean to the Sky Expedition that made a 1500 m (4920 ft) ascent of the Ganges from Calcutta. River running is now an established business in Nepal and, to a lesser degree, in India.

Commercial rafting

Commercial river running today is usually in large (six or twelve-person), virtually unsinkable, inflatable neoprene rafts. They are either rowed by a boatman with a large pair of oars mounted on a rowing frame, or steered by passengers with single-ended paddles — the type used in a Canadian canoe. Either way, the river usually does most of the work. The oars or paddles are for directional control and for positioning the raft in the safest part of the river. Life-jackets and waterproof kitbags are usually provided by the outfitter.

The quality and safety of white-water rafting is dependent on the level of the rivers. The seasonal variations are the biggest consideration, though flash floods

RAFTING TO CHITWAN

JONATHAN CHESTER

The excitement of rafting is some-thing even the least athletic or unadventurous can safely experi-ence whilst in Nepal.

The boiling rapids were fast ap-proaching as the boatman cried out 'hang on tight!'. Within seconds our eight-man inflatable raft was bucking and bouncing its way through a turbu-lent section of the Upper Trisuli River. Other than the occasional wave breaking over our bows, the experi-ence was just like a roller-coaster ride. The bonus in this case, however, was that instead of the backdrop of an amusement park we were passing foothills of the magnificent Nepalese Himalaya.

This was just the beginning of a three-day descent of one of Nepal's most fascinating rivers. Our desti-nation, Tiger Tops Jungle Lodge, lies in the heart of the Royal Chitwan National Park, some 110 km (70 miles) south-west of Kathmandu. Experi-enced oarsmen safely navigate these virtually unsinkable craft through rapids and rocks down to the more tranquil waters of the Narayani River, and so to the jungle of the lowlands.

Once the first section of heavy water was safely negotiated we sat back and absorbed the surroundings. The adrenalin had eased, but our boatman confided that this was only a tiny rapid and there was more excite-ment in store. All the supplies and lug-gage necessary for us to be self-

Some rafting companies offer trips where everyone participates in the paddling, but the river does most of the work.

sufficient during the journey were se-curely strapped down in watertight boxes or bags.

Soon another rapid came into view and, being more familiar with the pro-cedure, I ventured to photograph with one hand while clinging tightly with the other. Specially designed lifejackets are worn and should one be acciden-tally tossed out of the boat, it's simply a matter of floating feet first down-stream till you can be rescued. No un-intentional dips were taken on our trip and we were told they were a rare event.

After negotiating the second rapid with ease I became interested in big-ger waves and heavier water. Most rafters find the excitement addictive and much of our time was spent gazing downstream at regular intervals in an-ticipation of the next section of white water.

On the quieter sections of the river more attention can be focused on the unique wildlife. Rhesus monkeys are

easily disturbed, but the silent passage of the raft enabled us to approach a troop drinking at the water's edge for a close-up view. Many beautiful birds inhabit the banks of the river and the brightly coloured Asian kingfisher was a prized sighting.

Relaxation is the keynote of these trips and there is the opportunity to sunbake and soak up the mountain scenery while the raft slides effortlessly along. Soon another rapid approached and we were once again riding a liquid roller-coaster. The oars-man must manoeuvre the raft into the best line to take before we plunge into a standing wave, ensuring an exciting but untroubled passage. On smaller sections of white water passengers are given the opportunity of taking the oars. The force of the water and skill in judging a good line were soon ap-preciated as we strove to direct the craft. The flat water gave us a chance to develop the rowing technique and to work up an appetite.

A lunch-stop at the confluence of the Marsyandi and Trisuli Rivers enabled us to discover the contents of the giant ice-chest our oarsman had been using for a seat. Fresh salads and cool drinks appeared, enabling us to savour foods which are rarely found in Nepal away from five-star hotels. Whilst our hunger was soon satiated with the generous portions of delicious food, our thirst for more white-water adven-ture lingered on. No sooner were we again afloat than the roar of a rapid caught our ears, and we were once again in a section of wild water. Not the most settling of after-dinner exercises, but to enjoy every aspect of Nepal one must accept the rough with the smooth at any time.

The late afternoon sun gave the hillsides an orange hue as we made camp on a sandy beach. Stan, our boatman, and his assistant prepared another sumptuous meal while we pitched the two-man tents and laid out the thick foam sleeping-mats. For those more accustomed to the comforts of home, 'roughing it easy' would be a good description of the style of camping practised by Himalayan River Expeditions. Being more used to the rigours of backpacking and mountaineering, I found the facilities positively luxurious. Following the evening meal of tasty stew and apple pie we talked for hours on the problems of the world. Our world was so remote on the banks of this river that our only problem was to sleep sufficiently to enjoy the next day.

Back on the river again, the rapids became fewer and further between. A large whirlpool loomed up and we secured any stray belongings. Cameras and binoculars were returned to the waterproof metal boxes with which each person was issued. The water maelstrom provided the most exciting time of the whole trip. The raft climbed the standing wave, teetered on the crest and plunged down the other side. White caps broke over the bows, dumping buckets of water on those in the front. The turbulent waters soon gave way to a calm stretch, and after a few minutes bailing we were none the worse for our drenching. The river then became wider and the character of the surrounding countryside began to alter. Gone were the narrow gorges with villages clinging to the hillsides like vines to a tree. The suspen-

sion bridges spanning the river gave way to other means of crossing — ferry canoes ply between the banks, bridging communities on either side of the river.

Since the eradication of the malaria-carrying mosquitoes, hill people have been migrating from the overcrowded high country down to this broad valley. In the space of several hours we had journeyed from the foothills of the Himalayas to the plains known as the Terai. Once known as 'death valley', in twenty years this region has been cleared of much of the native jungle and is fast becoming the rice bowl of Nepal.

The village of Devght provided an interesting diversion from our watery world. Set at the confluence of the Trisuli and the Kali Gandaki Rivers, it has unique religious significance in the Hindu spiritual life. Each year in mid-January thousands of devotees make a pilgrimage to bathe where the waters coalesce, believing that in spite of all wrongs they may have committed, their sins will be washed away and a passage to heaven assured.

The highlight of the second evening was a campfire at which we were entertained by young singers and dancers from a nearby village. What their performance lacked in polish and technique was more than made up for by enthusiasm and spontaneity.

By the third morning the rhythm of the river had slowed considerably. The lazy pace and hot summer sun saw me taking to the water at regular intervals to cool off. Sheltering under an umbrella was the other way to escape the burning rays.

Flocks of brown ducks heading north to Siberia, black ibis and storks were observed but the gharial crocodile and gangetic dolphin weren't to be seen, though we were now well into their habitat.

By early afternoon we sighted the jungle of the Royal Chitwan National Park and soon we made a rendezvous with a landrover sent to ferry us from the river to Tiger Tops Jungle Lodge. The tall trees of the sal forest reached skyward from a carpet of leaves. Creepers and vines, characteristic of jungle fantasies, twisted between the two, and as we bounced along in our open-topped vehicle I began to realise this was a special place!

My first close-hand encounter with the realities of the jungle was atop an elephant. The problem of how one mounts one of these enormous pachyderms is solved by simply stepping off the first floor of the lodge balcony into the wrestling-ring-like saddle. The ponderous gait of these beasts is not unlike travelling in a car with uneven-sized square wheels. The first stop was at the river where all the elephants took on water. Up to 5 litres [9 pints] at a time is drawn into the trunk then sprayed into the mouth. Elephants are the most suitable means of transport in the jungle. River, marsh, thick grasses and trees presented little problem as the elephant ploughed its way along. The time slipped by quite quickly and soon we were heading back to the lodge. Rhinoceros, spotted deer, wild boar, jungle fowls and the beautiful Indian roller [bird] were all to be seen in the course of the ride.

All too soon my jungle sojourn came to an end. The thirty-minute flight back to Kathmandu was in sharp contrast to the three-day raft trip. The remoteness and isolation of Tiger Tops is not appreciated by the many visitors who fly to and from Kathmandu, and this is especially so of those whose homelands are the more crowded and developed countries of Europe. The raft descent and jungle interlude were equally exciting, both offering interesting insights into little known aspects of Nepal.

can be a problem any time of year. There is usually too much water during the monsoon. Post-monsoon is the best time to go. Winter is also satisfactory but can be somewhat cooler.

River trips of this nature are within the reach of families and travellers of all ages. Today, the two main rivers in Nepal are the Trisuli and the Sun Kosi, while in India it is also possible to raft the Ganges and in Ladakh, the Indus River. Most first-time visitors combine rafting with another activity such as trekking or sight-seeing rather than just going on an ex-tended rafting trip. Several days spent rafting down the Trisuli River is an ideal way to travel through the Chitwan National Park.

Skiing

Skiing has had limited popularity in the Himalaya, but the extensive high snowfields are now beginning to attract ski-tourers as well as downhill ski en-thusiasts. The only ski resorts of any note are in India at Gulmarg in Kashmir, Kufri near Simla and Solang near Manali. Though not well served by ski-lifts or facilities, they are good sites for skiing.

The beginnings of skiing
In 1912 army surveyor and (later) Himalayan geographer, Kenneth Mason, was the first person to take a pair of skis to India. He taught himself to ski in Kashmir. Eventually the sport gained an

Rafting the Trisuli River in Nepal is a popular way of getting to the Royal Chitwan National Park in the Terai.

(Right) Being astride an elephant in the elephant grass near Machan Wildlife Resort is the safest way of viewing the wildlife in Nepal's Royal Chitwan National Park.

off-season following amongst the British army and administrative staff on leave at the hill-station resort of Gulmargh. There was very little early skiing in other Himalayan countries prior to the boom in remote climbing and exploring.

In the 1970s mountaineers began to make traverses on crosscountry skis. Americans Ned Gillette and Jan Reynolds effectively circumnavigated Everest on skis in two separate expeditions.

With an official winter mountaineering season now part of Nepal's mountaineering calendar, ski approaches, complete ski-oriented traverses and extreme ski descents of very high peaks are becoming more an accepted facet of Himalayan climbing than a novelty. Logistically, such winter ski trips are even more of a headache than pre-monsoon or post-monsoon trips, as local means of transport – porters, yaks and mules – can rarely cope with deep snow. It is also now possible to take guided ski mountaineering expeditions to remote peaks.

Wildlife Camps

A visit to one of the commercial jungle lodges associated with a National Park reserve is one of the best ways of appreciating what the native flora and fauna of the Himalayan region may once have been like. More details on the wildlife are contained in the Introduction to the Himalayan Region, see page 95 ff.

The best known wildlife camps are in the Royal Chitwan National Park in the Terai region of Nepal. Chitwan, 165 km (102 miles) from Kathmandu, is 960 sq. km (370 sq. miles) of deciduous, sal forest and flood plain on the banks of the Narayani River. Formerly the exclusive hunting preserve of the Rana rulers of Nepal, the park officially came into being in 1973.

India's premier wildlife park is the Corbett National Park. Established in 1936 as the Hailey National Park, on the advice of hunter and naturalist Jim Corbett, the park is set in 520 sq. km (201 sq. miles) of the Siwalik hills of the Himalaya. The park is 300 km (186 miles) north of Delhi in the state of Uttar Pradesh.

No matter what activity takes you to the Himalaya, trekking, climbing, rafting or a visit to a jungle lodge, the better prepared you are the more chances you have of achieving your goals. Making sure you are fit and well equipped, and choosing an activity or trip appropriate to your level of experience, will make all the difference to your Himalayan experience.

PART TWO

Preparing to go

> After three hectic months of preparation we met in London, on the eve of our departure, for a final review of our plans. Only Jungle, who was to have spoken on the use of the radio gear and his own methods of route-finding, was absent. He rang to say that he had taken the wrong bus and was not quite certain of his whereabouts; but he had just caught sight of the North Star and expected to join us shortly.
>
> **W. E. BOWMAN**
> *The Ascent of Rum Doodle*, 1956

Proper physical, mental and logistical preparation is the key to a rewarding and successful trek or climb. In this section, we examine what you need to do in order to prepare for your trip.

CHOOSING A TREK OR CLIMB

Preparation for trekking in the Himalaya should begin months, perhaps even years, before a proposed journey. Studying reference books, guides or brochures (if taking a commercial trek) to see what the possibilities are is the first step. You also need to reflect on whether your experience and fitness match your aspirations. The more serious the undertaking the greater the preparation should be.

You will need to be aware of the seasons and weather to get the most out of your time away. There is little point in going to Nepal in September for instance, if you are hoping to see the rhododendrons in flower. More details about the seasons, climate, geography and the natural history of the Himalaya are contained in the section on page 86 ff.

How long can you be away for? This is one of the questions that must be answered early when planning a trip. Today an average organised trek itinerary encompasses a week to twelve days, although more serious journeys can extend from three to five weeks. If you have no experience of walking and would normally never consider hiking for four or five

(Left) At high altitudes the seasons become shorter and the flora blooms later, as seen here at the Baltoro Glacier in Pakistan.

(Right) Choosing the right season to visit a particular region of the Himalaya can be crucial for optimal trekking or climbing conditions. Bad weather can strike at any time in the mountains and plans often have to be altered to cope with sudden changes such as this September storm in Kashmir's Warvan Valley.

hours at a time, then even a week may well be more than you would find enjoyable for a first-time trek. In Nepal there are two-day and three-day treks which, combined with other activities such as rafting and a visit to the Chitwan Jungle Lodge, are far less arduous. Similar possibilities exist in Kashmir. If you are travelling on your own and have no fixed time-table, you have much more freedom. For possible destinations and treks see pages 116 ff.

Research

There is no better source of information about where and when to go than those who have already had some experience of your proposed destination. They will be able to advise you on climate, conditions and customs. Be careful not to take any one statement as gospel, however. Seasonal conditions, political factors and varying perceptions can make one appraisal totally different to another.

As well as adventure travel company brochures, there are now many excellent handbooks on trekking and travelling to particular regions and countries spanning the Himalaya. (See Suggested Reading List.) The relatively inexpensive yet very detailed Lonely Planet guides are excellent to carry with you. They are regularly updated, so make sure you work from the latest edition.

Other titles worth tracking down are *The Trekker's Guide to the Himalaya and the Karakoram* by Hugh Swift and *A Guide to Trekking in Nepal* by Stephen Bezruchka.

The Insight series of guides also provide excellent cultural, historical and political backgrounds to the Himalayan countries. Specific titles are available on Nepal, India and Pakistan. *South Asia*, for example, briefly covers these countries as well as Bhutan, Tibet, Bangladesh and Sri Lanka. The Insight guides also include a wealth of general sightseeing and travel information about the main cities and regional centres. If you are particularly interested in the natural history of the Himalaya, the Insight title, *Indian Wildlife*, is worth tracking down. Through essays and excellent photographs this looks at the native species and the major parks of the Indian subcontinent.

Back issues of the *National Geographic* magazine also provide worthwhile background information about the Himalaya. The November 1988 issue, for example, featured several articles on Nepal and a superb map of the Everest region.

Maps

There are several large fold-out maps that show the entire Indian subcontinent, such as the Bartholomew map of the Indian subcontinent. These are useful for getting an overall picture of the Himalaya but they are not particularly convenient to use when travelling. A more detailed country by country series of maps published by APA Press is available. The sheets for Pakistan, Northern India and Nepal are very useful for broad-scale planning. Broad-scale maps are sometimes available through consulates and embassies, but often a large atlas is just as useful.

More detailed route maps are available for specific areas but the coverage is very limited. The US Army Map Service (AMS) USO2 series covers a good deal of the Himalaya but is not readily available. Nepal has the most complete homegrown coverage. The locally produced and inexpensive Mandala dyeline trekking maps cover the main trekking routes with adequate detail, but are not always completely accurate. The German E. Schneider Research Scheme Nepal Himalaya 1:50,000 series is by far the most detailed and lavish but is available only for selected areas.

For further details about other background reading matter and the maps, consult the Suggested Reading List on page 222.

TRAVEL MATTERS

Losing your money and travel documents or having them stolen overseas, no matter where you are, can be disastrous. Cancelling credit cards or traveller's cheques and renewing your passport and visas can take days, perhaps weeks. In Asia all these chores are doubly difficult.

Travel Documents

Keeping your documents in the same safe place all the time helps you to avoid the stress of thinking they are lost when you have simply mislaid them. Keep documents in a money belt around your waist or hang them in a passport wallet around your neck underneath your clothing. The latter style is preferable to more easily retrieve tickets or your passport when they have to be presented. With a money belt, a mini strip-tease is sometimes required. Increasingly popular now for Western travellers in Asia is a small waist-pack, worn on the front rather like a Scotsman's sporran. These are large enough to carry sunglasses, a small camera, lipsalve and maps but they are not so big as to be uncomfortable.

When you're trekking it is usually not necessary nor very comfortable to wear a waist-pack or money belt. Carrying papers in a day-pack is usually safe enough. If staying in teahouses on a popular trail, however, you should be as cautious with passports and money as you would be in the cities.

Passports

If you are thinking of going trekking and do not already have a valid passport, apply for one well in advance of your likely departure date. Your passport will have to be submitted at the same time as visa applications and these can take some time to process.

Prepare a file of photocopies of all your documents including your birth certificate, citizenship papers, passport, visas, travel insurance forms and important addresses and so on and keep these separate from the real documents. If the originals are lost or stolen, it will be much easier to obtain replacements with the information contained on the photocopies.

Most of the time in Asia you will need your passport with you, either to change money or as proof of identify. Your passport number is also required on endless forms, especially in India. It is a good idea to commit the number to memory.

If your passport is lost or stolen, report it as soon as possible to the nearest police station and obtain a copy of the report. A further copy of this report must be submitted with an explanation of the loss to your country's nearest consular office or embassy. The delay in having a passport replaced can be reduced if you have evidence of citizenship and your passport details. Remember too that the chances of getting your passport back are increased if you have a local contact address noted in the passport.

Visas

A visa is a stamp on a page inserted in your passport by an authorising agent of another country giving approval for entry to that country once you arrive there. If trekking with an organised group, the trekking company will usually arrange the visas. Visa applications are made to the relevant consulate or embassy of the country or countries you are visiting and each country has its own specific application forms, procedure and costs. These can vary depending on your passport.

Visa regulations change from time to time and country to country. Allow yourself plenty of time to obtain the necessary visas as there are often delays with processing and postage.

Nepal

Nepalese tourist visas are valid for three months from the date of issue and permit a stay of up to thirty days. Two one-month extensions are possible but after each one you must leave the country. Re-entry to Nepal is only possible one month after the date of departure. Application forms must be filled out in triplicate with recent photos and submitted with your passport and a stamped self-addressed envelope with appropriate payment for the visa and sufficient postage to cover the cost of registered or certified mail.

Pakistan

A visa is required for entry to Pakistan and is valid for thirty days. Two forms must be filled out with a photograph for each. Extensions of your visa have to be applied for at the foreign registration office at the police headquarters where you are staying in Pakistan.

India

A tourist visa for India is valid for a three-month stay with multiple entries. The first entry into India should be within six months from the date of issue of the visa. Applications must be submitted with three recent passport-size photographs and a letter from your travel agent or airline, detailing your travel arrangements to and from India. India requires passports to be valid for six months from the date of application.

Bhutan

A visa is required for Bhutan but it is only possible to travel within the country in a group under the auspices of the Bhutan Tourism Corporation. It takes many months to arrange the details as all the paperwork is done in Thimphu (Thimpu), the capital of Bhutan. The Tourism Corporation needs fifteen days to process a tourist visa. This must be paid for on arrival at the border town of Phuntsholing or Paro, the airport site, a ninety-minute drive from Thimphu.

China

A tourist visa for China entitles the bearer to enter Tibet and Inner Mongolia. Visas are valid for three months from the date of issue and permit travel for a period of three months. A Chinese visa can take two to three weeks to be processed.

Travel Insurance

You are strongly advised to take out comprehensive personal travel insurance if going to the Himalaya. Many trekking companies make it mandatory to have such insurance. This can take the financial sting out of many of the untoward events that could happen. You are advised to be covered for cancellation or alteration of your travel arrangements, loss of deposit paid in advance, sickness or accident, medical expenses, transportation costs in case of death or accident, additional expenses caused by delays or unforeseen events, personal legal liability and lost or damaged baggage. Read the policy conditions carefully to ensure that your trekking activity does not render you ineligible to claim. Most (readily available) policies today will not pay claims arising from participating in mountaineering involving the use of ropes and guides. Others such as ISIS, the International Student Insurance Service, require that you pay an additional adventure sports premium, but this still only covers you for mountaineering and trekking not necessitating the use of ropes.

If you have an accident, become ill, lose your luggage, or have it stolen, obtain as much official documentation as possible and a police report at the time. You must file a claim within a finite period of your return, usually thirty days.

Most policies have several different tables of benefits with increasing premiums for the greater coverage and length of time that you are away. Make sure you are fully aware of the limitations of the policy before taking it out. Trekking companies often act as agents for a particular insurer that will give adequate cover for whatever you undertake with them. You are not obliged to insure with that company but it is usually the most convenient.

Additional Photos

Take along at least three additional passport-size photos as these may be necessary for a trekking permit. If you are visiting several countries the same number could be required three or four times over. In these circumstances a dozen extra photos are worth having. If you run out, it is possible to have more taken in major cities such as Kathmandu and Delhi, but having enough with you saves time and trouble.

An accident, even something as minor as a sprained ankle, can create problems in inaccessible regions. Sherpas or porters sometimes have to carry an injured person to the nearest transportation, which may be many days away.

Addresses

Before leaving home a little research to find the location and addresses of your country's embassies or consular offices for the countries you intend to visit could save trouble if you have your passport stolen or need urgent medical attention. The addresses of other countries' embassies you intend to visit may also be useful.

Money

When travelling in the Himalaya it is best to have money or access to money in a variety of different forms. Cash, credit cards and traveller's cheques are the ideal combination.

How much and what kind?

American dollars are the most useful foreign currency to have in Asia. It is a good idea to carry several hundred dollars for emergencies in $20 or $50 notes stashed in several different places in your wallet, hand luggage or checked baggage (for your flight).

It is also a good idea to carry $50 worth of your native currency in a range of notes. These notes can also be a good conversation starter in foreign countries.

How much money to take depends on how long you plan to be away, your style of travel and the type of shopping you plan to do along the way. If you are going on an organised trek, most expenses will have already been paid before you depart. In such circumstances $400 in traveller's cheques should be adequate for meals, incidentals and souvenirs for a month unless you plan to buy a painting, carpets or jewellery. Credit cards can also help in these instances.

If you are travelling on your own, Asia can be as cheap or as expensive as you want it to be. You can exist on as little as a few dollars a day staying in dormitory accommodation and eating from street stalls, or in major centres you can stay in five-star hotels.

Credit cards

In most Asian countries, major credit cards are accepted only in large centres or cities and even then only at better hotels, shops and restaurants. Credit cards, however, can provide a very useful backup service if you are faced with an unexpected outlay such as a helicopter charter or an expensive purchase like a carpet.

American Express is the most useful followed by Visa, Mastercard and Diners Club. American Express has the advantage of also giving you access to traveller's cheques and cash. Make sure your credit cards are cancelled immediately if they are lost or stolen. Keep their numbers recorded in a separate place.

Traveller's cheques

Traveller's cheques are still a safe and relatively convenient way of carrying money. Fortunately, in Asia (unlike many countries in the West) you are not usually charged a fee when you cash them. In most towns outside major Himalayan tourist centres such as Kathmandu or Srinagar, the only places that will take traveller's cheques are banks. This can be very frustrating if you're stuck without ready cash and you turn up at the door to find it's a bank holiday. This is where your US dollars (cash) may save the day.

It is best to have only well-known brands of cheques such as Thomas Cook or American Express. These are more readily acceptable in third world countries and the companies' network of local offices enable more prompt replacement if they are lost or stolen. Keep one or more separate records of your cheques (used and unused) in your hand luggage and/or baggage so that if they become lost or stolen you can easily provide details for replacement.

Carry cheques in a mixture of denominations ranging from $20 up to $100. This will save you having to change more than necessary. Cheques in US dollars or British pounds sterling are more widely accepted than Australian dollars, New Zealand dollars or some other currency.

When cashing traveller's cheques, make sure you keep the paperwork that goes with the transaction. In India this will have to be produced when paying for airline tickets, hotel bills or other major purchases. This stricture is an attempt to limit black market transactions which are rife in places such as Kathmandu, Delhi and Srinagar. When you cash traveller's cheques or foreign money for local currency, be sure to get clean, undamaged notes in plenty of small denominations. In many places torn or dirty notes may not be accepted for your purchases and away from the main centres change is almost impossible to obtain.

Luggage

Cases are unsuitable for using on a trek. It is best to leave home with your luggage in a lockable kitbag or rucksack.

If backpacking or travelling on your own, you will most probably be using a backpack or rucksack instead of, or as well as, a kitbag. Modern travel packs with zip-open fronts are popular but are less secure than a kitbag even if there is a provision for padlocks. Airline baggage conveyors have a habit of breaking or tearing pack straps and buckles. One solution to this is a pack where shoulder straps are hidden away behind a zippered flap. Another option is a lockable nylon totebag that your backpack will fit inside. Carrying a spare, lockable, lightweight duffel bag can also be useful.

If using padlocks, make sure you have several sets of keys and if you are travelling with a companion give one set to him or her. Combination locks are one solution to the key problem, providing you have a good memory. If you don't, make sure the combination is written in several handy (yet not obvious) places. The back of your passport is one possibility.

The usual free, economy class, checked baggage limit is 20 kg (44 lbs). You are also allowed one piece of hand luggage which is seldom weighed, though airlines are becoming very strict about dimensions. You are allowed to carry a bag not exceeding 56 cm x 36 cm x 23 cm (22 in x 14 in x 9 in). A small to medium day-pack is usually acceptable.

If you are close to the limit (20 kg) with your gear, you can wear boots and bulky jackets on the plane. On some internal air routes such as the flight to Lukla in Nepal, the baggage limit may be 15 kg (33 lb).

Porters' loads on organised treks are 20 kg and the cost of the trek is based on a finite number of porters. When you are trekking with an organised group you should attempt to carry less than 3 kg (7 lb) in your day-pack, or you may be unnecessarily exhausted by day's end.

Make sure all checked hand baggage is clearly labelled. It is a good idea to have your address written on or taped to the inside of your pack or duffel in case the external label is torn off and the bag goes astray. For more details on packs and bags, see the equipment section, page 80.

Do not carry pocketknives on you or in your hand baggage because they may be confiscated. Make sure they are in your checked luggage.

Airline Tickets

Keep a separate record or photocopy of your airline ticket details, number, date and place purchased and cost. If your tickets are lost or stolen, report the loss as soon as possible to the airline. If your ticket has not been used you will be given a refund after a 120-day waiting period.

In the meantime, you may well have had to purchase another ticket to get back home. This is where your back-up credit card comes in handy. In certain circumstances you may also be entitled to claim the cost of this ticket on travel insurance.

Driver's Licence

It is unlikely you will at any stage drive a car when travelling in the Himalaya. It is possible, however, to rent motorbikes in places such as Srinagar or Kathmandu. For this you will only need some form of identification but if you are involved in an accident or traffic infringement and you do not have an International Driver's Licence, it could be a problem. It is safer to have a licence which can also serve as an extra form of identification.

Mail

If travelling with an organised trek, direct your mail to the particular agency business address, where it will be held for you until your return. It is seldom feasible to have it forwarded.

If travelling on your own, post restante is not advisable because there is often very poor security. If you use American Express traveller's cheques or have an Amex card you can have your mail held at American Express offices which can be found in most major centres.

Security

There is a small but growing problem of theft from trekkers in the Himalaya. It is better to be cautious where you can. Regardless of whether you are on your own or with a group, do not leave possessions lying around, especially if camping near a village. Keep tents closed day and night and store valuables in your locked kit bag in the middle of the tent. Some people even carry their day-packs in front of them in crowded markets and wherever else they feel vulnerable to prevent pickpockets.

FITNESS

You don't need to be a superman or superwoman to trek or climb in the Himalaya. No matter what you propose to do, a gradual build-up of fitness is recommended, if you are not used to regular exercise. The fitter you are, the more resistant you will be to infections and disease and the more enjoyable your trip.

Experienced mountaineers typically spend several years building up for an expedition to climb an 8000 m peak. If you are currently unfit you should be prepared to train for three months if you plan a long, high-altitude trek such as to Everest Base Camp, the Annapurna circuit or the Baltoro Glacier.

If you do not have the time or enthusiasm for this sort of build-up, many shorter, less ambitious treks are equally rewarding. Better to go for a three- or seven-day trek at low altitude than risk your expensive holiday and perhaps your life on a foolhardy, over-ambitious goal.

Training

Performing any aerobic activity such as squash, swimming, cycling or jogging two or three times a week for at least an hour is an excellent form of training. On trek, however, you are likely to be going up and down hills much of the time, so make sure your training includes plenty of this type of activity.

Walking is an ideal opportunity to break in new boots which could help spare you the agony of blisters later on. If you plan to carry a heavy pack on trek, make backpacking part of your training routine. Rather than seeing the fitness build-up as drudgery, try to have some walks in interesting and scenic surroundings and to incorporate them as part of your relaxation at weekends.

Trip Grades

Organised trek brochures have trip grades that vary in name. By studying these carefully you should be able to determine where you fit and what you should be capable of undertaking comfortably. Even going on your own, these grades are a good indication of the relative difficulty of particular itineraries.

Example 1

A. Easy walking or rafting. Suitable for all ages; no special physical preparation.
B. Moderate walking up to seven hours a day below 2500 m (8200 ft) averaging 6 to 15 km (4 to 9 miles) a day. Physical preparation such as regular walking (uphill and downhill) is necessary.
C. Moderate and strenuous walking up to seven hours a day reaching 4500 m (14,760 ft), averaging 6 to 15 km a day. Daily ascents and descents may total 600 m to 1500 m (1968 to 4920 ft). Physical preparation necessary, such as jogging, sports, regular walking (uphill and downhill), for six to eight weeks before your trip.

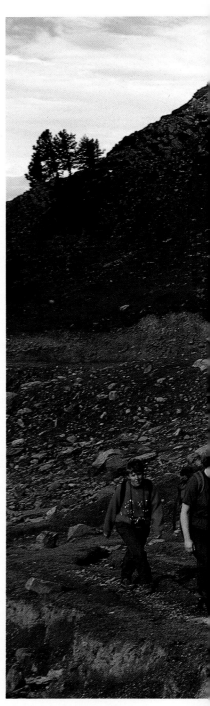

(Previous pages) In the Himalayan region aged local buses are the main means of transport to the roadhead for expeditions and trekking parties.

If travelling with an organised trekking group a small pack containing water bottle, waterproofs, warm jacket and first-aid kit is all that need be carried during the day.

D. Moderate and strenuous walking above 4500 m up to seven hours a day. Previous walking experience helpful but not necessary. Physical preparation as for grade C.

E. Strenuous walking up to seven hours a day, possibly longer. 6 to 15 km a day, maximum altitude 5500 m (18,040 ft). Previous walking experience and excellent physical condition important.

Example 2

Easy. For people who enjoy good health and do regular outdoor exercise, for example, walking, cycling, swimming, tennis and so on. Does not exceed altitudes of 4000 m (13,120 ft).

Moderate. You should be in excellent physical condition, regularly doing strenuous outdoor activities such as bushwalking, skiing and jogging. Sometimes involves solid walking to 5500 m (18,040 ft).

Strenuous. Requires a training programme of frequent strenuous exercise. Can involve basic ice-climbing and rock-scrambling but does not require previous experience. Involves walking above 5500 m. Previous trekking or walking experience an advantage.

MEDICAL MATTERS

Thanks to the splendid work of Prone the expedition was remarkably free from illness. All were fit and well, except . . . Prone, who was smitten with mysterious and complicated symptoms, namely: pallor, profuse sweating, pulse rapid and soft, temperature sub-normal, deep breathing and sighing, restlessness and thirst, cold extremities, faintness, dizziness and buzzing in the ears. Poor fellow, he was much distressed, both by his condition and by the fact that he was unable to diagnose his ailment. The problem was finally solved by Constant who produced a first-aid manual and pointed out that the symptoms were exactly those of haemorrhage, except that the last two were missing, namely: insensibility and death.

W. E. BOWMAN
The Ascent of Rum Doodle, 1956

Medical precautions for travelling to the Himalaya should begin at least three months before you depart. These should entail a comprehensive physical examination, a dental check-up, immunisations, the preparation of a first-aid kit and learning about the health problems you are likely to encounter.

While the chances of dying trekking are not very high, there is every likelihood that you will get sick at some stage. Chest, throat or stomach complaints are among the most likely problems and these are discussed further in this section.

The following advice and information is in no way a substitute for a good first aid book, as all the usual medical problems can arise, in addition to those specific to Asia or altitude.

Medical Examination

If you are signing up for an organised trek you are usually required to have a thorough medical examination. A special form is issued to be completed by a qualified medical officer. If you are travelling on your own a medical check-up is equally, if not more, important.

It is necessary to inform the examining doctor of your full medical history, medications and exactly what areas and altitude you are planning to trek to.

If you do not have a thorough medical, you could be endangering yourself and others who may have to cope with the consequences if you become ill.

If you suffer from a particular complaint such as diabetes, asthma, epilepsy or high blood pressure, or you have a bronchial disorder (such as chronic bronchitis or emphysema), heart condition, or even a recurring knee or ankle complaint, the far hills and high altitudes of the Himalaya may not be the place for you. You may still be able to safely undertake a more moderate trek at a lower altitude however, such as in the Annapurna foothills out of Pokhara or in the Vale of Kashmir.

If you do not have a regular doctor it may be prudent to seek out one who has some experience of trekking so that he or she will be more aware of what you are likely to encounter. Medical practices that cater especially to the needs of travellers can now be found in many major cities.

Your trek leader, if you are with a group, or your travelling companion should be made aware of any condition you suffer from and any medications you might be taking. It is also important to make him or her aware of any allergies to medications or foreign substances.

It is also prudent to carry a copy of your medical record with details of your blood group and allergies in case you should need emergency help. Leaving a copy of your itinerary and medical record with a close friend before you depart is also recommended.

If you normally wear glasses or contact lenses, make sure you take with you a spare pair and your prescription.

Dietary Considerations

If for medical or personal reasons you have specific dietary restrictions, you should advise airlines and the trekking company (if you are going on a group trek). In remote areas the choice of food is very limited, so you may not be able to keep strictly to your normal diet.

Dental Check-up

Dental care is not up to Western standards in any of the Himalayan countries. It is therefore wise to have a dental check-up well before you depart. In cold weather and at high altitude, fillings have a tendency to work loose. Once up there, you will be a long way from a dentist! Using an antiseptic mouthwash daily can help minimise caries or abscesses. A temporary filling material, Cavitt, might also be part of your first-aid kit, if on an expedition or trek in a remote area.

Immunisations

Virtually all remote areas in the Himalaya have primitive hygiene and sanitation. Cities and towns, too, have particularly poor public medical services. Before you go, make sure that all your immunisations are up-to-date, even though there are no official vaccination requirements for places like Nepal. Certain vaccinations, such as for cholera and yellow fever, are required by international health regulations, while preventative measures are advisable for diseases such as typhoid, tetanus, polio, hepatitis, rabies and malaria.

Your immunisation history must be recorded in a yellow passport-size booklet called International Certificates of Vaccination and should be carried with your passport when travelling between countries. These are available from some government health departments.

Cholera

You are not advised to have a cholera innoculation. The vaccine is not very effective and the chances of contracting the infection are small.

Hepatitis

Gamma-globulin injections are recommended. This serum is a collection of human blood proteins that is likely to contain antibodies against hepatitis A. Infectious hepatitis (as hepatitis A is also known), is the type caught from infected food and water or from contact with an infected person. This should not be confused with hepatitis B which is mainly transmitted by blood serum from non-sterile needles or through sexual contact (especially homosexual) with those living in highly endemic areas.

A small dose of Gamma-globulin (2 cc) given in one injection will give two months' useful protection while a larger dose (5 cc) will afford four to six months' cover. The injection should be delayed until several days before you depart, since it starts working immediately.

Malaria

When travelling through low-lying areas of the Himalaya, for example, the Terai of Nepal, you are at risk of contracting the parasitic disease malaria from anopheline mosquito bites. There is very little risk of contracting malaria anywhere in the mountains as the mosquitoes do not survive above 1000 m (3280 ft). No drug can give complete protection but several preventative measures can be taken.

The incubation period of malaria following the bite of an infected mosquito can vary from five to ten days to a year.

Early symptoms of malaria are fever with shivering, or feeling unwell, intense abdominal pain, vomiting and diarrhoea. If you suspect you might have malaria, have a blood test taken and seek medical attention urgently. Malaria can be a killer. Treatment should not be delayed if medical help is not available.

Treatment One gram of Chloroquine is the treatment, followed six hours later by 500 mg, and 500 mg on the second and third days. If you are in an area that has Chloroquinine-resistant malaria, one treatment of Fansidar can be safely taken. A new drug Lariam (Mefloquine) is also an effective treatment.

Precautions Precautions that can be taken to avoid being bitten include: wearing light-coloured clothing after dusk that covers your arms and legs; staying indoors and sleeping within insect-proof accommodation or under a mosquito net between dusk and dawn; using personal insect repellents (containing more than 20 per cent DEET) on exposed areas of the skin twice daily and using insecticide spray or coils to kill mosquitoes indoors.

The recommended prophylactic (preventative) tablets vary from doctor to doctor and country to country. Chloroquine and/or Maloprim (depending on the particular area to be visited) will give some protection against malaria. In certain parts of Asia malarial parasites are resistant to Chloroquine and so Maloprim must be taken as well. A prescription is required and the tablets should be taken once a week, two weeks before departure, throughout the period you are away and for four weeks after leaving the malarial area. The recommended dosage should not be exceeded and should not be taken on an empty stomach, but during or straight after a meal.

Meningitis

The meningococcus vaccine is recommended for travellers to Northern India, Pakistan and Nepal where recent outbreaks have occurred. Mencevax is one injection which should be administered two weeks prior to departing and it is effective for three years. People who have had their spleen surgically removed should have this vaccine as they have more chance of contracting the disease.

Polio

For people who have been immunised against polio as a child, an oral booster is recommended. This will be effective for ten years. People who have never been immunised or who have no record of it should receive three doses of polio vaccine, preferably at monthly intervals.

Rabies

There is now a vaccine which has few side-effects, that can be taken before you are exposed to rabies. This consists of three injections spread over a month. However, it is better to avoid animals as the vaccine is very expensive in Australia and difficult to obtain. It does not preclude the need for immediate treatment after being bitten by a rabid dog or monkey, but it reduces the treatment to two additional shots. If bitten, seek treatment immediately. David Shlim M.D., medical director of the Himalayan Rescue Association, does not recommend the pre-exposure treatment if you are in the Himalaya for a short period (less than a month) and mostly trekking at altitude.

Smallpox

Smallpox as a disease has been eradicated and vaccination is no longer required or recommended.

Tetanus

Most people were given this vaccine as a child. If you have not had a booster dose within the past five to ten years, it is advisable to have one before you depart.

Typhoid

Typhoid immunisation is recommended but protection also depends on exercising hygiene precautions. Two injections are given one month apart. Tablets are also available. Boosters should be given every three years.

Yellow fever

Yellow fever immunisation is not required by Himalayan countries unless you have been in equatorial Africa or America up to six days before arriving. The innoculation's immunity lasts ten years.

Tuberculosis (TB)

Tuberculosis is still rife in Asia. If you are spending time in crowded, poorly sanitised areas, have a Mantoux test before you go to establish whether or not you are resistant to TB. A B.C.G. inocculator is advisable if you are not resistant.

TB is transmitted by breathing in droplets expelled from an infected person sneezing in your presence. You are more susceptible if you are unfit and poorly nourished. Seek medical advice if you have a chronic cough and are very weak.

Common Complaints

Any overseas travel can be stressful, given the dislocation of crossing time zones, jet-lag, the fatigue of non-stop flying, not to mention the dietary impact of different food and drink.

The most common complaints you are likely to experience on the trail are blisters, stomach upsets, coughs, colds, joint strains and sunburn.

Blisters

Properly worn in, well-fitting boots, regular changes of clean socks, and the use of foot powder are the key to avoiding blisters. See the section for boots and socks under equipment, page 76, for more details. If you can feel a blister developing, stop and apply some moleskin or a sticking plaster. You need to treat such a problem immediately. Try to reduce the rubbing by adjusting your laces or changing your socks. With burst blisters, remove dead skin, apply some bland antiseptic and cover with a sterile non-adherent dressing.

Orthopaedic strains

Sore knees and twisted ankles are common trekking complaints. The best treatment is rest. If the joint is swollen, apply ice or snow and elevate. Aspirin will help reduce the inflammation.

Colds

Sore throats and colds can quickly develop into serious complaints unless they are carefully monitored. The Sherpa people of Nepal swear by copious quantities of garlic and chillies but these might not be to your taste. You are more susceptible to infections when you are run-down and not eating properly. Gargling aspirin or table salt dissolved in warm water or sucking on antiseptic lozenges will give some relief. If after three days you have no relief or are coughing up yellow sputum and have a fever, then a broad spectrum antibiotic course is recommended, especially for chronic bronchitis sufferers. It is quite common to develop a cough in the dry cold air of the mountains. Sucking on lozenges and inhaling eucalyptus vapour can bring some relief.

Stomach upsets and diarrhoea

Stomach upsets or pain can sometimes be caused by eating unusual foods. Before going trekking play it safe with the local cuisine.

'The runs', 'Delhi belly', 'Kathmandu two-step', no matter what you call it, diarrhoea is an extremely common complaint throughout Asia. Regardless of how careful you are, it usually catches up with you in the course of a long trek. Diarrhoea can occur in varying degrees of seriousness.

Infectious diarrhoea in most cases is short-lived and requires no treatment. Taking antibiotics before it is necessary is inappropriate and may even prolong the illness. The best treatment is rehydration with treated or bottled water or carbonated soft drinks. Maintaining adequate food intake is also important. No dairy products or alcohol should be consumed. Electrolytic salts such as Staminade are advisable if rehydration is necessary.

Some doctors recommend waiting two days and others four days. After that, if symptoms persist, you should then take a course of antibiotics. One dose of Bactrim DS every twelve hours for three to five days is suggested, or Augmentin (a penicillin drug) if you are allergic to Bactrim. Anyone allergic to sulphur drugs should take an alternative such as 250 mg of Tetracycline four times a day for five days. Lomotil can be useful if on a long trip. Giardia, an intestinal parasite that can cause rotten-egg stomach gas, burps and wind, vomiting and explosive runny stools is another all too common problem that strikes trekkers. This can usually be treated with 2 g (.07 oz) of Tinidazole but alcohol should never be taken at the same time, as it can cause severe headaches.

The most serious gastro-intestinal problem, amoebic dysentery, is diagnosed by loose stools which may contain blood and/or mucous, symptoms of fever, weakness and vomiting. This can also be treated with 2 g (.07 oz) of Tinidazole in a single dose repeated three days in a row, or by antibiotics such as Ampicillin.

Fever

If you contract a fever in the Himalaya and have passed through low altitude areas (less than 1000 m (3280 ft)), the possibility of having malaria should be seriously considered and if the fever persists you should seek medical advice.

Treatment for fever is focused on lowering the temperature and taking aspirin. Often the cause is a virus such as the 'flu for which there is no antibiotic treatment.

Dry skin

Dry skin and painful cracks in fingertips and lips are common. Applying moisturising (sorbolene or lanolin) cream to your hands and a chapstick to the lips helps.

Gynaecological matters

Women should be aware that high altitude can affect the menstrual cycle. This may mean missing periods and then having a very heavy flow when they start again. It is advisable to bring along extra tampons or sanitary napkins.

It is not advisable to take oral contraceptives if spending any length of time above 4000 m (13,120 ft). The pill is linked to increased incidence of blood clotting. It is best to discontinue taking it for several weeks before going to altitude.

It is worth carrying medication for monillia (thrush) and cystitis – both of which can cause discomfort. An attack of either in the midst of a trek, with no relief, could reduce your enjoyment of the trip.

Haemorrhoids

Haemorrhoids, or piles as they are commonly known, can trouble people if they are carrying heavy loads and over-breathing at high altitude. A suppository such as Anusol can give relief.

Snow blindness

Snow blindness is caused by ultraviolet rays burning the cornea of the eye. It does not usually become apparent until several hours after you have been over-exposed. Symptoms are bad headaches and a gritty feeling in the eyes. When on snow always wear dark sunglasses or goggles. Even in what might seem like cloudy or overcast conditions, it is still possible to have problems. Special glacier glasses are warranted if spending any length of time at altitude or above the snowline. If you have snow blindness, treat yourself with eye drops, cover the eyes with sterile pads, take painkillers and rest for a day.

Sunburn

At high altitudes in the Himalaya the earth's atmosphere is thinner and so more harmful ultraviolet radiation is present in the sun's rays. Prevention is the key to dealing with sunburn. In extreme sunny conditions carrying an umbrella and/or wearing a broad-brimmed hat and scarf, long trousers and a long-sleeved shirt will afford some protection.

The thin atmosphere in the Himalaya results in high levels of ultraviolet radiation. This, combined with the strong reflection from the snow makes it essential to wear good sunglasses and plenty of sun-protection cream when climbing and trekking.

Covering any exposed skin regularly with a 99 per cent protection (sun protection factor 15) sunscreen or sun barrier cream and applying a lipsalve or stick to your nose and lips is advisable.

These protective measures are particularly necessary if walking on snow when the sun is shining. The ultraviolet rays reflected from the snow can burn unusual places, such as the insides of your nostrils, beneath your chin and underneath your nose. If you become sunburnt, calamine lotion will bring some relief.

Nature's Annoyances

Fleas, lice and bedbugs are not uncommon in teahouses and local inns on trekking trails. The cheaper the accommodation and the longer the stay, the more likely you will be attacked. Fleas and lice can be minimised by washing yourself and your clothes regularly. Bedbugs can be reduced by sleeping inside your own sheet-bag or sleeping-bag, with a light on. Moving the bed away from the wall may also help.

Leeches

Leeches are a problem if trekking during and immediately after the monsoon. If you are climbing in the post-monsoon season, then you may have no choice but to make your approach during this time. Leeches lie in wait in low vegetation along paths and tracks for warm-blooded animals. They attach themselves to lower legs and ankles with amazing speed. They can work themselves through socks and the eyelets of boots, so regular inspections are advisable. If you feel unusual skin sensations anywhere on your body, stop and check.

Leeches can be removed by applying salt, alcohol, vinegar or a lighted match or cigarette. Avoid pulling them off by force as part of the head may be left in the wound, which can lead to infection. Leeches secrete an anti-coagulant. Even after they have been removed or fallen off, bleeding will continue. It is most import-ant to clean these wounds with soap and water to prevent them becoming infected.

Applying certain insect repellents to clothes and skin, or rubbing legs with tobacco juice will also keep them at bay.

Altitude or Mountain Sickness

Tilman, for all his strength and mountain-eering competence, appeared to be quite unable to acclimatise to high altitudes. It seemed that his ceiling was about 20,000 or 21,000 feet [6098 m] and on the sev-eral occasions when he went above that altitude he became ill. Though he was su-premely fit he was no better in this respect at the end of the season than he was at the beginning.

ERIC SHIPTON
Upon That Mountain, 1943

Acute Mountain Sickness (AMS) occurs if you ascend too rapidly to high altitudes. It is potentially deadly but can be easily prevented by understanding the causes, heeding any warning signs and taking the necessary precautions.

Acute Mountain Sickness is caused by the body's lack of adaptation to the de-creased amount of oxygen in the air. Though the proportion of oxygen in the air always stays the same, with an in-crease in the altitude the overall air press-ure decreases and so there is less pressure to drive the oxygen from the atmosphere into your lungs. To compensate for this your breathing and heart-rate increase. These and other factors lead to physio-logical problems where fluid accumulates in parts of the body where it should not.

You can have problems with altitude as low as 2500 m (8200 ft) but it is more likely to occur when you ascend above 3000 m (9840 ft). If you are trying to reach 5500 m (18,040 ft), you are considerably more at risk. The symptoms usually mani-fest themselves immediately, if not, within two to four days of reaching alti-tude. Anyone is potentially at risk, re-gardless of age, sex or level of fitness. In fact, the fitter you are the more suscep-tible you are. If you fly, ride or drive to a high altitude rather than walk you are more likely to have problems.

Younger people tend to be more sus-ceptible than older ones. Children are more susceptible to AMS and it is not wise to take infants to altitude as they are not always able to communicate the symptoms. Anyone who has problems breathing at sea level, has a heart con-dition, respiratory illness or is pregnant should not plan on going above 3600 m (11,808 ft). Over-exertion and dehy-dration can also contribute to AMS.

Mild AMS

In its most mild form, the symptoms are loss of appetite, headache, lassitude (weariness), swelling of the extremities, nausea, sleeplessness and irregular breathing. While these symptoms them-selves are not serious, they can quickly progress to a far more harmful condition. In the mild form they are annoying but can be coped with by taking aspirin.

Moderate AMS

As soon as these same symptoms pro-gress to where you become quite uncom-fortable, decisive measures must be taken. One or more of the following symp-toms may occur: severe headaches (es-pecially at night or in the early morning), that persist despite rest or aspirin; slurred speech; severe nausea; and vomiting. The individual may also become irritable, drowsy, attaxic (losing co-ordination), and even become comatose.

Severe AMS

With severe AMS there are the signs and symptoms of High Altitude Pulmonary Oedema and/or High Altitude Cerebral Oedema. They can occur individually or together and both can be fatal. They can either progress from mild AMS in a matter of hours or begin with very little warning.

If available, supplementary oxygen should be administered to anyone suffering from pulmonary or cerebral oedema, but ideally the sufferer should be moved to a lower altitude as quickly as possible.

High Altitude Pulmonary Oedema (HAPE)

HAPE, is a build-up of fluid in the lungs which leads to breathlessness, pink, frothy sputum cough and occasional blueness of the lips (cyanosis).

High Altitude Cerebral Oedema (HACE)

HACE is another abnormal shift of fluid, this time to the brain. HACE can come on from a worsening of AMS symptoms and can lead to unconsciousness and death in twelve hours if no treatment is given.

Treatment

There are three rules for treatment: (1) descent; (2) descent; (3) descent.

PETER HACKETT, M.D.
Mountain Sickness, 1984

Sufferers of moderate and severe AMS are no longer able to make rational decisions for themselves. Where it is available, extra oxygen should be administered and sufferers should begin to descend while they can still walk. If they cannot walk they should be carried by a yak, porter or mule. It is not advisable to wait for a helicopter, even if one has been requested. The more serious the symptoms the further the descent should be. A reduction in altitude from 300 to 500 m (984 to 1640 ft) can be enough but the main thing is to keep descending until there are signs of improvement. When the sufferer feels better he or she can ascend.

One 250 mg Acetazolamide Diamox tablet twice a day is sometimes taken as a preventative measure, or to treat mild AMS, but this practice should be treated with great caution. Common side effects of Acetazolamide are a desire to urinate, metallic taste and numbness (pins and needles). Though such medication can reduce some of the symptoms of mild AMS, some doctors believe that it may well disguise other important early warning symptoms. People who have taken diamox have still died from AMS. Sleeping pills and sedatives are also not advisable as they suppress breathing which could hasten the onset of AMS.

Dexamethazone has been used to prevent AMS and treat HAPE and HACE. This is particularly hazardous without medical supervision and is associated with a rebound of symptoms of AMS if regular treatment is interrupted.

Prevention

The best way to avoid Acute Mountain Sickness is to make a graded ascent and acclimatise properly. A recommended rate is a maximum 400 to 500m (1312 to 1640 ft) a day above 3000 m (9840 ft). If you fly to high altitude airfields, it is advisable to spend time acclimatising at that altitude on arrival, say, two to three days.

If headaches and other symptoms occur it should be assumed that it is AMS until shown otherwise. The rule for ascent is to remain at the same altitude until the symptoms go away but if they get worse then you should descend.

Keeping up your fluid intake will help to reduce the likelihood of AMS. A large urine output is part of the acclimatisation process and reduced urine flow is an early sign of AMS. The decreased humidity of cold, dry mountain air and sweating from the strenuous exercise of trekking and climbing can result in extreme dehydration. There should be a conscious effort to drink more water. Between 4 and 5 litres (8 and 10 pts) a day may be necessary but make sure the water is not contaminated.

Hygiene

Commonsense and care are the key factors in dealing with most hygiene problems in Asia or on trek. Treat all water supplies with suspicion. Do not take water into your mouth while under the shower, or clean your teeth with water from the tap. Better hotels will provide containers or thermoses of treated water for this purpose. In many towns and cities in the Himalayan region you can now purchase bottled mineral water. Bottled beer and soft drinks are usually safe to drink but be careful of *chang*, traditional Nepalese millet beer, as it is usually reconstituted with untreated water.

Avoid eating suspect food and drinking tap or stream water, wash your hands thoroughly with disinfected water before eating or handling food, keep your hands away from your mouth and treat any infections as soon as they appear. Do not trust ice cubes, unboiled milk, or icecream. Never eat salad vegetables unless you are sure they have been thoroughly washed with iodinised water.

On the trail recently cooked food and tea and coffee are generally safe, but the plates and glasses you use in teahouses are likely to have been washed in cold water. Local food is usually served on a bed of boiled rice. Eating just the food off the top of the rice is one way to minimise contaminants. Another is to use only your own utensils.

Water purification

Trekkers should get into the habit of always carrying a water bottle filled from a known safe source (or water sterilised by themselves) each day.

Boiling water for long enough at a hot enough temperature will kill most organisms that are likely to cause problems. At high altitudes water boils at a lower temperature and so it takes more time and fuel to make it safe. The best alternative is to add chemicals such as iodine, and with the right dosage this procedure can be simpler and just as effective.

Another recommended procedure is to start with 5 g (0.17 oz) of iodine crystals in a 30 ml clear glass bottle with a leak-proof inert substance (bakelite) top. Do not use plastic containers as the iodine will attack them. Top up the bottle with water, shake vigorously for sixty seconds, then let it stand for a few seconds to allow the heavy crystals to settle. The water in the bottle is now a nearly saturated iodine solution ready to treat your water supply. To a 1 litre (2 pt) waterbottle, add between 10 and 20 cc of the iodine solution (this is equivalent to between five and ten drops per litre). After twenty minutes the water will be disinfected. The effectiveness of the solution varies with the temperature and clarity of the water. At body temperature only 10 cc per litre is needed, but if it is near freezing or the water contains suspended matter, 20 cc per litre should be used. The iodine crystals should not be used directly, for too much iodine is highly poisonous. These steps can be repeated hundreds of times without replenishing the crystals. Tincture of iodine (four drops per litre of water of a 2 per cent solution of iodine left for half an hour) is also recommended. People with a thyroid dysfunction or iodine allergy should boil or use a chlorine treatment for water (such as Puritabs), although the latter is not effective against giardia.

Portable water purification filters are now also available from specialty outdoor equipment shops but these are bulky, expensive and not effective against the hepatitis virus. Micro-filters are very good at eliminating suspended particles and some organisms, but should be used in combination with iodine treatment.

Accidents

Accidents are more likely when trekking than in ordinary circumstances. Because of the rugged nature of much of the Himalayan terrain, narrow paths often hug the sides of steep rock faces and may even be built over sheer drops. When you are tired and feeling the effects of the altitude at the end of the day, your balance and judgement are not as sharp. Slipping over on an icy trail could easily result in a bad sprain or even a broken leg. Other problems can occur on crossing rivers and slippery paths in the monsoon.

Local people with medical problems seek help from expeditions and trekking parties, but there is often little that can be done except first aid.

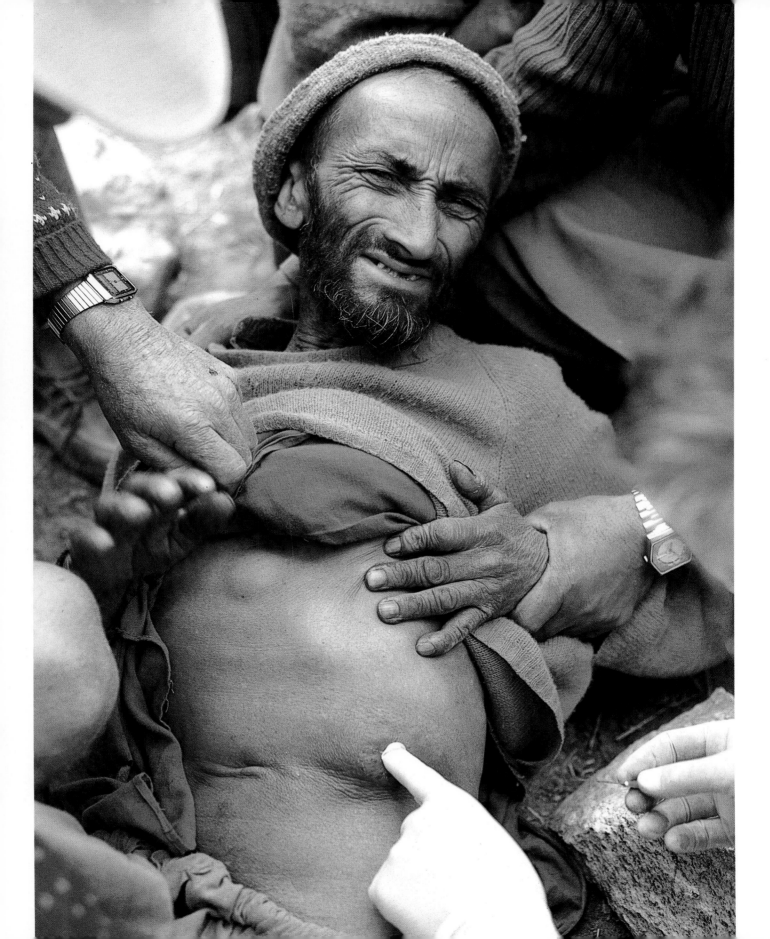

Storms in the mountains can happen at any time of the year. In winter at altitude the temperatures will be much colder and you have to be prepared for bad snowstorms. In October 1985, for example, eleven trekkers, two mountaineers, nine sherpas and twenty-two porters became trapped at 5000 m (16,400 ft) when an unseasonal storm dumped 3 m (10 ft) of snow on their camp high in the Annapurna Range. A storm of this magnitude is not uncommon, though trekking groups are rarely stranded in such a serious way.

If you are caught out in bad weather on your own and do not have the protective clothing and the experience to look after yourself, hypothermia and/or frostbite are potential problems.

Hypothermia and Frostbite

People who are older, thin and have a high metabolism (where they need to eat very regularly), are more susceptible to hypothermia. This is compounded by altitude/dehydration or any other illness. Hypothermia occurs when the body's core temperature drops. Below 32.2°C (90°F), hypothermia is very serious. Above this temperature rewarming can be achieved by removing the victim from the cause of heat loss and adding heat.

Wet, windy conditions are the most common cause of hypothermia and this condition should be suspected if someone is shivering, lethargic, stumbling, or complaining of the cold. As the condition progresses, the shivering may cease, judgement is lost and the sufferer will become oblivious to their plight. At this stage, immediate treatment is required if a fatality is to be avoided. A seriously cold individual should be treated very gently. Their rewarming should begin in circumstances that will not cause further heat loss. Seek shelter or at least get out of the wind. A tent or a teahouse is best. Heat up the surrounding air with a stove or fire, remove wet clothing and replace with dry.

Put the sufferer in one or more sleeping-bags with external sources of heat (hot water in a water bottle) applied to the armpits and groin. Putting someone else in the sleeping-bag is another possible way of adding external heat. Warm, non-alcoholic drinks can also help raise a very cold individual's core temperature.

To avoid hypothermia, keep well rugged up and wear gloves and hats if it is at all cold. Avoid getting wet through perspiration or rain or snow, or losing heat by the wind, by wearing proper shell garments (see clothing page 77).

Whereas hypothermia is the lowering of the body's core temperature, frostbite occurs when the extremities become so cold as to freeze. It is in effect a cold burn. This occurs most often to one's face, hands or feet. Frostbite should be suspected where there is a loss of feeling in the affected area after a period of feeling very cold. With exposed flesh (fingertips, cheeks or nose) the first stage appears white and waxy and later turns bluish. It is usually not possible to check one's feet as easily, especially if climbing, but if frostbite is suspected, remove boots and rewarm under a companion's armpit or next to any source of heat.

There are varying degrees of seriousness of frostbite. Rapid rewarming is the best treatment but if toes are badly frostbitten the sufferer becomes a stretcher case. If they have to walk to medical care it is better that the thawing be delayed. Massive blistering often occurs at the rewarming stage and then there is the risk of infection. Hospitalisation, or at the very least, sterile conditions, dressing and warmth, is necessary. Oxygen, if available, can be given and evacuation sought at the earliest opportunity.

Frostbite is not uncommon among Himalayan climbers but relatively unusual for trekkers. Proper use of the right clothing and care in judging the weather conditions can easily prevent problems of hypothermia and serious cold injury occurring.

Helicopter rescue in the Himalaya is carried out by the military on a user-pay basis. It is prudent to have insurance covering such a possibility as an evacuation can cost a minimum of several thousand dollars. The money often has to be paid before any flying will commence.

Simple mistakes, however, like not watching where you put your feet, or being distracted by looking through the viewfinder of a camera, are the most likely sources of danger on trek.

In a survey conducted by Dr David Schlim, results showed that the major cause of death to trekkers in Nepal in the three-year period from 1984 to 1987 was falling off the trail. In that time almost 150,000 people obtained trekking permits, over 100 were rescued by helicopter and twenty-three people died from one cause or another. The same sort of statistics probably apply to other countries of the Himalaya.

Rescue

> Pilots don't fly through clouds in the Himalaya, because the clouds have rocks in them.
>
> **ANONYMOUS**

The remoteness of most trekking areas and the minimal medical and rescue facilities in the Himalaya make even minor trauma potentially serious. If you can't walk and are not too heavy, a porter may be able to carry you. In certain areas it may be possible to ride a yak or mule.

If you are a stretcher case then it may be possible to obtain a helicopter but this option cannot be relied upon. Helicopters require favourable flying conditions, have very limited carrying capacity at altitude and generally cannot carry out rescues above 5500 m (18,040 ft). Himalayan rescue mission charges usually begin at $US800 an hour. The average helicopter rescue flight usually costs about $US1500 to $US2000 and in many cases the money must be deposited before the mission.

If you are trekking with an organised group then calling for a rescue helicopter is the responsibility of the leader, who will send a runner with a message to the nearest radio station or major centre. If you need to call a helicopter yourself, the request should be sent to your trekking agency or your embassy with details of your name, passport number, nationality, location and the injury (e.g. heat problem, frostbite, fracture). Messages can be passed via the police, military, National Park or airport radio systems depending on the nearest available. Several days may pass between sending a message and despatching a helicopter, providing there is one available.

If you are planning to trek on your own, it is a good idea to register with your country's nearest embassy, providing them with details of your rescue insurance if you have any, or to leave a sizeable sum of money with a reliable trekking agency. If you need help this information or deposit should speed it up.

The availability of aid and rescue facilities for trekkers and climbers varies greatly from country to country. Wherever there is a strong military presence, such as on the Baltoro Glacier in Pakistan, the chances of rescue are greatly improved.

Mountain rescue in the Indian Himalaya is handled by the Indian Mountaineering Foundation in conjunction with the Indian Airforce. Helicopters can take several days to arrange. The expedition or person being rescued is responsible for the cost.

In Nepal there are military and Royal Nepal Airlines helicopters that can be chartered. There is also the Himalayan Rescue Association (HRA), a voluntary non-profit organisation which was founded in 1973. The HRA maintains two trekkers' aid posts which are staffed during the pre-monsoon and post-monsoon trekking seasons by volunteer doctors. One post is at Pheriche (4200 m; 13,776 ft) on the route to Everest Base Camp in the Khumbu region and the other is at Manang (3500 m; 11,480 ft) below the Thorong La pass on the Annapurna circuit trek. The HRA maintains an office near Kathmandu Guest House in Thamel, where information on medical precautions for trekking can be obtained.

Edmund Hillary's Himalayan Trust Hospital at Kunde, near Khumjung in the Khumbu region, is another place where trekkers can seek medical help.

First-Aid

In trekking or climbing in the Himalaya you will be a long way from any reliable health care. In many situations you will have to deal with your own or others' medical problems. Besides having an appropriate first-aid kit, understanding the problems you are likely to encounter and knowing how to treat them is essential. In this book, however, it is impossible to go into these matters in any depth.

If you are trekking with an organised group, your leader or one of the staff will be carrying a comprehensive first-aid kit and they will have had some first-aid or paramedical training. There may even be a doctor or nurse in the party. You are advised to have your own first-aid kit, however, to deal with minor ailments. It is also essential for you to have a plentiful supply of any medications you use regularly or may need in the course of your time in Asia. It is also advisable to carry a prescription or written record giving generic names of these medications in case extra emergency supplies are needed. In most countries that span the Himalaya, drugs can be purchased without a prescription.

Travelling on your own is a more serious proposition and so your preparation must be more thorough. This might include learning first-aid yourself.

Medical Reading

In Stan Armington's Lonely Planet Guide, *Trekking in the Nepal Himalaya*, an excellent section on health and safety by Dr David Shlim covers diseases, treatments, a trekkers' first-aid kit and a list of medications and their use. Even if you are not going to Nepal, this section makes the book a worthwhile purchase.

Comprehensive medical handbooks for travellers are *The Travellers Health Guide*, by Dr A. C. Turner, and *Travellers Health*, by Richard Dadwood. *Medicine for Mountaineers*, by James Wilkerson, is an excellent self-help guide for groups travelling in remote areas without a medical professional in their party. It is perhaps too bulky to carry if you are on your own. *The Pocket Doctor*, by Stephen Bezruchka, and *Mountaineering First Aid and Accident Response* by the Mountaineers could more easily be carried with your first-aid kit, as could Dr Peter Hackett's *Mountain Sickness*, a lay person's guide to the prevention, recognition and treatment of Acute Mountain Sickness. One or more of these books should be studied before setting out for Asia. See Suggested Reading List.

After You Return

Some symptoms of disease, such as diarrhoea, are caused by organisms that have a long incubation period (such as intestinal parasites or worms), up to two or three weeks from the time of infection, which means you may fall ill after you return.

(Previous pages) The ascent of an 8000 m peak is the goal of many Himalayan mountaineers. From the summit of Broad Peak 8047 m (26,400 ft), Choglisa and a sea of mountains that form the Karakoram stretch to the horizon.

The more remote the destination, the more complete your first-aid kit and medical knowledge should be, especially if you are not with an organised trekking party or an expedition with a doctor.

Anti-malaria treatments should also be continued for a minimum of four weeks after you return from an 'at risk' area. If you come down with a fever within two years of your return from the Himalaya you should tell your doctor that you have recently been in a malarial country.

Health Care Checklist

Before you go

Anti-malaria tablets – begin course two weeks prior to departure
BCG
Dental check-up
Gamma-globulin injections
Mantoux test
Medical check-up
Vaccinations:
  meningitis
  polio
  tetanus booster
  typhoid
Prescriptions and additional course of usual medications.

Personal first-aid kit

Adhesive dressings or plasters
Antacid
Antibiotic broad spectrum
Anti-diarrhoea mixture
Antifungal powder for the feet
Antihistamine
Anti-itch cream
Antiseptic cream
Aspirin
Codeine
Contraceptives
Cough mixture
Crepe bandage for sprains
Decongestant
Dextrose tablets
Diamox (for altitude sickness)
Insect repellent or cream (containing 20 per cent DEET)
Iodine; Betadine
Laxative
Lipsalve
Mercurichrome
Moleskin (for blisters)
Nasal spray or drops
Opthalmic ointment
Pessaries (e.g. for thrush)
Soluble aspirin or paracetamol
Sunscreen
Tampons
Throat lozenges
Tinidazole (Fasigym) for giardia
Toilet paper
Vitamin tablets
Water purification tablets or iodine crystals

CLOTHING AND EQUIPMENT

Having proper clothing for a visit to the Himalaya can make all the difference between an enjoyable trip and a disastrous one. Depending on the time of year you go and the destination, temperatures can range from 40°C (104°F) during the day to –10°C (23°F) the same night and, if you are caught in a blizzard on a high altitude trek it may not rise above zero all day. A choking duststorm or monsoon rains can further tax your humour and wardrobe.

Preparation involves spending some time assembling a basic trek clothing kit. Good gear is expensive, but if it is looked after well, it will last for years. It should be looked upon as an investment in your holiday and, for more serious circumstances, cheap life insurance.

Where to Buy?

It is best to arrive in the Himalaya fully prepared for what you plan to undertake. If you buy at home you have the advantage of being able to shop around at leisure and select each item carefully. Specialty outdoor equipment stores in Western cities are the best place to purchase goods as they usually have experienced staff who can advise you on what you will need for a particular region or season. Army disposal stores are another possible source but the quality of the gear and advice is less reliable.

Getting properly outfitted all at once can be a very expensive exercise and much of the gear is so specialised that you may not have any further use for it once you return. Do not put your trip at risk, however, for the sake of a few dollars. Ask friends and family to see what you can borrow before you spend large sums of money. Some items you may be able to rent in the country of your destination or an outfitter could supply them if you are going on an organised trip. If you already have your own first-class gear do not leave it behind on the assumption that it will be supplied.

As a rule, good equipment and clothing is not available in Himalayan countries. Nepal is the one exception, however, where you could expect to be outfitted with Western gear. Second-hand clothing can be found in the trekking shops in the Thamel district of Kathmandu. Expedition equipment often ends up here only hours after it has been issued to local staff. Bargains can be found at the end of the season when everyone is heading home but when the demand is high, do not be surprised if shopkeepers quote you prices from the latest American mail order catalogue.

Hiring

While it is better not to take the risk of relying on buying basic gear in Nepal or any other country, many of the more specialised items, such as down jackets or sleeping bags, can be hired from the trek outfitters if sufficient notice is given. In Kathmandu shops will also hire out gear.

What to Buy?

Trekking is walking day after day from four to six hours for anything up to a month. Your equipment must be well-made, well-fitting and appropriate for the particular journey. The more serious the trip or climb, the more important the gear becomes. It is also most important to have the right equipment for a trek. Plastic double boots, for example, are quite unnecessary for the Annapurna sanctuary trek but they could be a toe-saving investment for an ascent of Island Peak.

If you are trekking on your own or with friends and carrying everything yourself, the sort of gear you need is the same as if you were bushwalking or backpacking at home.

The following basic checklist covers virtually everything you could possibly want for a safe and enjoyable trek under normal conditions. Certain items, however, are critical and so more detail is included to guide you in your decisions.

Footwear

Boots Starting from the feet up, it is essential to have well-fitting, waterproof,

lightweight walking boots or shoes that do not give you blisters. Buy them so that you can comfortably wear at least a pair of thin socks and one pair of thick socks. It is better to have them slightly big than too tight. Purchase boots well before your departure so that you can wear them in on your training walks. If buying plastic boots remember that, unlike leather, they have no 'give'. Ski shops sometimes have the equipment and experience to expand

The equipment considered necessary by today's Himalayan mountaineer is extensive and costly. Lightweight and efficient clothing and technical gear enables small teams to climb extreme altitudes quickly.

Well-fitting, sturdy footwear is essential for trekking. Lightweight waterproof boots (as seen here on a Nepali boy) are ideal.

the shell of plastic climbing or trekking boots where you have pressure points but this is a job that has to be organised well in advance in case several visits are necessary to get the right fit.

Running shoes or sneakers are quite suitable for some trails and to wear at camp at the end of the day. Even on the least serious treks this style of footwear is inadequate if you are caught in a storm.

Gaiters Snow gaiters, detachable calf-length canvas or nylon protective covers, are an extra safety measure. Supergaiters – extra long gaiters that fit snugly over the whole of the boot upper and seal the boot with a tight-fitting rubber strip – are an advantage for deep snow and enable a lower-cut shoe to be worn.

Socks Caring for your feet should include having several changes of thick and thin socks and being prepared to rinse them regularly. Thin polypropylene liner socks next to the skin draw away moisture and the polypropylene's slick fibres reduce the friction which causes blisters. A blend of nylon and wool is the best combination for thicker outer socks. For really cold conditions (below –10°C (23°F)) mountaineers sometimes add a vapour barrier sock which is nothing more than a thin, proofed, ripstop nylon liner worn between the inner and outer sock. An anti-perspirant powder applied to your feet each morning helps to reduce the clammy feeling from the moisture build-up.

Insulation

Freezing temperatures may be tolerable during a quick dash somewhere, but getting to the next campsite may require more time out in weather which could easily be life-threatening.

The secret to staying warm all day and yet still being able to control your temperature when working hard is to wear a series of layers rather than one heavy garment. Warmth is generated by your body. The job of good clothing is to prevent this heat from escaping and to keep you dry.

Underwear The most suitable layer closest to the skin is underwear that will draw away any moisture and minimise the clammy feeling when you sweat. A long-sleeved polo-neck top and a short-sleeved T-shirt together with a pair of longjohns in a thermal material and several pairs of your preferred underpants should be more than adequate for most treks or climbs. Over the years wool, silk, polypropylene and chlorofibre have been popular as a thermal layer but all these materials have certain shortcomings. Wool absorbs moisture; polypropylene must be washed regularly because it quickly becomes 'high' and loses its drawing properties; silk is very expensive and does not hold its shape; and clorofibre is difficult to launder.

New-generation materials such as capilene polyester or 'Drytech' seem to overcome these problems, but at a price.

Warm wear For the next layer, garments with a fur-like finish trap more air than just a single layer of cloth. This is important as the most effective insulation is trapped air. A woollen shirt or jumper has been the trusted second layer for generations of climbers and trekkers. Wool, however, absorbs moisture, becomes very heavy and takes a long time to dry. It took Norwegian fishermen to find an alternative and they and mountaineers have been using a synthetic wool-like fabric called 'fibre-pile' for over a decade. Today's most advanced synthetic fabric, Polarplus, offers the most in warmth for weight, fast drying, and hardwearing features, but the original Helly-Hansen nylon fibre-pile is also still hard to beat.

A worthwhile extra layer for any trek is a down or fibre-pile vest but if going to altitude, say above 4000 m (12,000 ft), a down or synthetic padded jacket is recommended. Down is still the warmest form of insulation for a given weight but has to be kept dry. Qualofill or dacron will not compress as readily as down but will retain insulating properties even if damp.

Trousers and skirts A pair of windproof trousers or a long skirt for women are best for walking in. Tracksuit bottoms are satisfactory at low altitude but above 4000 m fibre-pile pants, woollen breeches or ski warm-up trousers are recommended. Tight jeans are not at all warm if they get wet.

Shell garments

The outer layer of your clothing protection should consist of a windproof, waterproof parka (with a hood) reaching past the waist, plus a pair of overtrousers or bib-and-brace waterproof overalls.

Waterproof parkas When you are exercising you generate a certain amount of moisture from your skin. There are several waterproof fabrics that can also breathe. The best-known of these is Gore-tex. No garment, however, will be impregnable in all circumstances. Make sure that any breathing-fabric garment you buy has seams that have been covered by a waterproof tape. More traditional materials often represent better value for money and still give good protection. Oiled japara, PVC proofed nylon, and neoprene are all waterproof while 60/40 cloth (60% nylon, 40% cotton) is only windproof and showerproof.

Overtrousers Waterproof overtrousers or bib-and-brace overalls are essential if you have to travel in bad weather. Protection from a chilling wind is as crucial as staying dry. Overtrousers that have full-length zippers up the outside of each leg are preferable as they can be put on and taken off without removing your trousers and boots. Rainchaps are good if used in conjunction with a poncho or a jacket that comes down well below your waist.

Hand protection

A system of insulating layers works best for your hands, just as it does for the rest of your body. A light pair of silk or polypropylene gloves next to the skin allow you to manipulate fine controls such as those on cameras and videos without touching bare metal. In very cold tem-

peratures direct contact can result in a cold burn. For the next layer, wear a pair of thick woollen gloves or mittens large enough to go over the thinner liner gloves. If the mittens or gloves have a loop of thin elastic shock cord attached at the open end, they can dangle from the wrist when you need to wear just the liners. If it is snowing or very windy, you should wear a pair of waterproof mittens on top.

Headwear

In cold weather a woollen beanie or fibre-pile lined waterproof hat is essential as heat is quickly lost from the head and neck. A silk, woollen or pile balaclava is also a good investment.

In hotter conditions, a sunhat with a broad brim is equally important, to prevent heatstroke and sunburn. A cotton scarf or large handkerchief worn over the mouth and nose like a cowboy mask can give excellent protection from sunburn when walking in snow in bright conditions.

Accessories

An original Swiss Army knife is a useful accessory. Beware of imitations and choose one that has a lanyard attachment

(Above) The gentleman Himalayan climber of the 1920s, such as George Ingle Finch (shown here), wore a hat, tweed jacket, woollen sweater, socks and hobnail boots.

(Right) Whenever there is the likelihood of travelling over snow or on a glacier everyone must wear dark sunglasses to avoid snowblindness.

(Below) Plastic garbage bags are useful for waterproofing, but are no substitute for proper rainwear.

to help prevent theft or loss, and scissors, can-opener and screwdriver. Be careful not to carry such a knife in your hand luggage when flying.

Dark sunglasses, ski goggles, or special glacier glasses with leather sideflaps are necessary if there is any likelihood of spending time above the snowline. In bad weather goggles give added protection. If you wear prescription glasses, make sure the goggles will fit over the top of them.

Packs

Kitbags If trekking with porters or ponies the bulk of your gear should be carried in a sturdy kitbag that can be padlocked. Army, navy or airforce top-loading kitbags or duffels are ideal. Heavy-duty canvas or cordura nylon is the best material for kitbags.

On the backs of ponies and porters, kitbags come in for a great deal of punishment. Your closed cell sleeping mat is best arranged as a lining in the kitbag with your sleeping-bag and clothing then crammed inside this.

Rucksacks If you are trekking on your own a regular backpack or rucksack will usually be your main means of carrying all your possessions. A well-made, single-compartment, top-loading sack with a drawstring throat and internal frame is failsafe. Front-loading or multi-compartment travel packs with zipper openings are problems if the zipper gives up. The size of the pack depends on how large you are and how much you can carry. Expedition-style packs usually have a 60 to 80-litre capacity but with compression straps on either side the size of the pack can be tailored to suit the load. If you are going for a long time a porter can carry the rucksack fully extended while you carry just your day-pack. It is best to carry all your possessions inside your pack as this reduces the temptation for theft and the likelihood of something falling off unnoticed.

Two-person tents and foam mats are usually provided on organised treks. Campsites are set up, where possible, by the sherpas and staff near a village so the porters can find shelter and food.

Liner bags Large plastic or proofed nylon liner bags are also good protection against rain or stream crossings. These are used inside your rucksack or kitbag to add an extra layer of protection. There is nothing worse at the end of the day than finding you have a damp sleeping-bag. Large garbage bags can be used but these are not very durable, so take spares.

Day-packs A well-made day-pack with padded shoulder straps, padded back and waist belt is advisable, and a 30 to 40-litre capacity should be more than adequate to carry your waterproofs, waterbottle, camera, jacket or jumper and toiletries. A pack this size can also be used as hand baggage for air travel.

Sleeping gear

The choice of sleeping-bag and mat depends on personal preference and where you are intending to trek or climb. Some people are 'warm sleepers' and can be perfectly comfortable in a three-season bag (the one manufacturers recommend for spring, summer and autumn) even in the snow. Others might need to wear long underwear in an expedition sleeping-bag (about the warmest type made) under the same conditions.

The warmth of a sleeping-bag can be increased by the use of an inner sheet. Silk mummy-shaped sheets are popular with backpackers, but where weight is not so much of a consideration a cotton liner is just as good.

For an organised trek the agency usually provides mats and sleeping-bags but these can vary from just adequate to excellent. If you already have a good sleeping-bag, take it with you to avoid disappointment or discomfort.

Sleeping-bags If you decide to buy a sleeping-bag, check the conditions you might face with someone who has been to the area you are visiting. The sales staff of specialist stores may also be able to help.

When making a purchase, consider: type, quality and quantity of insulation (fill), shape, construction, fabric and additional features such as zips, draught tubes, hoods and draught collars.

High-grade down bags will be warmer for a given weight of insulation, last longer and cost more than a synthetic (dacron or Quollofil) bag. The latter, however, is less affected by the damp, a factor only to be considered if rafting. The quality of the down fill is classified by its loft (the volume occupied by a given weight of uncompressed down).

Sleeping-bags are usually mummy-shaped, rectangular or somewhere in between. With an integral hood the former is usually the warmer design but this style can be rather claustrophobic.

Sleeping-bags come with and without a side zip. Zippers add weight but they make a bag easier to get into and out of, are useful for temperature control and, with the right combination, it is possible to join two sleeping-bags together. A full-length zip should be covered by a draught tube to reduce the movement of cold air.

The warmer lightweight sleeping-bags have box-wall construction rather than sewn-through construction and are made from a high thread count, ripstop nylon that does not leak its down.

If you are trekking to altitude in the Himalaya and plan on camping, you could experience temperatures as low as $-10°C$ ($23°F$) or colder. Even expedition-rated sleeping-bags may be chilly if you are planning to climb in the Himalaya. This means a four or five-season bag should be considered. In the foothills, however, a three-season bag should be adequate.

Sleeping-mats Though closed cell foam sleeping-mats (such as Karrimats) are produced in a variety of lengths and thicknesses, they provide little cushioning. They are designed mainly to insulate you from the cold coming up from below. If your kit is being carried by a porter, weight is less of a consideration. In these circumstances it is better to have one that is full length, especially if you are to sleep on the snow. For high altitude climbing the thickest five-season model (good for the whole year plus snow conditions) may only just be adequate. Open cell foam mats are more comfortable than closed cell, but they are bulky and absorb moisture.

If you are not accustomed to sleeping on the ground or find it difficult, a lightweight air mattress may be preferable. Ordinary airbeds such as lilos are too heavy and do not give much insulation because the air inside is free to circulate. There are now several brands and models of self-inflating lightweight air mattress available, the Therm-a-rest being the most well-known. Whatever type you have, you must treat it with care as the mattresses are easily punctured. Don't forget to take a repair kit.

Preparation and experience are the key elements to ensuring a safe and comfortable trip. It is not enough to have all the right gear without knowing when and how to use it. If you are not an experienced outdoor person, it is safer to go with someone who is, or with an organisation.

Clothing and Equipment Checklists

Basic Trekking Kit

Day-pack
Duffel/kitbag or
  rucksack
Inner sheet
Sleeping-bag
Sleeping-mat/
  Thermorest
Beanie or warm hat
Cotton T-shirts – 2-3
Gloves
Lightweight walking
  boots
Mittens – woollen or
  fibre-pile
Over-gloves –
  waterproof
Over-trousers
Shorts
Skirt/culottes (for
  women)
Sneakers/running
  shoes
Socks – 4 pairs
Sunhat with
  brim/eyeshade
Swimming costume

Tracksuit (for sleeping)
Trousers – lightweight,
  loose-fitting
Underwear – 3-4
  changes
Warm sweater
Waterproof jacket with
  hood – thigh length
Wool shirt or fibre-pile/
  Polarplus jacket
Clothes washing kit
Handkerchiefs
Insect repellent
Personal first-aid kit
  (see health list)
Plastic bags – large and
  small
Plastic mug
Screwcap 1-litre (2 pt)
  waterbottle
Sewing and repair kit
Toilet paper
Toiletries
Torch – spare batteries
Towel (small)
Watch

Optional

Alarm clock
Binoculars
Books
Boot cleaning and
  waterproofing gear
Camera gear (see
  photography list)
Candle and matches
Cassette player and
  tapes
5 to 10 m (16 to 32 ft)
cord – of thin nylon

Compass
Inner-soles
Journal/diary
Maps
Musical instrument
Neck wallet or money
  belt
Stuff bags
Swiss Army pocketknife
Thongs/sandals
Umbrella

Camping Kit

Eating utensils
Stove pots

Tent

High-altitude/Winter Kit

(SUPPLEMENTARY TO THE
BASIC TREKKING KIT)

Balaclava
Dachstein mittens
Glacier glasses
Insulated parka – down
  or dacron
Long underwear –
  polypropylene

Snow gaiters –
  calf-length
Stout walking boots
Tent booties
Thick socks – 2 pairs
Woollen trousers

CLIMBING GEAR

Personal Kit

(SUPPLEMENTARY TO THE ABOVE KITS)

Belay/abseil device
Bivi bag
Carabiners –
  screwgate and plain
Climbing pack
Crampon protectors
Crampons
Double boots
Duvet
Extra sleeping mat
Harness

Head-torch
Helmet
Ice-axe
Inner gloves – 2 pairs
Insulated over-trousers
  – down/dacron
Prussic loops
Salopets
Snow goggles
Supergaiters

Optional

Altimeter
Ascenders
Avalanches
  transceivers
Down vest
Neoprene over-boots

North-wall hammer
Rescue pulley
Spare snow glasses
Thermometer
Thermos flask
Wind suit

Group Equipment

Bivi stove/s
Climbing rope/s
Cook pots
Deadmen
Fixed ropes
Friends
Ice screws
Jam nuts

Marker wands
Mountain tent/s
Radios – Government
  permission required
Rock pegs
Snow shovel
Snow stakes

Base Camp

Cook tent
First-aid kit
Pressure lantern

Repair kit
Stools
Storage tent – tarp

If climbing alpine-style everything must be lightweight but extremely sturdy to be able to withstand harsh and often primitive living conditions.

CULTURAL CONSIDERATIONS

Every Himalayan country is based on a traditional society which is governed by various ethical, spiritual and religious beliefs, customs and social mores. In India the caste system, dating back hundreds of years, is another governing factor.

When you visit the Himalaya for the first time much of what you see and experience will not always make sense. As a guest, however, you should try to be sensitive to local ways and values.

Some beliefs and customs are similar throughout Asia, and others are unique to a particular religion (be it Hinduism, Buddhism or Islam) or country. A brief survey of some of these will help avoid unintentionally offending local ways.

What to Wear

Generally speaking, people in Asia are very modest. Nudity is not acceptable in many countries and you should always wear some clothing when swimming. In most cities women should not wear short pants or have bare shoulders or heads in temples and shrines.

Photography

Unless you want a picture of a *saddu* or holyman who is traditionally paid for blessings, you should try to avoid paying for photographs. Be polite and ask for permission if taking close-ups and likewise always seek permission before photographing temples, *stupas* or monuments.

Tipping

Tips, gratuities, bribes or bakshish, no matter what you call them, are the same the world over. In the Himalaya, it is no different. If you have had particularly good service from trekking staff, a guide or driver, some form of additional payment should be considered. Wages are usually very low in these countries and what is a small amount to you could well be a handsome tip to a local.

On organised group treks the tradition is to contribute whatever amount you wish to a kitty which is handed over to the sirdar at the end of the trek. He in turn divides the amount, pro rata, among the staff according to their own system. Gifts of clothes and gear no longer wanted are also usually handled in this manner but you may prefer to give an item directly to an individual who has helped you in a specific way. The sirdar should always be consulted if there is any doubt about the protocol. On a group trek porters are not usually tipped in cash but cast-off clothing is usually welcome.

Giving away pens, balloons, sweets or similar Western trinkets indiscriminately encourages begging and the 'something for nothing' mentality amongst children and some adults. Such gifts are more appropriate if you have established a rapport with an individual over the course of hours or days.

There are ways of breaking the ice other than expensive handouts. Becoming involved in a ball game, playing cards or trying your hand at shuffleboard are possible conversation starters. Giving some pictures to a schoolteacher might be appropriate after a visit to a village school.

Bartering

There is often no fixed price for goods or services in countries spanning the Himalaya. This is especially so when buying in a market from a souvenir stall or paying for a taxi or *shikara*. Do not feel as if everyone is trying to rip you off. It is just the way business is transacted in this part of the world. Ask around or listen in to determine what the going rate is for a similar item or service. If you can enter into the spirit of haggling, it can be quite enjoyable. Never accept the first price offered. Your counterbid could start somewhere around 20 to 30 per cent of what you were first quoted. The final deal is often struck at 40 to 50 per cent of the first offer. If you are not getting much response starting at a very low bid, try walking away and see what response this brings.

If taking a taxi, shikara, ponyman or porter, always establish the price before you take anyone on or step into the cab. With a porter or ponyman establish whether food and accommodation is included, and the terms of payment.

Religion

Hinduism

There are several specific do's and don'ts that should be taken into account when travelling amongst Hindu people.

Avoid wearing or carrying anything made of leather into a Hindu temple. Beef is prohibited amongst Hindus and no female animal is killed for food. Most Hindus cannot eat food touched by a foreigner and no food or offering should be touched on its way to a shrine.

In India and Nepal always walk around a person – do not step over them. Do not offer anything with the left hand. This is traditionally reserved for cleaning oneself after going to the toilet. The right hand should be used to receive or give anything and if using your fingers to eat.

Buddhism

Always remove your shoes before entering a Buddhist *gompa* (shrine). Never touch a Buddhist child on the head or point the soles of your feet at a Buddhist.

Always walk clockwise around a Buddhist temple, shrine, *chorten* or *mani* wall. If passing a mani on the trail, keep it on your right. Prayer wheels should always be spun clockwise.

It is sacrilegious to remove any of the carved stones from mani walls. The inscriptions read 'Om mani padme hum', the Buddhist mantra which translates as 'The jewel in the flower of the lotus'.

Respect should also be shown to prayer flags no matter how tattered they seem.

Islam

Remove your shoes when entering a mosque. In Islamic countries, women should dress modestly in long-sleeved tops and long trousers or skirts. In mosques, women should also have their heads covered as well as their shoulders. In some shrines women are not allowed inside the inner sanctum.

Pakistani women seldom travel alone and it is offensive to Pakistani males to see European women travelling unaccompanied. There is virtually no open fraternisation between Pakistani men and women but men often hold each others' hands out of friendship and nothing more.

During the month of Ramadan, except at railway station restaurants, teashops and food stalls are closed between dawn and dusk. Once the sun sets, however, it is business as usual.

National Differences

India

Indians use the opposite head movements to Europeans in response to questions. For example, the head being waved from side to side means yes.

The Nepalese greeting *namaste* with hands clasped in front of your chest is also an Indian greeting. In Indian cities, shaking hands is accepted between males but Indian women do not shake hands. There is also much less open fraternisation between males and females.

Shoes should always be removed before entering houses and you should seek permission before taking photographs.

Pakistan

Because Pakistan is an Islamic state, alcohol is not freely available. To buy a

Travelling Sadhus making pilgrimages to many of the sacred shrines and holy sites in the Himalaya are a common sight in places such as Kathmandu.

drink in Pakistan you need to have a liquor licence and to get this you also have to have a tourist certificate. These are available from the Excise and Tax Office or from some larger hotels authorised to sell alcohol to non-Muslim residents.

Nepal

A Nepalese man dressed all in white should not be touched as he has had a death in his family and is considered contaminated. Most Nepalese remove their shoes before entering a house or a room. While this is not always practical every time you enter a village house when wearing heavy boots, it should be observed in the cooking and eating areas. It is also not polite to enter these areas without being invited. Do not stand in front of a Nepalese who is squatting on the ground eating. If you need to talk to him, squat by his side.

Any food or utensil touched by a used knife, spoon or fingers is considered contaminated. It would humiliate a Nepalese if such food were offered to him. No used dish should be used again without it being properly washed.

It is not considered polite to open a gift in the presence of the donor.

The most common greeting in Nepal is *namaste* or *namaskar* which is said with the palms of both hands pressed together in front of your chest. The translation from Sanskrit is 'I bow to the God in you'.

It is common to show respect to an older person by addressing them either as *daju* or *didi*.

Being sensitive to the unique aspects of other cultures can be achieved by following the guidelines above. It is far more valuable, however, to learn some background to the culture and religion of each country so that these guidelines can be seen in context. The enormous diversity of culture in the region is partly a function of the complex physical geography. These aspects, including the natural history of the Himalaya, will be dealt with next.

PART THREE

Introduction to the Himalayan Region

A basic understanding of the geography, natural history, politics, culture and religions of the Himalaya is helpful when trying to choose where and when to go. Once you have decided on a general area, researching the topography and weather of your specific destination will help you to be better prepared. On the trail, this background knowledge and an understanding of the culture will further help you to appreciate the countryside.

PHYSICAL GEOGRAPHY

The Himalaya is the most significant mountain chain on earth. It features the highest summits in the world, divides continents and dramatically affects the earth's weather patterns. The name Himalaya cames from the Sanskrit words *hima* (snow) and *alaya* (abode). The word Himalaya is often spoken and spelt as 'Himalayas'. Himalaya is plural and the 's' is therefore incorrect.

Though interpretations of boundaries vary, in its broadest sense the Himalaya stretches 2,500 km (1,553 miles) across Asia, from west of the Indus River in the

The Himalayas are young mountains, jagged forms not yet ground smooth by wind and rain. From the torpid plains of India they appear as white ghosts vibrating in the sun, a vague presence along the northern horizon that blends with the clouds, visible for a moment then lost again in the confusion of ice and vapour.

EDWARD W. CRONIN JR
The Arun, 1979

west, to the Brahmaputra River in the south-east. From south to north the Himalaya varies in width from 160 km (99 miles) to 320 km (199 miles).

Divisions

There are many divisions of this extensive chain of mountains and many separate names for the distinctive sections, but for the sake of simplicity, the entire length will be referred to in this book as the Greater Himalaya which expands the terminology adopted by Kenneth Mason in his definitive history of Himalayan exploration and mountaineering, *Abode of the Snow*. The Greater Himalaya in this definition embraces (from west to east) the Punjab Himalaya; the Karakoram; the Kumaun Himalaya; the Nepal Himalaya;

(Above) Vegetation in alpine regions of the Himalaya has not only to contend with a very short growing season and extreme weather conditions, but also the pressure of an ever-increasing demand for firewood and timber for building materials.

(Right) The geography of the Himalaya varies enormously from east to west and south to north. Ladakh in the Indian Himalaya, is in a rain shadow area and the few settlements such as Leh, in the desert mountains, exist beside streams fed from high snowfields.

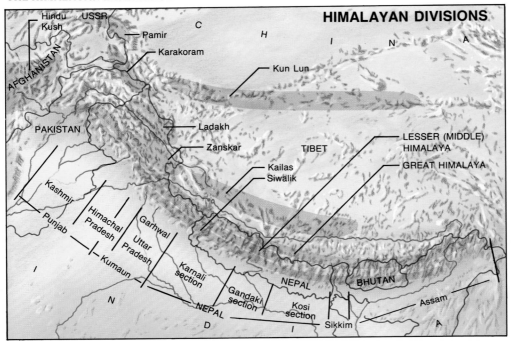

HIMALAYAN DIVISIONS

(Previous pages) The world's largest rivers of ice outside the polar regions, occur in the Karakoram. The Goodwin-Austen Glacier draws much of its supply of ice from K2, the second highest mountain in the world, and exhibits all the classic moraine features as seen here from the slopes of Broad Peak.

the Sikkim Himalaya and the Assam Himalaya. Geographers have further divided the Nepal Himalaya into three separate sections: the Karnali section; the Gandakhi section; and the Kosi section. These sections are named after the major rivers that drain them. Within this overall scheme each group of mountains is known as a *himal* and is sometimes named after one of its major peaks — Dhaulagiri Himal, for example.

As with any attempt to define there are always exceptions to the rule. While the Karakoram does not strictly follow the west to east pattern as it is to the north of the Punjab Himalaya and is more correctly known as a Trans-Himalayan range, for the sake of convenience, it is included as part of the Greater Himalaya.

Another exception to the west of the Punjab Himalaya is the Hindu Kush which merges at its eastern end with the Karakoram. While this is outside Mason's definition of the Great Himalaya it is still part of the almost continuous string of Asian mountains. The Hindu Kush lies astride the border between Pakistan and Afghanistan but the greater number of peaks are in the Chitral region of Pakistan. The highest peak in the Hindu Kush is Tirich Mir, 7349 m

(24,105 ft). The southern limit of this region is known as Nuristan, 'The Land of Light', made famous by Eric Newby in his classic expedition account, *A Short Walk in the Hindu Kush*. Because of the war in Afghanistan most of the Hindu Kush has been inaccessible to climbers, but trekking is still possible in the Chitral.

Aerial View

Seen from above, the Greater Himalaya resembles a giant crescent moon, 320 km (199 miles) at the widest point with a southerly extension in the west. Within this shape the detailed alignment consists of roughly parallel ranges running east-west. From south to north the pattern of the Himalaya is of three parallel ranges: the low hills of the Outer Himalaya rising out of the Indian Plain; the Middle or Lesser Himalaya; and the Inner Himalaya.

The Gangetic Plain, known as the Terai, is characterised by tall forests of deciduous sal and kapok trees and very hot weather in the summer months. The first relief of the Outer Himalaya is represented in India by the Siwalik Hills and in Nepal by the Churia Hills which rise abruptly to elevations from 750 to 1500 m (2460 to 4920 ft). For much of their length these hills are separated from the main

Himalaya by elongated duns — flat valleys, such as India's Vale of Kashmir and Nepal's well-known Chitwan Valley.

The middle Himalaya extends from Kashmir to Bhutan. In Nepal, these broken and undulating hills, known as the Pahar or Central Hills, vary between 600 and 2000 m (1968 and 6560 ft). This zone once supported extensive forests until woodcutters decimated them. The rock type is predominantly limestone.

The Inner Himalaya is distinguished by cloud-scraping peaks which are seldom less than 6000 m (19,680 ft). The highest summit is Mount Everest, 8848 m (29,021 ft), which forms the border between Nepal and Tibet. By traditional geographic conventions there are fourteen peaks above 8000 m (26,240 ft).

Formation

The structure of the Himalaya is the result of how it was, and is still, being formed. Between 70 and 80 million years old, the Himalaya is extremely young and geologically active. Geologists claim the mountains are growing at a rate of 15 cm (6 in) a year as the Indian plate moves northward and is forced under the Eurasian plate. These processes (plate tectonics) regularly subject the region to earthquakes (see diagram below). In 1934, 10,000 people were killed in a major earthquake in Nepal. This collision of continents is squeezing up sedimentary rocks that were once below the sea, and the resulting mountains now tower up to 8848 m (29,021 ft).

Glaciation

These great elevations set in motion active processes that shape the mountains and wear them down. Glaciers, avalanches, rockfalls and frost sculpture this landscape in far more dramatic and visible ways than in less rugged areas.

Snowclad peaks, visible from so many vantage points and trails, are among the main attractions of the region. The permanent snowline varies according to the summer temperatures, the amount of snowfall and the aspect. For example, the year-round snow line may be 750 m to 1000 m (2460 ft to 3280 ft) higher on a north-facing than a south-facing one.

This snow collects on the slopes and in high basins (*neve* fields) and as it is com-

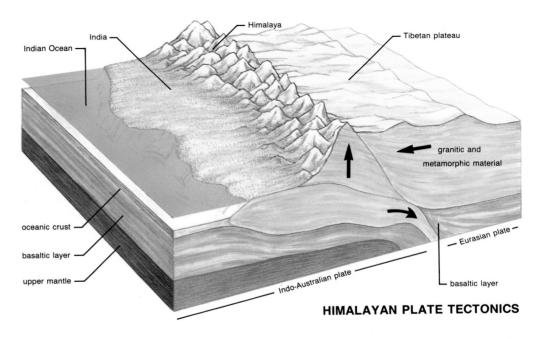

HIMALAYAN PLATE TECTONICS

pressed it transforms into ice. The ice flows down the slope under the force of gravity and the collecting basins merge to form glaciers, giant rivers of ice. Glaciers large and small occur throughout the Greater Himalaya. Glaciers flow down to lower and warmer altitudes where they melt. In the lower reaches they are often completely covered by moraine (rock and gravel). The Baltoro Glacier in the Karakoram is one of the most spectacular examples and, like so many of its counterparts, it is also a major access route to the inner mountains for trekkers and climbers. Glacier travel can be fraught with dangers in the higher neve areas because of hidden crevasses.

Rivers

Throughout the Himalaya the erosive power of water is evident but the overall Himalayan drainage pattern does not fit the classic form where the watershed lies along the mountain divide. This is because the rivers were there long before the mountains. The three main river systems of the Himalaya — the Indus, the Tsangpo (Brahmaputra) and the Sutljie — start north of the main mountain divide but find their way through massive gorges. The major river draining the southern side of Himalaya is India's most sacred, the Ganges. Deep gorges are also a feature of the headwaters of the Ganges's tributaries. The Kali Gandakhi has the greatest elevation difference of anywhere on earth. From river bed to mountain summit it is 5500 m (18,040 ft).

Throughout the Himalaya the rivers are important thoroughfares and trading routes, as are the numerous high passes that connect valley systems and cross entire mountain ranges. The Kali Gandakhi is an example of the river valley trading-route while the Nangpa La Pass was the route which the Sherpas took to cross back and forth from the Khumbu to Tibet .

While physical features of the Himalaya are vast and complex, they are relatively static. As better maps are made and more detailed accounts of exploration are written, people will be able to travel more assuredly from one place to another. The same can never be said for the weather, especially since global weather patterns seem to be shifting, bringing unseasonal storms and record rainfalls. A basic understanding of the seasons and probable weather patterns is essential, however, in order to select the best time of the year to visit a particular region.

CLIMATE AND SEASONS

The great height and sweep of the Himalaya governs the climate of the entire region and adjacent countries. There is always some part of the Himalaya that is 'in season' for the visitor.

Generally, the southern and eastern flanks of the Himalaya are influenced by heavy monsoon rains which greatly restrict travel and transportation in the wet and result in a great variety of luxuriant natural vegetation and farming possibilities. North and west the country is much drier as it is in a rain shadow.

Monsoon

The word 'monsoon' is derived from the Arabic *mausim* meaning 'season'. The monsoon is, in essence, a very large cycle of air that is energised by temperature differences between the land and the sea. The monsoon that affects the Himalaya is a rain-bearing wind that originates in the Indian ocean and flows northward in summer. As the season advances it gradually progresses westward. In Sikkim the monsoon usually arrives in early June. Nepal receives the rains slightly later and by the beginning of July the monsoon appears in Kashmir. The monsoon is usually over by the end of

The Eastern Himalaya, particularly Bhutan, Sikkim, and Nepal, are subject to heavy monsoon rains which call a halt to most trekking. Climbing expeditions however, often make their approach in the wet season to be acclimatised when the weather improves. The locals, such as these Nepali boys, are well-adapted to the weather.

September, but in some years a late monsoon may run into early October. It also takes some time for the ground to dry out, so reliable weather and good trail conditions do not usually occur before the second week in October.

Monsoon rains are not continual, but precipitation can usually be anticipated for several hours a day during September. There may even be the occasional fine day. At lower altitudes it can be very hot and humid. The vegetation becomes luxuriant during this time so that trails become overgrown and leeches become a regular annoyance. It is often very muddy and slippery underfoot. Good views are obscured by clouds most of the time. Many expeditions contemplating a climb in the post-monsoon season trek to the base of their mountain during the monsoon so that they are in position and acclimatised for when the rain abates.

In some areas, particularly Ladakh and the Karakoram, by the time the winds arrive much of their moisture has been lost. The average yearly rainfall at Leh, the main centre of Ladakh is 50 mm (2 in). Darjeeling, on the border of Sikkim at the opposite end of the Himalaya, has a yearly average of 3200 mm (128 in).

The mountainous areas of Ladakh and Pakistan are not affected by the monsoon but storms can still strike at any time. Some areas, such as Tibet, Zanskar and Ladakh, are in a rain shadow and so they are dry for much of the year and in winter are bitterly cold.

The Punjab Himalaya is mostly influenced in winter by westerly winds which bring moisture from the Atlantic Ocean, resulting in precipitation and snowfall, whereas the eastern Himalaya is relatively free from snowfall in winter.

Despite the fact that people had lost their homes and belongings, there was an air of gaiety about the village. Business sloshed on. Half-submerged rickshaws laboured through the streets bearing wealthy matrons, vendors floated wagons of oranges and soft drinks toward higher ground . . . Only when the water began to lap around their chairs would they move to the second storey or the roof.

STEVE McCURRY
Monsoon, 1988

Altitude

Altitude is the other main factor affecting the climate and weather of areas in the Himalaya. For every 100 m (328 ft) ascent, the temperature drops by 1°C (2° F).

The snowline this close to the equator is relatively high. In summer it can be as high as 6000 m (19,680 ft) while in winter it may come down to 4000 m (13,120 ft). Storms can occur at any time and it is wise to be prepared for snow on high passes.

When it snows in the Himalaya the amount and nature of the snow can be quite unlike that of any other part of the world. Up to 1 or 2 m (3.2 or 6.4 ft) can be dumped in a single storm and the snow can be so dry that slopes as low-angled as 15° may avalanche. Elsewhere in the world, 30° is regarded as the angle when snow becomes unstable. Once a storm passes the snow will ablate directly into the very dry air rather than melt, if the sun shines enough and the air temperature is above freezing.

If you are caught in a snowstorm, it is prudent to wait one or more days in a secure place until the storm finishes, to give the fresh snow time to ablate, melt or consolidate. Very dry snow on top of ice, old snow or vegetation is extremely unstable and will avalanche readily. Travelling through deep, unconsolidated snow is extremely exhausting and frostbite and hypothermia threaten the inexperienced or improperly clothed. (See page 75 ff.)

Trekking and Climbing Seasons

In monsoon areas the two best seasons for trekking and climbing are the spring pre-monsoon (March, April and May) and the autumn post-monsoon (September, October and November).

The pre-monsoon season is usually chosen for climbing as the weather is warmer, but for three weeks before the monsoon arrives the weather may be unsettled. This can sometimes be confused with the arrival of the monsoon itself.

The post-monsoon, autumn is the most popular time to trek, but if you are climbing on high mountains you will find the weather is colder and much windier than pre-monsoon. The post-monsoon is the best time for photography as the air is clear and the vegetation luxuriant in the lower regions.

By December temperatures begin to drop and snow can block the higher passes. In the winter trekking season the temperatures at altitude are tolerable when the sun is out. If it is windy and overcast, it can become cold very quickly, especially at night. The short span of daylight means you will also spend more time indoors or in your tent and you will need much heavier clothing. However, the trails are less crowded in winter, and if this is the only time you can get away it can still be a rewarding time to trek providing you are properly prepared. Some climbers are now deliberately choosing winter for the added challenge of cold, short days.

Because the monsoon has very little influence on the climate of Kashmir, the most suitable time to trek there is from May to October. This complements the gap in the trekking year in the eastern Himalaya. (See also Kashmir, page 141ff for more details.)

NATURAL HISTORY

The flora and fauna of the Himalaya are extremely diverse because of the area's great range of different ecological niches and habitats.

As discussed in the section on climate and seasons, the eastern Himalaya is much wetter and consequently has more luxuriant vegetation than the western half and to the north of the main mountain divide there is a rain shadow.

Zonation

In terms of habitats, traversing from the jungles of the Terai to the mountain tops is like going from the equator to the poles. Thus overlying the pattern of regional variations brought about by the topography and climatic differences, there is an altitudinal distribution of animals and a vertical zonation of vegetation. The transition from one zone to the next is often very gradual but where there is a change of aspect (whether the slope faces the sun or is away from it) the changes can be pronounced. Broadly speaking, as you ascend there are four major vegetation zones that can be distinguished.

Tropical

The lowest is the tropical and subtropical jungle which occurs in the lowlands and hills up to about 1200 m (3936 ft) in the eastern and central Himalaya. Here the deciduous sal tree, *Shorea robusta*, is the dominant species. This zone is the home of subtropical fauna: tiger, one-horned rhinoceros, deer, water buffalos, and consequently the major wildlife lodges.

Temperate zone

The temperate zone occurs between the altitudes of 1200 m to 2000 m (3936 ft to 6560 ft) in the central hill region. It is the home of lush evergreen forests of conifers, oaks, a variety of shrubs and the famous rhododendrons. Sir Joseph Dalton

Hooker, Charles Darwin's contemporary, made the first detailed study of Himalayan flora in the nineteenth century. He travelled through Sikkim from 1848 to 1850 and discovered twenty-two new species of rhododendrons or 'rose-trees'.

The rhododendron, the national flower of Nepal, is known locally as the *laliguras.* They range in form from low shrubs to massive trees up to 20 m (66 ft) in height, and flourish in complete forests that bloom from February to April. Easily transported as a shrub, the rhododendron is one of the most well-known floral exports of the Himalayan region. There are over eighty species that flourish in the eastern Himalaya. Their profuse flowers vary in colour from deep crimson, to red, to pink and yellow. Treks are often run to see the rhododendrons in flower.

The main tree species in the forest of the western Himalaya are conifers, among which are the blue pine, *Pinus excelsa*, and the mighty Himalayan Cedar, *Picea smithiana*, which is commonly known as the 'deodar'.

Sub-alpine zone

Stunted wind-blown birch, rhododendron and juniper make up the sub-alpine zone which is a transition between the temperate and alpine zones. In the north-western areas the rhododendron is replaced by poplars and willows.

Alpine zone

The alpine flora and fauna zone occurs from the tree-line (above 3500 m; 11,480 ft) to the permanent snowline and is characterised by alpine meadows. Limited as it is by a short growing season and little moisture the flora is characterised by hardy grasses and ground cover plants that form carpets of flowers in spring.

Meadows of wild flowers are another attraction for trekkers in the alpine regions of the Himalaya. The Valley of the Flowers, in the Garhwal, is one such destination. In the western Himalaya this zone is considerably drier than the east and the plant life is accordingly more sparse and hardy. Sagebrush is the main species of the barren screes of the Karakoram region.

Yak, sheep and goats are traditionally pastured. The native species include the red foxes, ibex, pikas, marmots, bharal.

Insects, crustacea, microscopic plant-life, lichens and mosses can be found above the snowline in certain circumstances while larger mammals and birds pass through very high regions when migrating or moving from one hunting area to the next.

Fauna

Trekkers in the wild may occasionally be able to glimpse species that are closely identified with the Himalaya. Many species, however, now exist only in National Parks and reserves, or in the inaccessible remote areas.

Birds

The birdlife of the Himalaya is extremely diverse. Nepal alone has over 800 species and the total number of different species for the subcontinent is over 1250. The bird types of the Himalayan region more closely resemble those of the Indo-Chinese region to the east, than the species found on the Indian continent. The southern boundary of the Himalayan region is the 1000 m (3280 ft) contour. More common indigenous species of the mountains are babblers, finches, pheasants — many of the world's most impressive pheasants come from the Himalaya. Around villages and trekking camps of the high hills ravens, large black crows, snow pigeons and choughs are visible. Less common are griffons and lammergeyers, bearded vultures, that have been sighted as high as 9000 m (29,520 ft).

Birdwatching is a rewarding pastime to combine with trekking in the Himalaya. The best times to trek with this in mind are spring and summer when the birds are at their most colourful. The types of species you are likely to encounter will very much depend on the nature of the habitat. Forests will have a very different avifauna to alpine meadows.

No matter where you trek, a pair of binoculars and a field guide such as Flemming's *Birds of Nepal*, or Woodcock's *Collins Handguide to the Birds of the Indian Sub-Continent*, are worthwhile additions to your kit.

Endangered species

Hunting and poaching have all but wiped out numerous native species from the Himalayan region. Snow leopards, for their pelts; musk deer, for their pod of musk scent; Marco Polo sheep; thar; ibex; bharal and markor, for their horns, and many more are endangered. It is said the Himalaya is the habitat of more endangered mammals than any other area of the Indian subcontinent.

The mountains will remain magnificent even without the wildlife, but when the last snow leopard disappears from the icy crags, an intangible aura of mystery will vanish too.

GEORGE SCHALLER in GALEN ROWELL'S
Throne Room of the Mountain Gods, 1977

(Left) The Impeyan pheasant, monal or danphe, as it is variously known, is the national bird of Nepal. These magnificent pheasants haunt alpine meadows and are regularly seen above Namche Bazaar, in the Khumbu region of Nepal.

(Above) The Himalayan thar, a close relative of the goat, is found throughout the Himalaya. They rarely venture far above the tree-line, but are pictured here against the back drop of the Twins near Kanchenjunga in eastern Nepal.

In many places native species suffer because of the extreme competition for space. Forests are felled for agricultural land and these animals are then forced to feed on crops and prey on domestic animals. They soon become the target for farmers' guns.

Impeyan pheasant One of the most colourful animals you may see on trek in the Khumbu is the national bird of Nepal, the *monal* or impeyan pheasant, also known as the *danphe*, the bird of nine colours. The impeyan is hunted as a popular game bird and its habit of damaging fields makes it unpopular with farmers.

Snow leopard The famed snow leopard, *Panthera uncia*, is easy prey for hunters. It is prized for its thick spotted grey and white pelt. Now very rare, the snow leopard's range is from 1850 m (6068 ft) to 5550 m (18,204 ft) and each animal roams over a very great hunting area.

Mountain sheep Occurring in the Hunza region of the western Himalaya, the very rare Marco Polo sheep have the greatest horn length to body weight ratio of any sheep in the world. These magnificent spiral horns have long made them highly prized by trophy hunters. This, combined with the very harsh desert conditions

The king's hunting reserve where, during the Rana era of Nepal, big game hunts were carried out, is today the Royal Chitwan National Park, which is dedicated to the conservation of the species that were once ruthlessly slaughtered.

under which they live, has led to their near extinction. Other Himalayan sheep and goats facing a similar fate are the bharal, and the urial or shapu. The latter lives in the rolling hills of the Karakoram and Indus catchment basins. The bharal, a goat rather than a sheep, likes grazing on open slopes and can be found throughout the Himalaya from Ladakh to Bhutan.

Musk deer The musk deer inhabits the birch forest of the temperate zone. The male with long tusk-like canine teeth has the highly prized scent gland. The musk from one mature deer is worth more than a year's wage for the average Nepalese. The musk is prized by the Chinese for folk medicine and as an aromatic with supposed aphrodisiac properties.

Bears Three species of bear inhabit the Himalaya: the sloth bear lives in the foothills; the black bear wanders the lower forested slopes while the giant brown bear prefers the open ground above the tree-line.

Indian rhinoceros The endangered, one-horned Indian rhinoceros, *Rhinoceros unicornis*, is only found in numbers in the grassland and riverine forest of the Terai,

at Chitwan, and in Kaziranga, in Assam. There are about 400 at the former and 1200 in Assam. Despite the rhino being free from the threat of big-game hunters in these parks, in Asia their horn is so highly prized, for medicinal purposes, poachers are a serious problem. In Chitwan a detachment of the Nepalese army have helped to reduce the poaching but the rhinos go wandering beyond the bounds of the park, damaging farmers' crops in their wake. Some attempts are being made to relocate rhinos to other parks in India.

Tiger Once subject to the ravages of the big-game hunts of the days of the British Raj, the Bengal tiger is now less under the threat of extinction thanks to the conservation efforts of Project Tiger. The loss of the Bengal tiger, the symbol of Indian wildlife, would be a tragedy for the continent and humankind but this almost came close to happening. At the turn of the nineteenth century it is estimated that there were 40,000 tigers in India. In 1972 an all-India census showed only 1800 but by 1984 this climbed back up to over 4000. Today the entire world population of all species of tigers is estimated at only 6000 to 8000 beasts.

Tigers live in a wide range of habitats including Himalayan forests and the Terai. Today tigers can only be seen safely and reliably in the wild in the main National Parks in the Terai at Chitwan and Corbett.

Yeti The yeti, also known as the abominable snowman, is probably the most infamous creature associated with the Himalaya, yet there is no scientific proof to date that such a beast exists. This fabled creature is said to live between 2000 m (6560 ft) and 3500 m (11,480 ft) in the thick forests of the eastern Himalaya. Wall paintings in temples and monasteries show two types, one that looks similar to a large monkey and the other resembling a bear. The smaller yeti is said to feed on humans while the larger eats yaks.

The strongest evidence for the existence of the yeti are photographs and observations of tracks in the snow between 5488 and 5793 m (18,000 and 19,000 ft) by mountaineers, Eric Shipton and Dr Michael Ward, in the vicinity of the Menlung Glacier in 1951. Their photos showed a 30-cm (12-inch)-long footprint that matched no known animal and which appeared to be made by a beast that weighed more than 91 kg (200 lbs). One suggestion is that the yeti is a relative of a huge anthropoid *Giantopithecus*.

With the native fauna and flora of the Himalaya drastically affected by human settlement, agriculture, grazing and hunting, the destruction of habitats in the region is now a very serious issue. Conservation efforts are long overdue and made difficult by the great poverty of the region.

Conservation

While trekkers and climbers often contribute to the local economies of the Himalayan regions through employment of porters and payment for accommodation in certain areas, they can also add to the environmental problems. The

> Even in the Himalayas, man in his numbers and constant hunger can overwhelm the tallest mountains in the world.
>
> **EDWARD W. CRONIN JR**
> *The Arun,* 1979

mushrooming number of teahouses and lodges built using scarce timber and the timber fuel they use to cook and heat with open fires, is contributing to deforestation of regions such as the Khumbu and the Annapurna in Nepal.

In some places such as the Annapurna region, many hectares of rhododendron forest is lost every year for fuel. Trekkers should be sensitive to these problems and strictly observe recommendations about using kerosene for cooking.

Population pressure is extreme in virtually all countries along the Himalayan chain, but certain pockets of natural vegetation are being conserved and management plans conceived for regions under the greatest threat.

The Sagamatha National Park in the Khumbu region of Nepal is the most well-known example and one of the most important to be protected for tourism, trekking and climbing. Within its boundaries lies Mount Everest. The Sagamatha Park came into being in 1976 and was declared a World Heritage site in 1979 in recognition of the cultural significance of its Sherpa culture, its flora and fauna and the presence of the world's highest mountain.

The Annapurna region has also recently become the focus of attempts to redress the steadily deteriorating environment. Conceived in 1985, the Annapurna Conservation Area Project is attempting to link conservation with human development in the region of the most intense tourist and local pressure. Employing a multi-land use concept, the scheme is trying to have local people make management decisions rather than have directions imposed by the government or park rangers.

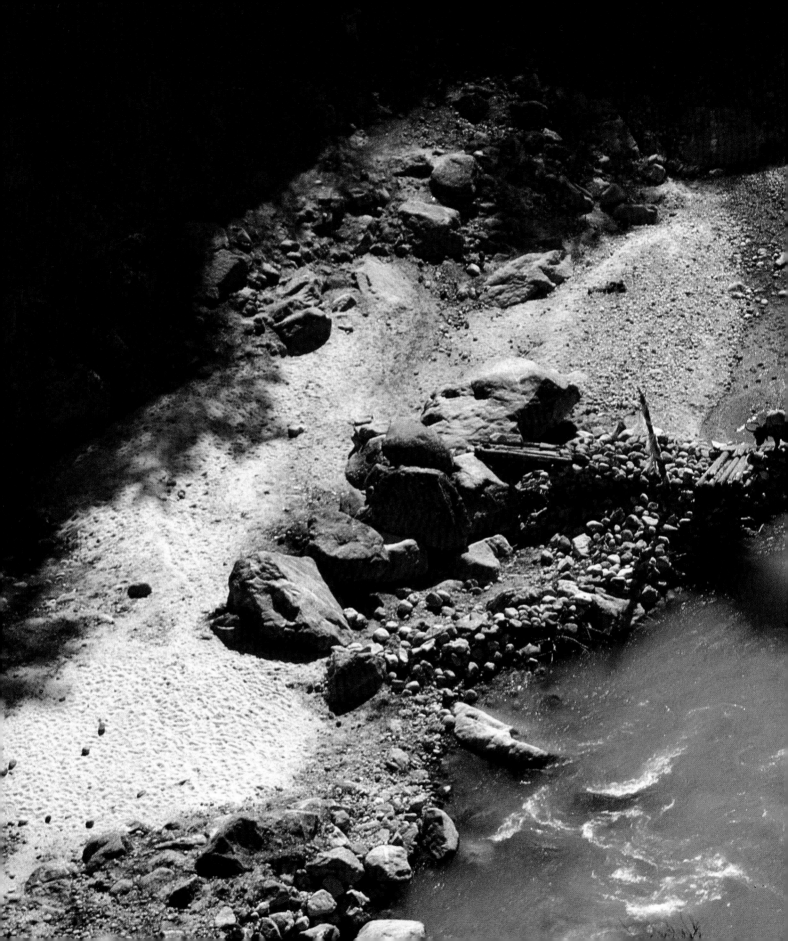

Nepal's other premier park is the Royal Chitwan National Park in the Terai. The jungle vegetation is home to the Indian one-horned rhinoceros, the Royal Bengal tiger, the sloth bear, wild boar, deer, leopards, crocodiles and over 300 species of birds. Nepal also has the Langtang National Park, the Koshi Tappu Wildlife Reserve and a dozen other smaller ones.

Bhutan is the most conservation-conscious of the Himalayan countries. More than 20 per cent of it is protected, and it has completely banned hunting and timber felling.

India's main National Parks in the Himalayan realm are the Corbett National Park in Uttar Pradesh, the Dachigam National Park in the foothills of the Ladakh Range, and the Kanchenjunga National Park in Sikkim.

Pakistan has the Khunjerab National Park and Kirhan National Park.

While National Parks, conservation areas and reserves are essential to give endangered species a chance of survival, the deforestation of the Himalaya through increasing population growth is the most serious single problem facing the region. No matter where one goes in the high mountains of the Himalaya, climbers and trekkers can help minimise the negative impact of their presence by adopting the following guidelines: try to avoid using firewood and do not have hot showers; carry out or dispose of responsibly any rubbish or packaging, tins, bottles etc; do not upset the local economy by paying too much for food or services; set examples of responsible conservation practices for the locals and support National Parks. If you are to make the most of a trek, then understanding the human face of the mountains is as important as a knowledge of the natural world .

The rapidly expanding local population, combined with an increasing number of trekkers and climbers, is leading to rapid deforestation in parts of the Himalaya, such as Nepal. Timber is cut to make way for agriculture, and for fuel and building materials.

(Previous pages) The Dudh Kosi in the Khumbu region of Nepal has to be crossed several times on the trek up to Namche Bazaar. Monsoon storms regularly wash away bridges and change the course of rivers, undermining the often precipitous track.

RACES AND RELIGION

And now approached the yellow silk-lined palanquin of the Living Buddha, gleaming like gold in the sunlight. The bearers were six-and-thirty men in green silk cloaks wearing red plate-shaped caps. A monk was holding a huge iridescent sunshade made of peacocks' feathers over the palanquin. The whole scene was a feast for the eyes — a picture revived from a long-forgotten fairytale of the Orient.

HEINRICH HARRER
Seven Years in Tibet, 1953

Races

The varied cultures are as much part of the area's attraction as its dramatic landscapes and mountain scenery. From one end of the Himalaya to the other there is an enormous diversity of culture and people. There are nineteen principal ethnic communities in the realm of the mountains with corresponding differences in language and religion. The most well-known ethnic communities are the Mongols, Tibetans, Sherpas, Kashmiris, Newars, Indians, Gurungs and Pathans, while the Turkomans, Kazakhs, Bhotias, Nuristanis and Hunzakuts are some of the more obscure examples. Even though traditional ways are fast being eroded by outside influences, there are still such enormous contrasts between the lives of the mountain people and westerners that the brief insights gained on a trek or visit can be immeasurably enriching and give a new perspective on life.

Some understanding of the more distinctive ethnic groups is a great advantage when trying to understand the colourful culture of a country such as Nepal. Rieffel in *Namaste Nepal* lists twenty-four ethnic groups on the basis of geography alone but there are also Hindu caste divisions. These include the Brahmins — the highest caste who were traditionally priests — the Chetris — rulers and warriors — and the Newars, possibly the first ethnic group to settle in the Kathmandu valley.

The geographically defined ethnic groups are equally interesting. Gurkhas are known to many as the regiment of fierce soldiers of the British and Indian Armies. Fewer people would know that the Gurkha name originated from the Gurung people of Nepal who live in the shadow of the Annapurna massif.

Most people have also heard of the Sherpa people of Nepal's mountainous Solu Khumbu area. The Sherpas are of Tibetan stock, practise Buddhism and speak Tibetan. They migrated south from the Tibetan Plateau roughly 600 years ago and lived as traders. The decline of trade was followed by the growth in mountaineering and trekking and today these hardy people find work as guides and high altitude porters.

Local people from mountain areas of the Himalaya supplement trading or subsistence agriculture by working as guides, cooks and porters for expeditions and trekking groups. The Baltis in the Karakoram work as porters, while the Kashmiri ponymen provide a similar service in Kashmir.

The Himalayan ranges also act as a natural barrier to the free exchange of culture. This has resulted in tribal mountain people developing and retaining strong individual cultures. At a national level the sovereign kingdoms of Nepal and Bhutan are independent and until quite recently so too were Sikkim, Ladakh and Spiti.

The south to north cultural transition in Nepal is an example of a pattern that is repeated time and again in other areas of the Himalaya. The lower areas, the Terai, are populated by the dark skinned Tharu

people who originate from India. The middle hills, such as the Siwalik and Mahabharat Ranges, are dominated by mountain tribes that speak Nepali. The higher regions are populated mainly by those who speak dialects of Tibetan and practice Tibetan Buddhism (Lamaism).

Religion

The religions with the largest number of followers in the Himalayan region are Hinduism, Buddhism, and Islam. Other influences and minority religions are Shamanism, Sikism, Jainism, Judaism, Parsism and Christianity, but these do not have very many followers in the realm of the mountains.

Broadly speaking the distribution of faiths follows national boundaries. Tibet, for example, almost exclusively follows Tibetan Buddhism (Lamaism), a particular form of Buddhism also found in Ladakh, Sikkim and Bhutan. Islam is the state religion of Pakistan, while Nepal is the only remaining Hindu monarchy in the world. Buddhists and Hindus co-exist peacefully in India and Nepal and there are temples in these countries sacred to followers of both religions. India is the stronghold and source of Hinduism.

Hinduism

Hinduism is a complex religion and a school of philosophy that provides a complete basis for social mores and structures. The three main gods honoured are: Brahma the creator, Vishnu the preserver or renewer; and Shiva the destroyer. Each of these gods has many different incarnations and their wives, sons, daughters, and the birds and animals they ride are also deities to be worshipped.

Hinduism offers salvation through proper conduct which traditionally was bound up with the caste system. As old as Hinduism itself, the hereditary caste system grew from a fourfold structure of: Brahmans, the scholars and priests; Kshatrya, the warriors; Vaishya the shop-keepers and merchants; and Sudros, the farmers, servants and labourers. Today there are over 3000 different castes. Every Hindu is born to one of these castes according to how he or she lived his or her previous life. The most lowly individuals, the untouchables or outcasts include anyone who has violated the caste system. Hindus are only allowed to marry within the same caste. The untouchable lowly position was addressed by Mahatma Gandhi who renamed them the Harijans (the chosen ones of god). While the Indian Government outlawed the caste system with the coming of independence it is still a fact of life for many Hindus.

The most enigmatic aspect of the Hindu religion to westerners is the rich idolatry, symbolism and worship of inanimate objects. The ritual slaughter of animals, bathing in sacred but polluted rivers such as the Ganges, the pilgrimages and numerous wandering holy men, the Sadhus dressed in ochre robes — all these aspects are as bewildering as they are colourful.

The sacred texts of Hinduism are the Vedas, the Upanishads and the Bhagavad Gita. Salvation for a Hindu is to be freed from the cycle of rebirth. This is known as Mosksha. The conditions of one's next birth are based on the collective results of one's actions in a previous life (Karma).

The most visible aspect of Hinduism to travellers is the *tika* that devoted individuals wear on their foreheads. This is usually a spot or mark of coloured clay and offering, such as a rice grain.

In Nepal Hinduism is interwoven with Buddhism which results in a high degree of religious tolerance. Some temples are sacred to followers of either creed.

Buddhism

Buddhism emerged from India in the 6th century BC. The founder, Siddhartha Gautama, was born near what is today known as Lumbini, in the western part of Nepal's Terai. At the age of twenty-nine Gautama abandoned his life of luxury and

(Previous pages) Traditional life is one of the main attractions of remote areas in the Himalaya. The village people of the Warvan Valley are a refreshing contrast to the bustle of Indian cities such as Delhi and Srinagar.

became a religious hermit. After five years of wandering he became enlightened and was soon referred to as Buddha (the Enlightened One). He began preaching the 'Middle Path' to salvation. He taught that everything in the world is subject to change (the law of impermanence) and that nothing happens by chance (the law of causation).

His teachings conveyed the philosophy that all suffering comes from over-indulgence in our desires. If we can suppress these desires we will eventually achieve Nirvana. This is where we become free from desire and delusion. The key to enlightenment is the eightfold path of right thinking, behaviour, understanding, concentration, alertness, purpose, vocation, effort. Buddhist morals are very close to Christian ones.

Buddha taught that salvation could be attained without the formal rituals of Hinduism but in the time since his death, Buddhism has developed many rituals of its own. There are two main branches of Buddhism: Hinayana (the small vehicle) and Mahayana (the big vehicle). The version that became popular to the north, especially in Nepal, is Mahayana. Buddhism is closely linked with Hinduism in practice as well as spiritually. Hindus regard Buddha as the ninth incarnation of their god Vishnu. Some also regard Christ as another incarnation.

Tibetan Buddhism (Lamaism)

In Tibet, Buddhism took on aspects of the ancient Bon religion and Trantism. The former was practised by shamans and involved the worship of gods in inanimate objects such as trees, rocks, etc., while Trantism is, simplistically, a belief in the occult forces of magic and superstition.

Tibetan Buddhism was introduced in the 7th century AD and four main sects developed over the centuries: The Gelugpa or Yellow Hats, the Kargyupa or Red Hats, Nyingmapa or Ancients, and Sagyapa or People of the Earth. The Dalai Lama, the spiritual leader of Tibetan Buddhism, is a Yellow Hat whose government is in exile in Dharamsala, India.

The Panchen Lama ('the Master who excels among those who know'), the second most important leader, was still based in Tibet, but his death in February 1989 leaves a vacuum until his next incarnation can be discovered. A party of senior monks will travel among the Tibetan people in search of a successor among the children who display superior intelligence. The eventual successor will be the child who can recognise certain religious objects that belonged to the earlier Panchen Lama. This same process is used to identify a new Dalai Lama.

Tibetan Buddhism stresses meditation as a way of tapping into universal cosmic forces. Meditation techniques include the chanting of a mantra (the most famous being, 'Om mani pad me hum'), or focusing on a sacred diagram or mandala, and are learned from a personal teacher.

Apart from Tibet itself, Tibetan Buddhism has its strongholds in Ladakh, the Kumbu region of Nepal, Bhutan and through the presence of refugees and the Dalai Lama in Himachal Pradesh in India.

Islam

The third main religion of the Himalaya is Islam which is Arabic for 'submission' to the will of God. Islam is the state religion of Pakistan. Many Kashmiris also follow the prophet Mohammed (Muhammad). Muslims believe in one God, Allah, whose law was revealed to Mohammed and is laid down in the Koran.

Five times a day a devout Moslem will pray before Allah on a prayer rug facing Mecca, the sacred city of Islam. The calls to prayer to the mosque by the Muezzin are a feature of every Islamic city.

Born in Mecca in 570 AD, at the age of 40 Muhammad was called upon by a messenger from God to proclaim his glory. Once in his life a true follower of Islam will make a pilgrimage to Mecca and following this is entitled to advertise this fact by dyeing his beard with reddish-brown henna. Unlike the Hindu devotee, all Muslims believe they are born equal and have a strong sense of brotherhood. The Islamic religion has helped to diminish the rigid caste system of India but it is highly anti-feminist in its fundamental form. Women are rarely seen in the remote villages and in the cities they are almost always in purdah.

Muslims are called on by their faith to proselytise, even by force if necessary. There are two factions of Islam. Today 90 per cent of Muslims are Sunnites while the remainder are Shiites. The latter division are a majority in Iran.

Muslims have a very fatalistic view of life. The phrase 'en shalla' ('if God is willing'), is heard time and time again when trying to organise anything in an Islamic country.

During the month of Ramadan, Muslims fast from sunrise to sunset. Exceptions are allowed to this rule for those who are sick, travellers and soldiers on active service. The end of the month of fasting is acknowledged by wild celebrations.

The mixture of religions throughout the Himalaya is very complex and always in a state of flux. The suppression of Buddhism during the cultural revolution in Tibet resulted in dramatic changes to the culture of the region and led to an exodus of refugees into Nepal and India. A similar change occurred in India and Pakistan during the partition in 1947. The fusing of these new settlements and people has also resulted in changes in the language.

Language

A first-time visitor to Asia may be concerned about not speaking the native languages. In the Himalaya this is rarely a problem because English is so widely spoken by officials and people connected with tourism. Even so, you are more likely to enjoy your time if you have some understanding of the local tongue.

Whenever I slip, Tensing views me balefully. He speaks no English or Chinese, I no Tibetan or Nepali. When the strain of silence becomes too intense, he breaks into an improvised Hindi — garbar karta hai, ekdum slip *(make confusion, completely slip)*; or rasta bahut badmash *(path very rascal)* — which proves something I have often thought; that those who don't know a language properly are often the most expressive in it.

VIKRAM SETH
From Heaven Lake, 1983

The main languages and dialects spoken in the Himalaya are Urdu, Hindi (Hindustani is a combination of the two), Nepali, Tibetan and English. Other important regional languages are Balti, Burushaski, Kashmiri, Khowar, Ladakhi and Dzongkha.

Hindustani

Hindustani is the lingua franca, the universal means of communicating on the Indian subcontinent. Hindustani was originally the language of the bazaars of Delhi and was derived from Western Hindi. Its currency spread when it was adopted by troops of the Mogul Empire.

When spoken, Hindi and Urdu are very similar languages with the sentence structure, grammar and sound system being virtually identical. Hindi is spoken by over 150 million Indians while Urdu is the official language of Pakistan. The differences between these languages stem from their different origins.

Hindi is based on Sanskrit and is written in the Devagari script while Urdu comes from the Persian and Arabic languages and is written in Arabic script. Today many Hindi and Urdu words are common. Often, in commerce and technology Hindi has assumed English words.

While Hindi is the national language of India, there are fourteen other regional languages protected by the constitution and, excluding dialects, 220 spoken languages in the Indian subcontinent.

Kathmandu has many statues of Hindu gods. In Nepal, like many other parts of the Himalaya, centuries of cultural tradition have led to the co-existence of Buddhism and Hinduism. Some temples and sites are sacred to Buddhists and Hindus.

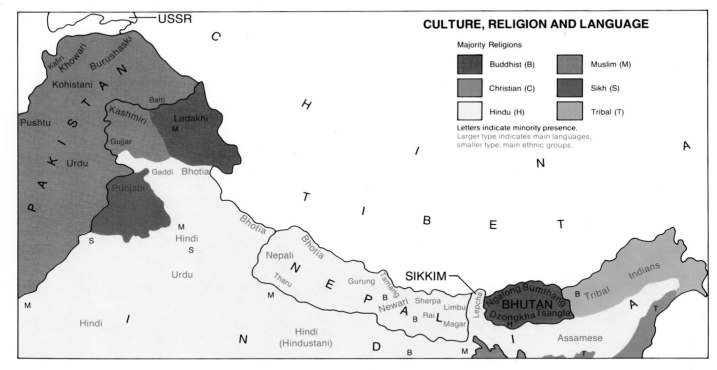

You are most likely to encounter Punjabi and Bengali en route to the Indian Himalaya.

Nepali

Nepali, the main language of Nepal, is related to Hindi, and is spoken by 18 million people. It is useful in Bhutan, Sikkim and Darjeeling and is very easy to learn. Nepali is the native language of high castes in Nepal such as the Brahmans and Chetris. Other ethnic groups have their own language but can also speak Nepali.

Written Nepali is in the Devagari script, the same form of writing used for Hindi and Sanskrit languages. This script is phonetic with a fifty-letter alphabet, each letter making a single sound. Transliteration is required for Nepali to be written in English which is the reason why so many alternative spellings occur.

Tibetan

Tibet is the most difficult region of the Himalaya to get by with just English. Few speak English and there are many dialects of Tibetan.

Balti

Balti is the language of Baltistan which lies to the east of the Indus centred on Skardu. Anyone visiting the Baltoro Glacier will be in the heart of Baltistan. Balti is a western dialect of Tibetan.

Burushaski

Burushaski is spoken in the districts of Hunza and Nagir in the northern territory of Pakistan. It is unrelated to any other Asian language.

Dzongkha

The national language of Bhutan is Dzongkha which is spoken mainly in the western part of the country. Bumthangkha is spoken in the central region while Shorchopka is spoken in the east, but English is widely spoken by officials and educated people.

Kashmiri

Kashmiri is spoken by the villagers and hill people of Kashmir but most of these also speak Urdu or Hindi. English is also widely spoken in Kashmir.

Khowar

Khowar, regarded as one of the Dardic language group, is spoken by the Kho people in the district of Chitral in the northern territory of Pakistan, and also in the Ghizar and Yasin Valleys of the adjacent Gilgit district. A glossary of Khowar can be found in Hugh Swift's *The Trekker's Guide to the Himalaya and Karakoram*.

Ladakhi

Ladakhi, a western dialect of Tibetan, is spoken only in Ladakh. It is in the same category as other western dialects of Tibetan, namely, Balti, Lahauli, and Purak (spoken in lower Ladakh). Even though it is a dialect of Tibetan, and written in Tibetan script, Ladakhi is sufficiently different that natives from each area often speak Hindustani with one another. The one Ladakhi word definitely worth learning is *jullay* which is the universal greeting that can mean, hello, goodbye, how are you or just simply greetings.

Spellings

One direct result of the variety of Himalayan languages is the multiplicity of acceptable spellings that appear in books and on maps through transliteration. Simla or Shimla, Ghorapani or Ghorepani, Thyangboche or Thengboche — which is correct? The spellings of place names and geographic features and even the names of such places or features vary enormously throughout the region. There are often not one but several alternatives. This is most common with features that straddle borders. Such vagaries make the job of traveller, mapmaker and author more challenging. Most of the variations arise from the anglicisation of native names. Changes in national government policy have sometimes made a traveller's geographical knowledge redundant overnight, as was the case in China where spelling was changed from the Wade Giles romanisation system to Pinyin, and Peking became Beijing.

Just as high level politics has a considerable bearing on national education policy, official languages, and even systems of spelling, so political considerations are the very heart of the relationships between countries. Some understanding of the various alliances and tensions, and their historical antecedents, puts many aspects of the Himalayan states in perspective.

POLITICAL GEOGRAPHY

The treaty of Amritsar was wonderfully imprecise. 'All the hilly or mountainous country, with its dependencies, situated to the eastwards of the river Indus and the westward of the river Ravi was ceded to the Maharaja.'

JOHN KEAY
When Men and Mountains Meet, 1977

The USSR, Afghanistan, Pakistan, Tibet/China, India, Nepal and Bhutan straddle or are adjacent to the greater Himalaya. Internal political considerations are at least as important as geographical limitations in determining where one can trek or climb. The relationship between countries also dictates which borders can be crossed.

Today there is an extremely delicate balance between these countries, which is hardly surprising given the region's turbulent history. Wars, invasions, partitions and truces have been a feature of the Himalaya for thousands of years and this trend continues. As tensions increase, strategic areas, even entire countries, sometimes become closed to travellers. The opening and closing of Tibet and China in the 1980s has greatly affected people's travel aspirations.

Closed Regions

A closed region with an exotic culture can be an attraction in itself. In many instances recently it has been a geographic feature that has been the prime attraction causing adventurers to circumvent political obstacles. The earliest attempts to climb Mount Everest, for example, which straddles the border between Tibet and Nepal, were from the north, because at the time Nepal was closed and had been for over a century. In 1951 King Tribhuvan put an end to Nepal's Rana regime, the rule by hereditary prime ministers, and their policy of total isolation.

The first ascent of Everest was eventually made via Nepal and since then this tiny kingdom has been opening its doors to visitors at an ever-increasing rate. Politically, Nepal is a buffer state between China and India. Nepal's relationship with India has fluctuated greatly over the years. With no real power itself it has had to try to maintain cordial relations with both its neighbours—a diplomatic balancing act, because these countries have been estranged.

Contemporary strained relations originate from when China marched into Tibet in 1951. Skirmishes then occurred in the common border area of East Ladakh. In 1959 when the Dalai Lama fled to India relations took a further turn for the worse. China subsequently invaded the Aksai Chin region, the most north-easterly portion of the Indian state of Jammu and Kashmir. Though claimed by India this area is under Chinese administration.

Trekkers and visitors are currently prohibited from the country adjacent to the border of the Aksai Chin region. These restricted areas are rigidly enforced and applications for special permission to enter can take anything up to six months to be reviewed and the answer is usually no. The Indian side of this border is not the only restricted area. Much of the other side of the border in China and Tibet has been closed to travellers for years.

The people of Kasgar in China's westernmost province Xinjiang (Sinkinang), which can now be reached by the Karakoram Highway from Pakistan, have quite different facial features to the Hunza people.

Though intrepid mountaineers such as Bruce, Finch and Mallory opened up a route through Tibet to the north side of Everest in the 1920s and 1930s, this limited accessibility changed dramatically when the People's Liberation Army of the Chinese Communists moved into Tibet in 1951. For nearly a decade the occupation force interfered little with traditional ways, but the social character of the region altered dramatically and religious freedom became nonexistent in 1959, causing the Dalai Lama's exit.

Since the cultural revolution, from 1966 to 1976, there has been a gradual relaxation of restrictions in Tibet. In 1978 China opened its doors again and by 1980 a flood of mountaineering expeditions were climbing in China and Tibet but at a cost (up to five times the price of an equivalent peak elsewhere in the Himalaya). China then saw the foreign exchange to be earned from organised trekking parties and eventually lone travellers were also admitted. Disturbances in Tibet in 1989 saw it again closed to westerners.

It seems that constant, sometimes violent change, is as much a part of the Himalayan political scene as it is of the mountain landscape. The creation of new independent states and disappearance of others is a continual factor. Sikkim, for example, was until 1975 a separate kingdom, though India had controlled its foreign affairs and defence from 1947 when it took over these roles from the British. In 1975 the monarchy was abolished and today it is a state of the Indian Union. Special permits are required to enter Sikkim and Darjeeling.

The partition of India in 1947 saw the creation of Pakistan, with states in the East and West. This later divided into two countries, Pakistan and Bangladesh. The latter country however is outside the confines of the Himalaya and so beyond the scope of this book.

Trans-Himalayan Links

Foreign aid and the use of the military have led to the construction of two major north-south highways. It is now possible to cross from Nepal into Tibet and on to Lhasa via a road opened in 1985, built with aid from the Chinese and Swiss Governments.

Equally important for travellers is the Karakoram Highway that runs from Rawalpindi in Pakistan northwards across the Khunjerab Pass to Khasgar, the fabled city of China's Xinjiang province. For much of its length in Pakistan the Grand Trunk highway shares a narrow gorge with the Indus River. The Karakoram Highway follows the route of a major branch of the ancient Silk Route that in earlier times ran from the Mediterranean to China and eventually Japan.

While the opening up of China and Tibet has enabled access to the north side of the Himalaya, access has been reduced in the far west.

The Hindu Kush has been closed for a decade because of the war between Russia and Afghanistan. Although this is currently moving towards settlement, it could be some time before safe travel there is again possible.

Mountaineers have always led the way for trekkers into closed regions or countries, but where there are border conflicts then access is usually not possible into that specific area. A sizeable portion of the Himalaya has been and still is disputed territory. As recently as 1983 Pakistan and India have skirmished over part of Kashmir and the two nations maintain sizeable forces along what is known as the line of control. Several battles have been fought between the two countries.

In the eighties however, Pakistan has pursued a policy of non-alignment and attempted to improve relations with India, China and Iran. It has acquired a more fundamental Islamic profile but the death of President Zia in 1988 could result in changes.

While the larger countries of China, India and Pakistan all have development programmes to help the poorer and more remote mountainous regions, foreign aid is also very important in helping local people. To cater to tourists as well as their own development needs, many mountain areas such as Nepal's Khumbu are becoming increasingly westernised but in so doing they are rapidly losing the unique qualities that early travellers prized so highly.

Bhutan was the last Kingdom to grant access, albeit limited to foreigners. Tour groups were first admitted in 1974 and trekking parties two years later. Today parts of Bhutan are opening up to trekkers and climbers but at a very great cost.

In general political tension seems to be decreasing the length of the Himalaya, and there is hope that even more areas will become open to trekkers and climbers. This may help to reduce the environmental pressure on the most popular regions. Places such as the Hindu Kush, Nuristan and Arunachal Pradesh may one day again be possible destinations.

We shall now study each country in more detail to look at a few of the possible options available in each of the major trekking and climbing regions.

TIBET AND TIBETAN BUDDHISM

LINCOLN HALL

Lincoln Hall has come to have a deep respect for and understanding of the Tibetan people and religion as a result of his numerous visits to their country and his own study of and meditation upon the Dharma.

It is ironic that Tibet's wish to remain isolated from the world had much to do with her demise at the hands of the Chinese. Tibet had no interest in the machinations of the world at large, having no need for trade and no concern with imperialism, war, and the exploitation of other national states. Her army was small, ill-equipped and poorly-trained; an adequate force for parades outside the Potala in Lhasa, but useful for very little else. Tibet had long been a Buddhist country – not just a place where Buddhism was the state religion, but a country where virtually the entire population practised the religion, where every action was based on Buddhist faith. Since the 16th century this responsible task has been performed by the Dalai Lama, who is groomed for his position of penultimate authority from the age of two or three years (that is, from the time his reincarnation is recognised by the most senior and holy monks).

The fourteenth Dalai Lama, though only a teenager in 1950, attempted co-operation with the invading Chinese army because he believed in non-violent solutions to all problems, even invading armies. The Chinese promises of modernisation at first seemed like welcome news, since the Dalai Lama had planned to implement such a programme upon reaching his majority. These, however, were just the first of many promises the Chinese were to break; it was soon apparent that China's immediate aims were strategic. Highways were extended from China across Tibet to Ladakh, thus giving China military access to western India.

Contact with the compassionate, non-violent Buddhist religion can be nothing but uplifting. This, combined with Tibet's reputation as a land of mystery, has made it a popular destination, despite the hardships of travel there.

Most travellers will be overjoyed simply to be in Tibet. Though rugged and desolate, it is undeniably beautiful. The harder the journey, the more worthwhile it seems to be. The holy mountains and lakes which dot the vast pastures of the high plateau give an air of freedom that cannot be tasted anywhere else in the world. Perhaps it was this purity that enabled Tibet to hold out against the intrusive modern world.

The long-forbidden 'land of snows' was the last of the ancient civilisations to fulfil the age-old pattern of disintegration at the hands of barbarians. The difference with Tibet is that the invaders came in tanks, and bombed monasteries from aeroplanes, a far more efficient but less colourful way than Genghis Khan's.

Over the last two or three years Tibetans have been given the freedom to 'practise' their culture. One suspects that the Chinese, while firmly holding the reins, appreciate the tourist value of quaint folk history. Such decisions, indeed all decisions of importance, are made in Beijing, or by Chinese officials in Lhasa. Tibet as a country governed by the ethics of Buddhism no longer exists, and it is difficult to see how Tibetan society can continue to evolve. To visit Tibet is to see history passing, as the cement shoes set around the culture's feet.

While the 100,000 Tibetans in exile continue to identify themselves with Tibet, many have given up hope of returning to their homeland. Others believe that Chinese communists are no more than the darkest cloud amongst the many invaders that have come and gone in Tibet's long history. Faced with a determined programme by the Chinese to eliminate the religion, the Dalai

Lama's exiled government in Dharamsala has turned its eyes outward, and is teaching the Tibetan interpretation of Buddhism to the world. This programme continues despite the Chinese about-face, and will ensure the survival of the Tibetan creed. Tibetan lamas, as the priests are known, have revitalised the religion in the Buddhist kingdoms of Nepal, Sikkim and Bhutan, and have established Tibetan Buddhist centres in many Western countries.

Tibetan Buddhism is properly known as Vajrayana from *vajra*, meaning 'to all that is pure and indestructible'. A sub-sect of Mahayana Buddhism, Tibetans see compassion as the chief virtue, and their ideal is the Bodhisattva, an enlightened being who renounces heavenly bliss in order to help all sentient beings evolve spiritually. Vajrayana is a practical form of mysticism which expounds precise techniques for attaining wisdom, the goal being the negation of ego, and hence entry to the bliss of one's own divinity. One of these practices is the visualisation during meditation of the countless 'mythical Buddhas' which embody all the aspects of Buddha. Vajrayana is the way of power and of transformation: the power to master good and evil, and the transformation of inward and outward circumstances into tools by the power of the mind. Such accomplishments are not for the casual, but only for those who devote their whole being, experience and environment – good and evil equally – to the task of attaining Buddhahood.

With Buddhahood comes an understanding of reality which shortcuts the hundred-year steps of experimental science. Every person has the potential, but few the discipline to achieve this ultimate understanding. The techniques of Vajrayana are very powerful and, wrongly applied, can lead to madness. Consequently, protective

Tibetan culture and religion has been suppressed for decades in Tibet yet it flourishes in refugee camps in Nepal and Northern India — especially Ladakh. The recently completed massive statue of Matryia (the coming Buddha) at Tikse Monastery is one such example.

secrecy has long cloaked Tantric Buddhism, as Vajrayana is also known, from the inquisitive. Those curious enough to practise seriously soon appreciate the worth of the precautions.

Scientists have in the past dismissed mystical interpretations of the universe, but nuclear physicists in particular are beginning to see the meeting of the two paths, and how Vajrayana leads beyond to explain the unexplainable. A true scientist rejects only hypotheses that have been tested and proven wrong. Vajrayana is ready for any test, and has been for a thousand years.

For many foreigners, Tibetan Buddhism is not just a casual dalliance but a lifetime commitment, with an increasing number of westerners taking the monastic vows of the lamas. The pragmatic nature of Buddhism appeals to the Western intellect, its solution to the world is complete – not an answer but an attitude – and its message of non-violence and compassion attracts many who are disillusioned with the arms race and the gross injustices between the modern and third worlds. Any philosophy which can help us deal with these problems is surely worthy of support and respect.

An author, mountaineer and adventure travel guide, Lincoln Hall was also a leading climber on the 1984 Australian ascent of Mount Everest and wrote the highly acclaimed account of the expedition, *White Limbo* (Weldons, 1985). Lincoln is also author of *The Loneliest Mountain* (Simon & Schuster, 1989), the story of the Bicentennial Antarctic Expedition's first ascent of Mount Minto in the Antarctic. He is now writing a novel about Tibet's guerilla war against the Chinese communists.

PART FOUR

Himalayan Countries

'Fashion your life from a chain of deeds like a garland is fashioned from a chain of flowers.' And here was a chain of sunlit mountains above a sea of cloud.

PETE BOARDMAN
Sacred Summits, 1982

Details in this book about the areas of the five countries that touch on or completely include the Himalaya — Pakistan, India, Nepal, Bhutan and Tibet — are of necessity very brief. Like much travel-related information, they can very quickly become outdated. It is also almost impossible for one person to visit all the places referred to in this section.

The ebb and flow of the political tides in the region are particularly rapid, especially in Tibet and border areas between India and Pakistan. The Manali to Leh road in India has recently been opened to organised groups of foreign travellers, but they must have a police escort. This means a circuit from Kashmir to Ladakh and down to Himachal Pradesh is now possible which greatly improves the scope for travel in the Indian Himalaya.

Lhasa was the scene of anti-Chinese riots in March 1989 where up to sixty Tibetans were killed. All westerners were ordered to leave Lhasa, but how long this situation lasts is open to speculation.

Within months the Tibetan fracas was overshadowed by the student protests and subsequent massacre in Beijing. This brutal show of force sent shock waves through China and around the world. Climbing and trekking in China and Tibet will no doubt be restricted if not forbidden for some time.

Use the following chapters as a planning guide, but seek up-to-date information from travel agents, tour companies and recently returned travellers to make sure you are on the right track concerning when, where and how to go.

The cultural diversity of the Himalayan region is one of its enduring features and attractions. The wizened Ladakhi women (right) who still dress in traditional fashion, practise Tibetan Buddhism while a little to the north-west in Pakistan (below) the Baltistanis are Muslims.

PAKISTAN

> As I studied the maps, one thing about them captured my imagination. The ridges and valleys that led up from Baltistan became increasingly high and steep as they merged into the maze of peaks and glaciers of the Karakoram and then suddenly ended in an empty blank space. Across this blank space was written one challenging word, 'Unexplored'.
>
> **ERIC SHIPTON**
> *Blank on the Map, 1938*

It is remarkable to think that only fifty years ago many parts of the Greater Himalaya were unknown. Today trekkers and climbers regularly visit the Karakoram, the Himalaya and the Hindu Kush ranges in the northern section of Pakistan, wedged between Afghanistan, China and India.

The Karakoram is particularly significant for climbers as it boasts K2, the second highest mountain in the world, as well as four other 8000 m peaks and numerous small but technically demanding rock spires. For trekkers the main attractions of the Karakoram are mountain vistas and the formidable reputation of the treks. The Hunza region, part of the western extremity of the Karakoram, is gaining a reputation for having some of the most beautiful and unspoilt landscapes in the Himalaya.

Nanga Parbat, the most westerly of the 8000 m peaks is the focus for climbing and trekking in the western end of the Himalaya proper. The Hindu Kush, further to the west again but regarded as a separate range, has some notable treks in the region known as the Chitral. Access to this area is limited because of the sensitive political situation in Afghanistan on the western border.

Trekking in Pakistan is less developed than in Nepal or India. You can join an organised trekking group outside the country, but if you go on your own you will not find the same level of support or experienced trekking agencies in Pakistan as elsewhere in the Himalaya. If you trek on your own you must be self-sufficient as the country is often very harsh, with few hotels and teahouses. There are no facilities in Pakistan for commercial skiing or rafting but there is plenty of scope for small groups and expeditions who wish to make ski traverses.

Pakistan is an independent nation which has only existed since the partition of India in 1947. The Indus Valley, however, which lies mostly in Pakistan, has seen the rise and fall of many civilisations since 3000 BC. Pakistan's name was invented by one Choudhury Rahmat Ali, a Cambridge University student. It stands for 'land of the pure' and combines the initials of Punjab, Afghan Province and Kashmir with the ending of Baluchistan.

The notion of the division of India into two separate states, Hindu and Muslim, was first proposed in 1930. At the time of the eventual partition in 1947 there was a mass migration of some 12 million refugees. Muslims crossed into the northeastern and the north-western extremities of the subcontinent and the Hindus into the central Indian portions. In 1970 there was a further split when the eastern side became Bangladesh and the western side remained as Pakistan. Modern Pakistan is a cultural crossroads with strong Islamic influences.

Entry Details

When entering Pakistan, you will need to deal with bureaucratic formalities in the twin cities of Islamabad and Rawalpindi, regardless of your final destination. Karachi is the main point of entry for international flights, so if you are arriving by air you will need to take a connecting flight to Islamabad.

PAKISTAN AT A GLANCE

Area
803,950 sq km
(310,325 sq. miles).
Population
80 million.
Government
Democracy, led by President Benazir Bhutto.
Capital
Islamabad, 16 km (10 miles) from Rawalpindi.
Population: Islamabad 201,000; Rawalpindi 806,000.
Flag
L.h.s., white vertical rectangle; r.h.s., white star and crescent moon on green background.
People of the Himalaya
Punjabis, Baltis and Hunzas.
Language
Urdu, the national language; Pushto in the North West Frontier Province; Punjabi in the Punjab; tribal languages in the hills.
Religion
Islam – State religion.
1% – Hindu.
Highest point
K2, 8611 m (28,244 ft) — world's second highest mountain.
Currency
Rupees and paise (100 paise = 1 rupee).
1989 approximate:
US$1.00 = Rs 14.00
AUS$1.00 = Rs 12.30
UK£1.00 = Rs 19.50.
Time
Pakistan is five hours ahead of GMT.
Portion in Himalaya
States of North-west Frontier, Northern Area and Azad Kashmir.
Best time for trekking and climbing
June to September.

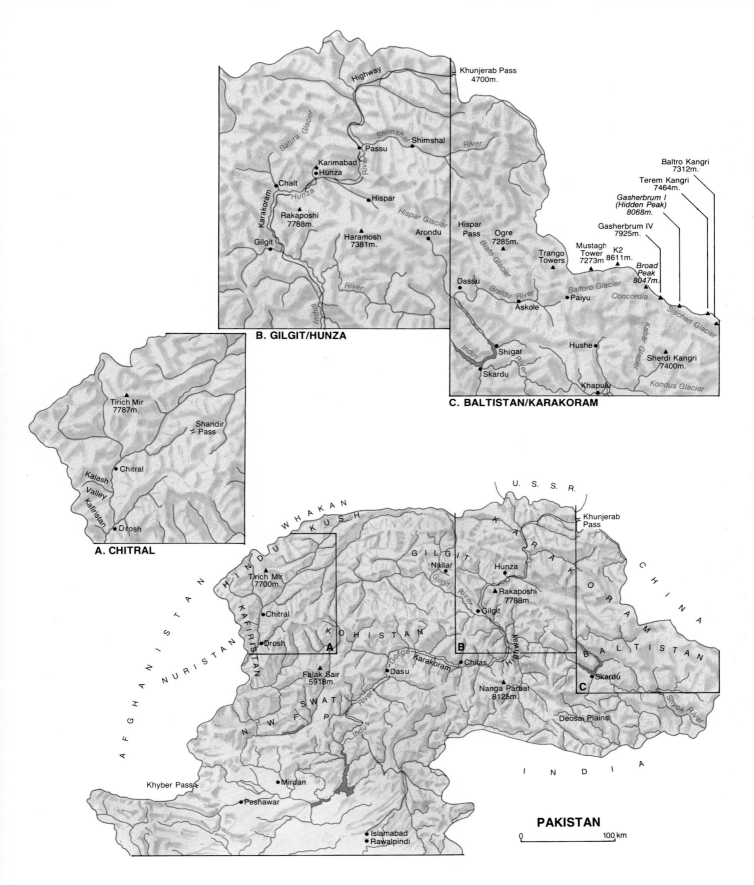

B. GILGIT/HUNZA

Khunjerab Pass
4700m.

Highway

Battura Glacier

Shimshal

Passu

Karimabad
Hunza

Chalt

Karakoram

Hispar

Hunza

Rakaposhi
7788m.

Gilgit

Haramosh
7381m.

Arondu

Hispar Glacier

Hispar
Pass

Ogre
7285m.

Biafo Glacier

Trango
Towers

Mustagh
Tower
7273m

K2
8611m.

Baltro Kangri
7312m.

Terem Kangri
7464m.

Gasherbrum I
(Hidden Peak)
8068m.

Gasherbrum IV
7925m.

Broad
Peak
8047m.

Dassu

Braldu River

Askole

Paiyu

Concordia

Siachen Glacier

Kabar Glacier

Indus

Shigar

Hushe

Sherdi Kangri
7400m.

Skardu

Khapulu

Kondus Glacier

C. BALTISTAN/KARAKORAM

Tirich Mir
7787m.

Shandir
Pass

Chitral

Kalash
Valley

Kafiristan

Drosh

A. CHITRAL

HINDU KUSH

WHAKAN

U. S. S. R.

GILGIT

KARAKORAM

Khunjerab
Pass

Naltar

Hunza

CHINA

Gilgit River

Tirich Mir
7700m.

Chitral

AFGHANISTAN

Rakaposhi
7788m.

Gilgit

BALTISTAN

KAFIRISTAN

Drosh

NURISTAN

KOHISTAN

Karakoram

Chilas

Indus River

Gorge

Skardu

Falak Sair
5918m.

Dasu

Nanga Parbat
8125m.

Shyok River

SWAT

N. W. F. P.

Indus River

Deosai Plains

INDIA

Khyber Pass

Mirdan

Peshawar

Islamabad

Rawalpindi

PAKISTAN

0   100 km

For those coming overland from India, the access is limited to either the Lahore-Amritsar railway or a nearby road link that crosses the border at Wagah. The Karakoram Highway is now open to travellers wishing to enter Pakistan from China in the north.

Pakistan regulations prohibit the importation of liquor into the country. Trekking and mountaineering parties, however, often take in foodstuffs which sometimes include alcohol. This tends to be overlooked by the customs authorities.

Rawalpindi/Islamabad

Islamabad, the new federal capital of Pakistan, is 15 km (9 miles) from the old military city of Rawalpindi/Islamabad on the grand trunk road between Peshawar and Lahore. Most of the colour and life of the adjacent cities is to be found in the Rawalpindi sector which is where many of the best hotels are found. Most trekkers and expeditions base themselves at the Flashman's Hotel in Rawalpindi where there is a tourist information centre. How-

ever, for official business, such as obtaining visa extensions or trekking permits, you will need to go to Islamabad.

Islamabad is a completely planned city in the style of Canberra or Brazilia with modern buildings and paved streets. Its very formal layout and grid of tree-lined boulevards and buildings is in stark contrast to the usual chaos of Asian cities.

Trekking

Pakistan is much less popular for trekking than India or Nepal. The countryside is often inhospitable and in general the people are not as friendly as in other parts of the Himalaya. The Islamic culture means that Pakistanis tend to be more distant and reserved than, say, the Nepalese.

Most of Pakistan's trekking agencies are in Rawalpindi and Islamabad (see addresses on page 217 for details). The semi-governmental Pakistan Tourism Development Corporation (PTDC) is one of the best sources of information as it has offices in most major centres.

(Previous pages) While the Baltoro Glacier trek to Concordia and K2 Base Camp is one of the most gruelling commercial treks in the world, it maintains its popularity because of the unsurpassed mountain scenery. The porters are smiling because they are close to the end of their journey.

While the mountains of the Karakoram are the main attraction for trekkers and climbers in Pakistan, there are cultural sights in almost every region. The ancient Askandria Fort is just a short climb above Skardu, the main town of Baltistan.

Organised treks in Pakistan concentrate on the Baltoro Glacier, though some companies offer departures to trek in the Hunza region of Nanga Parbat (The Fairy Meadows Trek) or its southern face (the Rupal Face). Nanga Parbat, 8126 m (26,653 ft) is the furthest west of the 8000 m (26.240 ft) peaks and is considered by many to be the western limit of the Himalaya.

There is plenty of scope in Pakistan to organise your own trek or small-scale expedition. It is not advisable for women to travel on their own as this can offend the Islamic cultural traditions (see cultural recommendations on page 83). The books most helpful for Pakistan are Hugh Swift's *The Trekkers' Guide to the Himalaya and Karakoram* and José Roleo Santiago's *Pakistan — A Travel Survival Kit.* (See Suggested Reading List.)

PERMITS

Treks in Pakistan are divided into three categories — open, restricted 'specified' routes and restricted 'unspecified' routes. In the open areas it is possible to trek without a permit or a guide, providing the route is below 6000 m (19,680 ft). These treks are easy walks of one or two days, or a week at the most. The restricted treks are those where the route goes above 6000 m and where trekking is moderate to strenuous. Treks last from two weeks to a month. The restricted zone applies to areas in prohibited border regions above 6000 m where trekking is strenuous and takes over a month. A permit, porters, and a guide are prerequisites.

Information about treks is available from the Tourism Division of the Ministry of Sport and Tourism in Islamabad (see Address Appendix) or from Pakistan embassies. Permits for approved treks in the regulated zones (Chitral, Gilgit and Skardu) are also obtainable from the Tourism Division. You also need to register with the foreigner's registration office of the local police when you arrive in the region where you plan to trek.

Climbing

Climbing in Pakistan has become extremely popular in recent times with over fifty expeditions each year going into the Karakoram. The modern era of exploration began there in 1954 when foreign expeditions were again given permission to enter, but there are still many areas out of bounds. Permits are needed for expeditions to mountains above 6000 m (19,680 ft).

PERMITS

Mountaineering in Pakistan is controlled by the Tourism Division of the Ministry of Culture and Tourism of the Government of Pakistan. (See page 217 for addresses).

Applications for a peak permit for all peaks above 6000 m except K2 have to be sent to the nearest Pakistan Embassy between January and October, a year in advance of the expedition. For permission for K2, two years' advance notice is required. The minimum size permitted for a climbing expedition in Pakistan is four people (excluding the liaison officer) and no member is permitted to take part in more than one expedition per season. Winter expeditions are now also permitted in Pakistan but in these instances the minimum number of people has to be six, all local staff must be paid at double the summer rate, and porters are required to carry only 20 kg (44 lbs) instead of the summer load of 25 kg (55 lbs).

Expedition porters must be insured and kitted out with tennis shoes, woollen socks and sunglasses while the liaison officer must be provided with a full expedition kit. The expedition is entitled to ask for the clothing to be returned but this seldom happens.

A deposit of $US4000 must be placed with the National Bank of Pakistan in Islamabad in case a helicopter rescue has to be mounted. The alternative is to have a letter guaranteeing any such payment from a registered travel agent in Pakistan or your own country's embassy.

Regions

The best regions to trek and climb in Pakistan are in the Northern Area and the North-west Frontier. The Northern Area, the main region, includes Baltistan (which incorporates the Karakoram), Gilgit and the Hunza. The Chitral and Swat districts of the Hindu Kush are the most notable parts of the North-west Frontier for trekking and climbing.

NORTHERN AREA

Much of the Northern Area of Pakistan is mountainous desert, very sparsely populated. The few villages are found in an oasis of green valleys and on river- banks or on the snow-fed side streams (*nalas*) that descend from steep gorges. Most nalas have alluvial fans at their exit onto the broader river valley and the villages have irrigation channels that often run long distances to water-fields of mustard and wheat. The local lifestyle of subsistence farming is often very primitive with little or no comforts in the more remote settlements, and it is almost impossible to buy any provisions.

To get to the Northern Area trekking and climbing districts from Islamabad, flights can be taken to either Gilgit or Skardu. Road travel to these destinations is via the Karakoram Highway that snakes through the spectacular Indus River Gorge. Travelling the Karakoram Highway to or from the mountains, even for just a sightseeing trip, is well worthwhile. The best time to visit is May or August as it can be extremely hot in June and July.

Karakoram Highway This road connects Pakistan and China and follows the path of the ancient Silk Route over the 4700 m (15,416 ft) Khunjerab Pass. It is the same path that Marco Polo reputedly travelled some 700 years ago. The terrain is extremely rugged and the route hazardous. At times the so-called 'highway' is little more than a one-lane track hewn out of solid rock on the side of a narrow gorge. In these and many other precarious situations one mistake from the driver would end in a sheer drop into the Indus River. From Islamabad to the Chinese border is 883 km (548 miles). In good conditions the journey up the Karakoram Highway from Islamabad to Kasgar in China takes four or five days. Little wonder that constructing the road took some 15,000 workers twenty years. It was finally opened to tourists in 1986. A Pakistan bus or mini-bus takes you as far as the border and then a Chinese bus picks you up on the other side.

On the route north from Islamabad the first major mountain of the Himalaya is the famous peak of Nanga Parbat.

Nanga Parbat Nanga Parbat derives its name from the Sanskrit words *nanga parvata*, which mean 'naked mountain'. The mountain is part of the Punjab Himalaya and is regarded as the western end of the Himalaya. It is 8125 m (26,650 ft) and was first climbed in 1953 by a German team only five weeks after Hillary and Tensing reached the summit of Mount Everest. The Germans were led by Dr K. Herlingkoffer who subsequently led expeditions up all three of Nanga Parbat's faces — the Rupal Face, the Rakhiot Face and the Diamir Face.

Reinhold Messner, arguably the world's leading Himalayan mountaineer, and his brother Gunther took part in Herlingkoffer's 1970 attempt on the Rupal Face. After reaching the summit, Gunther Messner became delirious and eventually separated from his brother and died, possibly in an avalanche. Before this there had been a mix-up over which coloured flares should have been fired off to give the weather report. Messner subsequently blamed Herlingkoffer for a series of mistakes contributing, so he claimed, to his brother's death. The matter ended up in Bavarian law courts and became a highly publicised case that was eventually settled in Herlingkoffer's favour.

The Karakoram Highway runs alongside the Indus River for much of its route northward through Pakistan. Close to the Chinese border it is a highway in name only (right). This main trans-Himalayan link follows a branch of the ancient Silk Route and passes through many different cultural areas. People of these regions such as the Balti (below) and those from Gilgit, can be differentiated by the style of their woollen berets.

Diamir was an earlier name used for the mountain. This name in the Dardi language (the Dards are a race living between Kashmir and the Hindu Kush) means 'dwelling place of the fairies'. One of the treks in the region is to the north face of this legendary mountain and the alpine-forested Fairytale Meadow, so named because the locals believe that this, too, is inhabited by fairies. The trek is in an open zone, so no permit is needed. The round trip takes four or five days and begins from Rakhiot Bridge on the Karakoram Highway. There is also a longer circuit of the mountain which takes you beneath the sheer 5000 m (16,400 ft) Rupal Face. This trek and others in the region are usually approached from Gilgit. To the east of Nanga Parbat is Baltistan.

Baltistan Region Once part of Ladakh, Baltistan extends more than 100 km (62 miles) either side of the Indus Valley. The Karakoram is the northern boundary and the southern and western limits are within the Deosai Plains. Baltistan consists of five valleys: Shigar, Skardu, Rondu, Khapulul, and Kharmang. The region is home to the hardy Balti people who are often employed as porters for trekking and climbing parties on the Baltoro Glacier. The Balti porters are notorious for driving a hard bargain and strikes commonly feature in expedition accounts. Galen Rowell's superbly illustrated book *In the Throne Room of the Mountain Gods* tells the story of an abortive attempt to climb K2 against a historical background depicting mountaineering in the Baltoro and its people.

The Karakoram The name Karakoram comes from the Karakoram Pass (5575 m; 18,286 ft), where the term means 'black earth' or 'black gravel'. The Pass is the highest point on what was once one of the main trading routes between India and China.

The Karakoram, or Trans Himalaya Range as it is also known, is a formidable place to trek or climb. Barren and sparsely populated, it has few of the civilising aspects trekkers can find in Kashmir or Nepal. There are no local village hotels, teahouses or lush green meadows. Despite their austerity, the mountains of the Karakoram are a powerful lure for climbers and trekkers.

The Karakoram Range extends 350 km (217 miles) and abounds with geographical extremes. It has the world's largest glaciers outside the polar regions: the Saichen ('Great Rose', 72 km; 45 miles); the Hispar (61 km; 38 miles); the Biafo (59 km; 37 miles); and the Baltoro and Batura (both 58 km; 36 miles).

Skardu The town of Skardu is the main staging-post for the Karakoram, and the district headquarters of Baltistan. Skardu is accessible daily by air from Islamabad. It takes twenty-five to thirty hours via the Karakoram Highway.

Skardu is located on the bank of the Indus River just 8 km (5 miles) above the confluence of the Indus and the River Shigar. With its altitude of 2286 m (7498 ft) and cooler climate, it is the best place for trekkers and expeditions to buy provisions and sort out details before heading into the hills. Jeeps, tractors with trailers and drivers can be hired here to take you to the various roadheads.

The K2 Hotel on the outskirts of Skardu is where most expeditions stay while they organise their equipment for the walk into the mountains.

Kondus Glacier A popular Baltistan trek in the open zone goes up the Kondus Glacier to the base of K7. The round trip takes some seventeen days. From Skardu you must hire a jeep to take you to Khaplu on the banks of the Shyok River. From here it is about a two-week round trip up the Kondus River valley to the base camp of K6 at the junction of the Kondus and the Kabar Glacier. There are many other trekking possibilities in the region but most are in restricted areas where a guide, permit and sometimes a liaison officer are required. The trek up the Baltoro Glacier is one of these.

Baltoro Glacier Access to the Baltoro Glacier is via the Shigar Valley and the villages of Shigar and Dassu (Dasso). The road is gradually being pushed further towards Askole, the last main village on the way to the Baltoro Glacier. Progress with the road is slow because of the border tensions between Pakistan and India in the Saichen Glacier region. The Baltoro Glacier, 58 km (36 miles) long, is bounded by ten of the world's thirty highest peaks. Four of them are over 8000 m (26,400 ft), including K2, the second highest mountain in the world.

The Baltoro Glacier trek is the most popular trek in Pakistan and also one of the hardest regularly offered by adventure travel companies in the Himalaya. The trek has achieved notoriety because of the many earlier climbing expeditions to the region, and because of K2, the second highest and one of the most difficult summits to climb.

Adventure travel brochures do not mince words in describing it: 'The most spectacular trek in the world'; 'the grade of the trail makes walking to Everest Base Camp look like a picnic'; and 'this is definitely not a trek for the faint-hearted'. Veteran trekkers who have already been round Annapurna or crossed from Kashmir to Ladakh may well have the Baltoro trek at the top of their 'to do' list.

The trek to Concordia or K2 Base Camp and back can take anywhere from twenty-four to thirty days. From the roadhead above Dassu the route follows the Braldu

Skardu, the administrative centre of Baltistan, is the main centre for trekking and climbing in the Karakoram. It can be reached from Rawalpindi/ Islamabad by bus via the Karakoram Highway in a day and a half or by air very quickly.

(Previous pages) The Fortress on the side of the Baltoro Glacier is just one of the many impressive rock faces and spires that have led this region to become the mecca for alpine big-wall climbers.

into the Braldu River above Askole. Above Payu on the main route is the Baltoro Glacier proper and the terrain is very rough. The trail is poorly marked and it is a gruelling walk over glacial moraine or glacier ice all the way.

For all these hardships there is the outstanding mountain spectacle of scenery of the Paiju Towers, the Trango Towers, the Lobsang Spires, the Mustagh Tower, Masherbrum and the Gasherbrums. The focus of the trek is Concordia — the dramatic junction of the Goodwin-Austen and Baltoro Glaciers. Within this small area is the most concentrated grouping of high mountains in the world. Broad Peak — 8047 m (26,394 ft); Gasherbrum II — 8035 m (26,355 ft); Gasherbrum III — 7952 m (26,083 ft) and Gasherbrum IV — 7925 m (25,994 ft).

K2 Base Camp is another day's walk to the north underneath the looming bulk of Broad Peak. At busy times during the climbing season there may be six or more mountaineering expeditions in the vicinity of Concordia and K2.

K2 (Chogori, Goodwin-Austen, Qogir Feng) The world's second highest mountain, K2, is widely regarded by mountaineers as being much harder to climb by its most straightforward route than Mount Everest is by its easiest route (Hillary and Tensing's original South Col line). K2 is not visible from any inhabited place which is why it has no local name. The most regularly used local alternative is Chogori, which in Balti means 'great mountain'. The peak is also sometimes referred to as Mount Goodwin-Austen, after Lt Goodwin-Austen who explored in the region in 1861. K2 is renowned for its cold, ferocious blizzards that have caused the deaths of some of the world's leading mountaineers in recent years.

In 1987 scientists from the University of Washington in Seattle proposed that K2 was in fact 8858 m (29,054 ft) high rather than the accepted 8611 m (28,244 ft). Their calculations, based on satellite

River. At the height of summer (June and July) the temperatures in the river gorge can reach over 40° C (104° F). Under these conditions most trekkers begin walking at about 5 a.m. to avoid the heat. The campsites along the route are rather limited and garbage is becoming a problem here as it is on other intensively used routes in the Himalaya.

Beyond this point trekkers need a permit and a liaison officer, so the Baltoro is hard to penetrate. Occasionally individuals or pairs can mix in with a climbing expedition provided the liaison officer does not object. The best and safest option is often a group trek.

A permit is not needed, however, to head up the Biafo Glacier which flows measurements, suggested K2 might be taller than Mount Everest at 8848 m (29,021 ft). This was later disputed and so far Mount Everest still holds the crown.

While K2 has drawn trekkers and climbers to Pakistan, many have returned time and again to the lesser-known spires and peaks found in subsidiary areas that offer very stimulating challenges in their own right. The other main glacier coming into the Braldu River, the Biafo, is one such area.

Biafo-Hispar Circuit The start of this trek is the same as for the Baltoro Glacier but it turns up the Baifo Glacier. The advantage is that it is a round trip. It is a strenuous trek, probably best done on skis early in the season.

The Biafo Glacier passes beneath the Ogre, 7285 m (23,895 ft). Both are famous for being the site of an epic retreat in 1977 when Doug Scott, abseiling from the summit, slipped and broke both legs. On the descent his partner, Chris Bonington, also slipped and broke some ribs. The team were six days struggling to get back to base camp, five of them without food.

The other rock peaks of the Biafo Glacier, especially the Latoks, are particularly challenging though not as high as those on the lower Baltoro Glacier. Continuing over the Hispar Pass to the Hispar Glacier, the lower part of the descent to the Hunza is over extremely rugged moraine. Less well-known than Baltistan for trekking, the Hunza region lies at the north-west extremity of the Karakoram.

K2 (also known as Mount Goodwin-Austen) is the second highest mountain in the world, yet it is not visible from any inhabited place, which is why there is no widely-used local name.

he Balti people of Askole eke out a ving from one of the harshest physical nvironments in the Himalaya.

etables and the high iron content of the Hunza water. This, however, is no longer believed to be the case. The Hunza people are mostly followers of the Ishmailis Muslim sect who worship the Aga Khan.

The Hunza valley has been opened only in recent times but now the Karakoram Highway (KKH) winds through its length on its way to the Khunjerab Pass, at 4700 m (15,416 ft), and the border. The Hunza has a number of shorter treks which commence from the main town of Karimabad. The 600-year-old Balti castle above Karimabad was originally the residence of the Mirs (former kings of the Hunza).

Popular treks in the Hunza are shorter routes. The Batura Glacier and Shimshal treks both begin from Passu further north on the KKH. The latter is a strenuous five-day route through an open zone to an altitude of 320 m (1050 ft) to the village of Shimshal. The Passu Batura trek is a week-long route over the Passu and Batura glaciers. The landscapes away from the Hunza valley floor are extremely barren, rugged hillsides often rising to snowcapped peaks.

Hunza Region The Hunza valley, north of Gilgit, was once famous for the longevity and hardiness of its people which was attributed to their diet of fruit and veg-

Gilgit Located on the Karakoram Highway, Gilgit is a major regional centre for trade and administration. With a bustling bazaar, Gilgit is an important staging-post for trekking and climbing. In the shadow of Domani (one of the three peaks of Rakaposhi), Gilgit, at 1453 m (4766 ft), is the capital of the northern areas of Pakistan. The trek from Gilgit to Rakaposhi Base Camp is in an open zone and so no permit is necessary. It is a moderate walk and takes ten days. Rakaposhi, at 7788 m (25,545 ft), is the twenty-seventh highest mountain in the world.

Two other treks are from Naltar just north of Gilgit to Pakore to the north-west and from Naltar to Chalti to the east. Both are seven-day moderate to strenuous treks in the open zone. At the conclusion of these treks, the jeeps can be taken back to Gilgit.

A rough and tumble version of polo is the favourite sport of the town which is host to a tournament in the first week of November each year. Polo, in fact, originated in the Gilgit region and *polo* means ball in the Balti language. It was the British who exported a tamer version of polo to the outside world. The wilder local version is a subjugated form of tribal warfare complete with raucous bands egging on their teams. Spectator involvement is every bit as enthusiastic as that of European soccer crowds.

The traditional, almost universal headwear of the people of northern Pakistan is the Gilgit hat, a soft woollen beret. There are distinct regional variations, however, which identify the wearer with a particular place.

Gilgit has grown rapidly since the highway was completed in 1975 and this has helped open the region. Gilgit itself is an oasis of green at 1400 m (4592 ft) in an otherwise extremely stark landscape. From Gilgit it is also possible to take a rough jeep-ride to the west up the Gilgit River valley and over the Shandir Pass to the Chitral. This journey is offered as an organised tour by some companies.

NORTH-WEST FRONTIER

Peshawar is the entry-point for the Chitral region of the North-west Frontier. This ancient city of the Pathans is 172 km (107 miles) west of Rawalpindi and Islamabad. From Peshawar it is possible to fly to Chitral in fifty minutes. Going by road via Dir takes a long day.

The states of Chitral, Surat, Hunza and Ngir were once semi-autonomous. It was only as recently as 1974 that the Hunza, for example, came under full Pakistan jurisdiction.

In general, climbers and trekkers are not permitted to venture within 30 km (19 miles) of the Chinese and Afghanistan borders (except if crossing borders such as on the KKH). The restriction (on the disputed territory with India) is not closer than 15 km (9 miles) to the ceasefire line.

Chitral Region The Chitral Valley is the main accessible part of the Hindu Kush Range for trekking and climbing. The dominant peak of the region is Tirich Mir at 7787 m (25,541 ft) which dominates the 320 km (199 mile) valley. Bordering Afghanistan, the Chitral did not become a district of Pakistan's North-west Frontier province until 1969.

Another major attraction of the region is the people of the Kalash Valley, 40 km (25 miles) from Chitral on the eastern border of Nuristan in Afghanistan. The 3000-strong Kalash tribe, or 'wearers of the black robe' as they are known, is a primitive, pagan tribe supposedly descended from soldiers of Alexander the Great's army. The Kalash women dress in long black gowns with elaborate headdresses decorated with cowrie shells for the main religious festival, Chaomos, which coincides roughly with the winter solstice. The Kalash religion is the last remnant of the pre-Muslim culture of Kafiristan which Muslims called the 'Land of the Unbelievers.' From 1895 to 1898 most of the people of Kafiristan were converted at knife-point to Islam, and only the Kalash people escaped this fate because they were under the patronage of the British who controlled the Chitral at the time.

The Kalash people worship elaborately carved effigies, partake in wine and attach religious significance to livestock, especially goats, all of which is contrary to the neighbouring Muslims' faith. Permits, which can be obtained in Chitral, are necessary to visit the Kalash Valley.

Chitral Bazaar is the starting-point for walks in the region. There are several moderate treks that can be taken in the side valleys. In the north the region is extremely barren but to the south the climate is like Kashmir's. For six months of the year many of the valleys are snowbound. The villagers survive only because extensive irrigation in summer ensures that their carefully protected orchards provide fresh fruit. The best time to visit the Chitral is July and August.

Shepherds graze their goats on the flanks of the Hispar Glacier, one of the many rugged landforms of the the Hunza region of northern Pakistan.

Swat Valley South-east of the Chitral is the lush green Swat Valley. In what is regarded as the lesser Himalaya are a variety of trekking routes of up to a week's duration and two peaks for smaller climbing parties — Falak Sair at 5918 m (19,411 ft) and Mankial at 5715 m (18,745 ft). Swat Valley can be reached by road either from Islamabad or Peshawar via Chakdara, or by plane from Islamabad. The Swat Valley has a rich archaeological history centred on the ancient capital of Mingora, with Hindu and Buddhist ruins.

Mingora and its twin town, Saidu Sharif, are the main centres for the region. In the latter, the Swat Museum contains the best collection of Gandhara sculpture in the world.

Swat was once the kingdom of Gandhara and home to 1400 Buddhist monasteries at the time of Christ. The Kushans, as they were known, decorated their monasteries and stupas with statues of Buddha that were sculpted in a fusion of styles from Greek, Roman, Persian and Indian sources. The Kushans were first to represent Buddha in a human form.

Trekking in the Swat district takes you through pine-covered ridges and alpine meadows. Swat is readily accessible and the best trekking is in the Ushu and Gabrial Valleys, but in the northern areas the Pathans are untrustworthy and it is best to trek with a reliable guide or outfitter. The local people in these harsh mountainous areas can be suspicious of outsiders, but if you are friendly and attempt to communicate in their own language you will quickly win their confidence.

Generally speaking, trekking is not as popular in Pakistan as in Nepal or India, but the large number of climbing expeditions visiting this country each year shows that the Karakoram has much to offer the more serious trekking and climbing parties. Climbers usually lead the way for trekkers and with the streamlining of the permit system there is excellent scope for both walking and small-scale mountaineering.

'YOU COME BACK!'

GREG CHILD

Mountaineer, Greg Child, enjoys more than high peaks in the Karakoram.

Some might call a traveller's fondness for Pakistan an acquired taste; tor most of Pakistan, from the ocean port of Karachi to the Karakoram Range — a distance of 1500 km [932 miles] — is flat, harsh desert. It is not until one reaches the hills a few hours north of Islamabad that a shimmering, hazy suggestion of snowcapped peaks interrupts the seared landscape of brown earth and browner rivers. In the maze of valleys in the mountain foothills live the people of the Karakoram; beyond the foothills a monumental ripple in the earth's crust — a knot of winding glaciers and fang-like towers up to 8000 m high — divides Pakistan from China and India. This range is the Karakoram.

In the shadows of the great Karakoram peaks many different cultures have evolved, for not only does the Karakoram divide Pakistan from its neighbouring nations, but its gorges, glaciers and peaks divide the mountain tribes. Tribes separated by a river or a range may speak a different dialect, belong to a different sect of Islam, or adopt a different dress or set of customs. Life in a Karakoram village is not

An insignificant spire on the shoulder of the 8047 m (26,394 ft) Broad Peak would elsewhere be a climber's dream.

easy. Winters in the Karakoram are long and cold, summers are arid. The isolated pockets of greenery surrounding the villages are hard-won from the land. The water which irrigates village crops is captured from mountain streams by means of elaborate viaducts and channels that crisscross cliffs and hillsides. Electrical power, piped water, sewerage, schools, or hospitals are virtually non-existent.

Those who visit the villages of the Karakoram leave convinced they have met the toughest people on earth.

Perhaps the toughest of this tough breed are the Balti, who live a few days' walk from Skardu along the Braldu River, which is fed by the Baltoro Glacier which, by and by, leads to K2, the world's second highest mountain. It is said that the people of the Braldu Valley secretly settled the land in the last century, to escape the taxes of the rulers of Baltistan. Even today, in their simple homes of mud-brick and riverstones, surrounded by wheat fields and herds of goat, sheep, and yaks, the Balti barely eke a living from the land.

My encounters with the Balti began in 1983, during a mountaineering expedition to Broad Peak, an 8000 m (26,240 ft) peak on the Baltoro Glacier. Prior to the expedition I had read much about the Balti in books about the great expeditions. Those books painted the Balti as a people who, to put it mildly, knew how to drive a hard bargain with an expedition. Years of being cut off in their isolated valleys had made them suspicious of outsiders, for, to the Balti, outsiders had always meant trouble.

Only a few decades before my visit, Hunza raiders had frequently swept down the passes to pillage the Balti's villages, while the first expeditions brought with them the military and government scrutiny, and the strange ways of foreigners.

So it was with some preconceived notions about our 100 Balti porters that I began the trek up the Braldu Valley. Ahead of us, burdened by our 25 kg [55 lb] loads, were our porters, clad in ragged homespun tunics and flimsy rubber boots. They led us into the poplar-lined cobbled streets of Chongo Chakpo and Askole, places where the way of life had scarcely changed since medieval times.

Beyond the last village and the curious attentions of dozens of ragamuffin children, we climbed onto the rubble-strewn Baltoro Glacier. On this popping, crackling, constantly moving ice-river we camped each night in desolate but inspiring places, flanked by turrets of rock and ice.

During these nights the porters huddled together, wrapped in blankets, squatting beneath tarpaulins draped over circular rock shelters, brewing their sweet, strong tea, singing away the cold nights, and puffing cheroots of wild tobacco or the noxious K2 cigarettes. It occurred to me during this expedition that to the Balti, locked as they were in life-long toil with the land, we westerners with our wealth and our modern trappings must seem a strange sight, and that our plans to climb an 8000 m mountain must seem an extravagance of lunatic proportions with no practical purpose. Certainly the porters are mainly in it for the money. But, as I noticed, the mountains moved the Balti too.

The oldest porters had been on many expeditions, in fact some were portering for the Karakoram pioneers when I was still in nappies. They knew the routes each expedition had climbed and the names of the famous climbers. They were proud of the craft of portering. As we neared the highest peaks, around the great glacial intersection called Concordia, I watched the old hands take the novice porters aside and teach them such things as how to shape a walking stick for chopping steps in the ice, or how to find the right path on the glacial vastness. And in the evenings, after their prayers and chants to Allah, the elders would point to the peaks and give each one a name: Masherbrum; Trango; Gasherbrum — the 'beautiful mountain' that shines gold at sunset; Chogolisa — 'the bride peak'; triple-summited Broad Peak; and tallest of all, K2. As the porters spoke about the mountains I saw that they stared at them the same way we climbers stared at mountains. They, no less than us, appreciated the rugged geometry of the Baltoro.

Near base camp, snow left from winter lay knee-deep on the glacier, making the journey arduous for those breaking trail. The climbers took turns in front, until a young Balti from Askole, named Musa, insisted on taking the lead. With no reason other than the desire to share with us the adventure of finding a safe path through crevasses and rushing glacial streams, Musa, carrying a full load, led us to base camp, proud to show us he was as much a mountaineer as any of us.

Expeditions and treks are simply encounters with memorable people in remarkable settings. Later that season of 1983, Musa, curious about our progress on Broad Peak, appeared in base camp bearing gifts of a chicken and eggs — a walk of five days. In gratitude, we gave him the fabric from a wind-torn tent that he happily presented to his father, Ali, who, toothless and ancient, manned the cable bridge across the Drumordu River, a tributary of the Braldu. By the time we passed by Musa's and Ali's households, the tent had been sewn into clothes for Musa's children.

In 1986 and 1987, en route to and from Gasherbrum IV and K2, at the Drumordu bridge old Ali and I have sipped tea in his cave-shelter and traded — me exchanging a flashlight bulb or a cigarette lighter for a meal or some fuel. Whenever Ali sees me he exclaims happily in broken English, 'you come back!' — pleased I have returned to his valley to try another peak and, on my way home, happy to see I have survived a summer at altitude. At each meeting we try to see that the other goes away with the better trade, but old Ali always wins on the way out, by sending word ahead to Askole for his household to give me one final gift of mulberries, apricots, or eggs.

Standing on the high summits of the Karakoram, as I've been lucky enough to do a few times, gives one a view across a land beautiful for its starkness. It is a place where one sees geological time etched across gorge walls and mountain faces, while, in the villages, time as we know it in the West stands still. The lushness of the occasional alpine meadows and villages seems all the more lush against the hostile surroundings. Whenever I run into old Ali on the banks of the Drumordu, his kindness seems like an oasis too. I have a feeling that he'll always be there, every time I return, and that he's there right now, even as you read this, pulling travellers across on the cable bridge.

Based in the US, Australian Greg Child is one of the world's leading all-round climbers. He is also highly regarded as a mountaineering writer. His first book, *Thin Air* (Patrick Stephens, 1988), recounts his Himalayan exploits.

INDIA

> Yet a special joy had been with me throughout the pilgrimage and during all my time in Kashmir. It was the joy of being among mountains; it was the special joy of being among the Himalayas. I felt linked to them; I liked speaking the name. India, the Himalayas; they went together.
>
> **V.S. NAIPAUL**
> *An Area of Darkness, 1964*

India is a vast country with a population to match; over 800 million people. The Indian Himalaya is similarly vast, though it is divided by Nepal into the Western Himalaya and the Eastern Himalaya. The former includes the states of Jammu and Kashmir in the north-east, Himachal Pradesh to the south and, further south again, Uttar Pradesh. The Eastern Himalaya includes Darjeeling and the states of Sikkim, and Arunachal Pradesh.

Given the great distances between Western and Eastern Himalaya, it is not surprising that there are different gateway cities and that travellers generally visit either the Western or the Eastern Himalaya at one time.

Despite over 200 separate languages being spoken in India, English is sufficient for most day-to-day needs, thanks to the legacy of the colonial era. Hindi is the predominant native language in the north-west of India. In Muslim regions such as Kashmir, Urdu is more widely spoken. Bengali is the main language of Calcutta.

In specific areas of the Indian Himalaya, languages such as Kashmiri, Ladakhi and Sikkimese predominate. When travelling in a group with a guide, language is seldom a problem. But if you are off the beaten track on your own, a friendly smile and a phrasebook (see Suggested Reading List) will suffice.

Trekking

There is no system of trekking permits in India. However, some states such as Jammu and Kashmir require trekkers to register with the Tourist Office. Otherwise you can usually go anywhere in the mountains providing you do not cross into restricted areas adjacent to the Northern border. This is denoted by the so-called 'Inner Line' which varies in position. Details of the restricted zone can be obtained from the State Government tourist office in the respective region or from the headquarters in Delhi. Sikkim is the one exception to the rule where a permit is required to trek.

For details on specific regions and trekking routes, Garry Weare's *Trekking in the Indian Himalaya* is recommended, as is Hugh Swift's *The Trekker's Guide to the Himalaya and Karakoram*. But any such guide can quickly become dated, so it is always best to seek up-to-date information from consulates, adventure travel companies or recently returned trekkers.

India has been promoting climbing and trekking through a series of mountaineering and tourism meets with the world's leading climbers.

Climbing

Climbing in India is controlled by the Indian Mountaineering Foundation (IMF) which came into being in 1957 through the patronage of the then Prime Minister, Pandit Jawaharlal Nehru. Capitalising on Tenzing Norgay's success with Edmund Hillary on the first successful ascent of Everest in 1953, Nehru also set up the Himalayan Mountaineering Institute in Darjeeling, Tenzing's home town. The Institute offers mountaineering training courses for Indians and foreigners. Other mountaineering institutes are now also to be found at Manali in Himachal Pradesh and Uttarkashi in Uttar Pradesh. The latter is named after Pandit Nehru.

INDIA AT A GLANCE

Area
3,287,590 sq. km (1,269,010 sq. miles).

Population
760 million, growth rate 2.1%, 1/6 world population.

Government
Parliamentary democracy – Federal Republic of India. 22 states, 9 union territories. Prime Minister – Rajiv Gandhi.

Capital
New Delhi, population 6,000,000.

Flag
Three stripes cross wise. Saffron yellow, white (with blue ashoka wheel) and green.

People in the Himalaya
Kashmiris, Ladakis, Tibetan refugees, Sikkimese.

Language
Hindi (national language); 14 other languages spoken by 30% of population and recognised by the constitution.

Religion
82% Hindu; 11% Muslim; 2.5% Christian; 2% Sikh; 1% Buddhist; 0.5% Jain.

Highest and lowest points
Sea level to Nanda Devi — 7817 m (25,640 ft).

Currency
Indian Rupee (1 Rupee = 100 paise).

Time
Indian time is 5½ hours ahead of GMT.

Portion in Himalaya
The states of Jammu and Kashmir, Himachal Pradesh, Darjeeling, Sikkim, Assam and Arunachal Pradesh.

Best time
April and May – pre-monsoon; September and October – post monsoon.

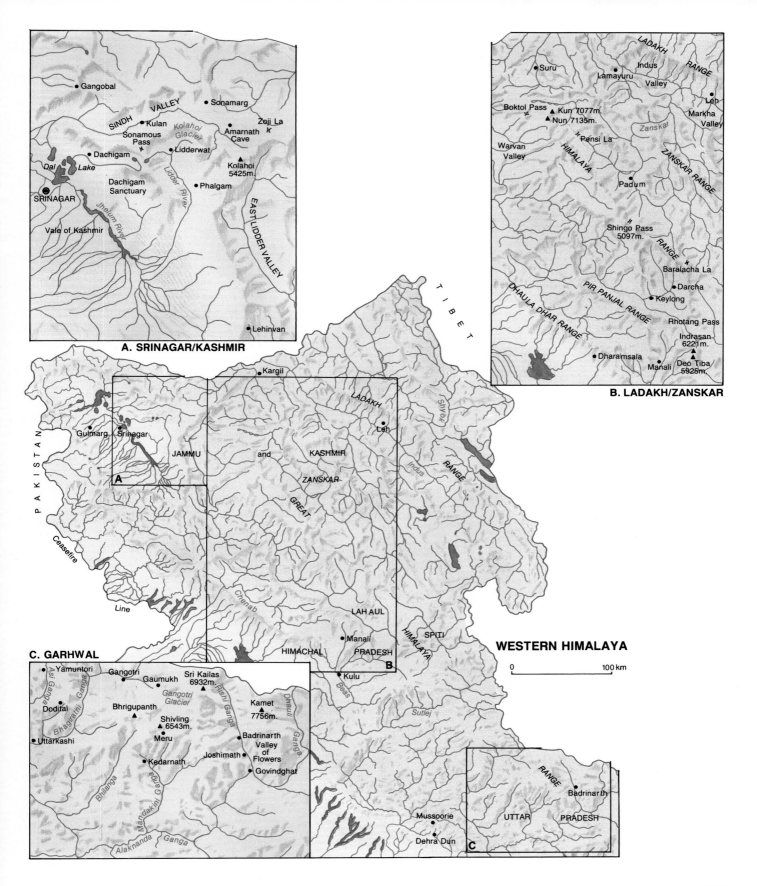

A. SRINAGAR/KASHMIR

Gangobal
SINDH VALLEY
Sonamarg
Kulan
Kolahoi Glacier
Zoji La
Sonamous Pass
Amarnath Cave
Dachigam
Lidderwat
Dal Lake
Kolahoi 5425m.
Phalgam
SRINAGAR
Dachigam Sanctuary
Jhelum River
Lidder River
Vale of Kashmir
EAST LIDDER VALLEY
Lehinvan

B. LADAKH/ZANSKAR

LADAKH RANGE
Suru
Lamayuru
Indus Valley
Leh
Boktol Pass
Kun 7077m.
Nun 7135m.
Markha Valley
Zanskar
Pensi La
Warvan Valley
HIMALAYA
ZANSKAR RANGE
Padum
Shingo Pass 5097m.
RANGE
Baralacha La
Darcha
PIR PANJAL RANGE
DHAULA DHAR RANGE
Keylong
Rhotang Pass
Indrasan 6221m.
Dharamsala
Manali
Deo Tiba 5925m.

WESTERN HIMALAYA

Kargil
TIBET
LADAKH
Leh
Shyok
PAKISTAN
Gulmarg
Srinagar
JAMMU
and
KASHMIR
ZANSKAR
GREAT
Indus
RANGE
A
Ceasefire
Line
Chenab
LAHAUL
HIMALAYA
SPITI
Manali
HIMACHAL
PRADESH
B
Kulu
Beas
Sutlej
0   100 km

C. GARHWAL

Yamuntori
Gangotri
Gaumukh
Sri Kailas 6932m.
Asi Ganga
Dodital
Bhagirathi Ganga
Bhrigupanth
Gangotri Glacier
Rishi Ganga
Kamet 7756m.
Dhauli Ganga
Uttarkashi
Shivling 6543m.
Meru
Badrinarth
Valley of Flowers
Bhilanga
Joshimath
Kedarnath
Mandakini Ganga
Govindghat
Alaknanda Ganga

RANGE
Badrinarth
Mussoorie
UTTAR   PRADESH
Dehra Dun
C

Permits

In India, to climb anything that looks like a mountain higher than 5000 m (16,400 ft), you must have permission from the IMF. There is no category of trekking peaks as is the case in Nepal. The IMF has its headquarters in Delhi where all the paperwork has to be directed when trying to obtain a permit (see page 217 for the address). At least six months' notice is required when booking a peak. The usual rules and regulations about rates of pay, food, clothing and insuring staff and porters apply, as in other Himalayan countries, and a liaison officer is compulsory for each group. The IMF works closely with the Indian Airforce which carries out any helicopter rescues.

Between seventy-five and a hundred expeditions climb in India each year. Peak fees in US dollars for 1989 were:

Below 6000 m (19,680 ft)	400
6001–6500 m (21,320 ft)	600
6501–7000 m (22,960 ft)	900
7001 m and above (22,960 ft)	1200
Nun and Kun	1500
East Karakoram	2000

A number of peaks in the Indian Himalaya are also climbed by commercial expeditions or guided parties. The main ones are Trisuli, at 7120 m (23,354 ft) in the Garhwal, Nun at 7135 m (23,403 ft) in Zanskar, and Stock Kangri at 6121 m (20,077 ft) in Ladakh.

Western Himalaya

The Western Himalaya has the most variety and scope for trekkers and climbers. Kashmir, Ladakh, Kulu and the Garhwal are all worthwhile visiting and all are easily reached from Delhi.

DELHI

A legacy of the British Raj, Delhi has been India's national capital since it moved its administration from Calcutta in 1911. Delhi is one of nine Union Territories and twenty-two states that make up the Indian Union. As the seat of the Lok Sabha (lower house) and the Rajya Sabha (upper house) it is the political focus of the subcontinent and has importance beyond what its size and population would otherwise warrant.

The commercial heart of New Delhi for visitors is the Connaught where many of the modern tourist shops and hotels and restaurants are. The main shopping street, Janpath, has numerous curio shops.

Several days can be spent sightseeing around Delhi and becoming accustomed to the heat and the ways of Indian bureaucracy. The Red Fort is a must for any tour, while the nearby Jami Masjid, the Friday Mosque, is the largest in India. Both sights are part of old Delhi and help give an insight into the true India.

AGRA

A visitor to Delhi and the Himalaya is well advised to take at least a day trip to Agra to see the Taj Mahal and other historic monuments. Agra is 200 km (124 miles) south-east of Delhi and can be reached by taxi, bus, train or plane.

COMING AND GOING

To be at the airport at eleven for an aircraft that leaves at midnight; and then to wait until after three in the morning, intermittently experiencing the horrors of an Indian public lavatory, is to know anxiety, exasperation and a creeping stupor.

V.S. NAIPAUL
An Area of Darkness, 1964

To get to the main centres in the Western Indian Himalaya (Srinagar, Leh, Kulu or the Garhwal) from Delhi takes at least one or two days by bus or train, or a one or two-hour flight on one of two internal airlines. It is also possible to go by taxi, though this is expensive unless the cost can be shared.

Delhi is also often a staging-point for the entire Himalaya with trekkers and climbers going overland or by plane to Kathmandu or Calcutta, either on their

(Previous pages) The shikara, a gondala-like craft, is the traditional means of transport on the lakes and waterways of Srinagar, the main city of Kashmir. Merchants and water taxis visit the hundreds of houseboats that are moored on the banks of Dal and Nagin Lakes seeking customers.

On your way to or from the Himalaya, several days can be fruitfully spent sightseeing in and around Delhi. The Mausoleum of Humayan was built prior to the Taj Mahal at Agra and is well worth a visit.

way to the Kumaun Hills and the Garhwal.

Land Travelling overland to the Himalaya from Delhi by bus, taxi or train could be an adventurous experience in itself. You will learn more about the cultural side of India than you could on countless plane flights.

Indian main roads are always crowded with traffic, from trucks with teetering loads, overcrowded local buses, and wobbling bicycles to all manner of foot traffic including horses and carts, water buffaloes and even the odd sacred cow. For drivers, negotiating such traffic is taxing, but even being a passenger can be an exhausting business. The roads are rough and horns are continually blaring as faster traffic tries to overtake underpowered or ancient vehicles. Not surprisingly, self-drive cars are almost unheard of in India. Taxis or chauffeured cars are the most reasonable and relaxing form of road transport for sightseeing.

Government and private bus services run between New Delhi and many of the major hill towns which are the staging-points for treks. Direct services run to Simla, Mussoorie, Jammu (which then connects with Srinagar) and Hardwar, with connections to the Kulu Valley and Dharamsala. Luxurious buses may even have airconditioning and videos.

Railways For Kashmir an overnight train service runs to Jammu where there is a bus that connects with Srinagar. By alighting from the same service at Pathnankot and catching local buses, hill stations in Himachal Pradesh such as Dharamsala and Chamba can be reached.

way to or from their home port. Indian Airlines and Royal Nepal Airlines fly to both these cities from Delhi. Rail connections are not so straightforward to Nepal as the closest station is at Birganj, from where you must take a bus to the border town of Raxaul before taking another to Kathmandu. From Raxaul to Kathmandu takes at least six hours by bus. Most people on a tight timetable elect to fly from Delhi to Nepal.

Air Plane travel to the Western Himalaya from Delhi is relatively inexpensive and can help maximise the time you have to spend in the mountains. It can also help minimise the chance of getting caught in any of the random terrorism carried out by militant Sikhs in the Punjab.

Indian Airlines flies daily to Srinagar via Jammu and also offers a direct service. Leh is the highest commercial airport in the world and is serviced daily by Indian airlines. Vyadoot, the third-level carrier or feeder airline, flies smaller planes via Chandigarh to Bhuntar (the airport for the Kulu Valley) and to Dhera Dun, the gate-

JAMMU AND KASHMIR

The state of Jammu and Kashmir (usually referred to by the abbreviation J & K) is the most northerly and beleaguered of India's states. The famous Vale of Kashmir comprises only a small portion of the state while Ladakh covers more than 70 per cent of its area.

AMIDST THE KASHMIR MOUNTAINS

GARRY WEARE

Trekking in the Himalaya can bring unexpected rewards, as Garry Weare relates on a trip he made in Kashmir.

The elderly shepherd surveyed our campsite.

'You have no sugar in your tea, you have no horses, you have no wives. You must be poor man.'

Our initial meeting had been a classic case of misunderstanding. The shepherd, living in the high remote valley in the Kashmir Himalaya, had encountered our motley trekking party. In our exchanges, we had not appreciated his order of priorities, neither had he appreciated ours. For him, wandering the mountains was his livelihood, migrating each summer in search of rich grazing pastures for his goats. For us it was a holiday, a trek which freed us from the material pressures of our world, a trek into a mountain region we felt privileged to visit.

We had arrived a week earlier at the alpine village of Phalgam, some 90 km [56 miles] by road from Srinagar, the capital of the Indian state of Kashmir. From Phalgam we planned to hire horses and assistants, and trek off along the mountain trails that would take us across the Kashmir Himalaya into the Buddhist region of Ladakh. It was easier said than done.

In 1976, any trek beyond the confines of the more accessible Kashmir valleys was fraught with difficulties.

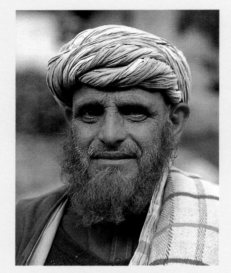

The henna dyed beard of a Gujar shepherd in Kashmir signifies he has made his pilgrimage to Mecca.

The horsemen had little inclination to go further than the nearby Lidder valley; for them Ladakh might have been on another planet. There was no way that they would come, and local guides warned us off what they considered to be a most foolhardy adventure. We tried to secure the services of the local Tourist Officer. We showed him our detailed maps outlining the route and the contours. We showed him our boots, rucksacks and revealed our innermost need to trek through these mountains. He seemed puzzled. The map rotated some 180 degrees; he again looked blankly at us. He remained silent for a while. We waited for the pronouncement.

'Why not go by bus?'

It was indeed a case of Kashmiri lateral thinking. Our problems, as far as he was concerned, were over. We could get to Ladakh the easy way. A tourist bus now plied the road from Srinagar to Leh, the capital of Ladakh; it would not be necessary to trek. With the road we were familiar; with our need to trek, the Tourist Officer was unfamiliar. And that was the conclusion of our meeting.

We were, however, not to be defeated. We had planned our adventure for months. If we could not hire horses, we would have to backpack each stage. The thought of straining up those passes with huge packs was not appealing, yet we had no alternative.

That evening we repacked, stored our excess gear in a local lodge and began to calculate the provisions we would need to get us from Kashmir to the first main settlement in Ladakh. From there we hoped we could sustain ourselves buying local food. Each time we distributed our loads, more was left behind. Luxuries were discarded — the likes of Shipton and Tilman would have been proud of us — as we debated the necessity of carrying that extra portion of oatmeal or rice.

Yet our plans were modest. It was decided to leave the next day. We would follow the ancient pilgrim route to Amarnath for the first two stages, trekking up the East Lidder Valley to the sacred lake at Sheshnag. We would then leave the main pilgrim trail and ascend a moraine-filled gully to the Gul Gali Pass and gain our first views of the inner Himalaya. From the pass we would be a couple of stages from the Kanatal Valley, and from then on, it would be only a few stages trekking across the glacial heights of the Boktol Pass into Ladakh.

These trails were by no means unexplored. The British, in the early part of this century, had crossed these valleys either on tours of duty or as part of an extended summer's leave. One could imagine the Forest Officer on his tour of duty staying in the modest 'dak bungalow', or camping in a huge canopied tent in a remote alpine valley. Those on vacation would not have been far behind. Tents are still displayed, complete with bath tub and dresser, in the Phalgam Bazaar. They would have been hired for the season as the party wandered off perhaps to Ladakh and then on to the Kulu Valley and back to Shimla by the autumn.

We compared our notes with the guidebooks written between the wars. Stages were outlined from Kashmir to the Karakoram, to Skardu and Gilgit, and to outlying regions of Ladakh, a testimony to a bygone age.

Since 1947 much of the territory of the Maharajah's state of Jammu and Kashmir had been partitioned to Pakistan. The region of Baltistan and the Karakoram was now distanced by ceasefire lines and disputed international boundaries, while India's sensitive border regions of Ladakh were closed to foreigners until 1974. Since then, a generation of Kashmiris had lost the feeling for the mountains; a generation of cooks, guides and horsemen had little knowledge of the remote trails more than a few days distant from Phalgam.

After a week we reached the shepherd encampment at Humpet. We were tired. It had been a long haul that day and we looked forward to relaxing and savouring the rarified mountain air. We pitched our camp near to a cluster of shepherd settlements and it wasn't long before the headman, accompanied by his many offspring, wandered down to pay his 'Salaams'. We acknowledged his greeting and without further ceremony he squatted and cupped his hands next to our modest fire. His eyes did not miss a thing as he silently surveyed our modest belongings. Neither did ours, for the shepherd helped himself to a mirror and admired his luxuriant red beard.

We offered him tea. He politely refused, until custom demanded acceptance. He sipped the brew infrequently and with obvious displeasure.

'You have sugar?' he asked. We shook our heads and entered into a rather involved explanation. We were backpacking. We were going light and sugar was a luxury, an extra weight to carry. Red Beard nodded. He fell silent for a time, then pointed his head towards a nearby ridge where his horses were grazing. He then asked after ours. We again explained the fundamentals of backpacking. Red Beard's curiosity was aroused. The enquiry continued. The next subject inevitably was women and the possession thereof. He seemed bemused by the fact that we were all males, in our 20s, and yet none of us were married. For a man who had an arranged marriage at 14, this sounded a little strange. Indeed, by the expression on Red Beard's face, this whole episode was one that he found totally bewildering. He looked down, stroked his beard, and made the following summary of his findings.

'You have no sugar in your tea, you have no horses, and no wives, you must be poor man'. With that he left.

Red Beard reappeared early the following morning. Without ado he presented us with a small calico bag, filled with sugar. As we thanked him his eldest son appeared, leading two horses. He pointed up-valley and explained that we could take them as pack animals on to the next camp at the head of the glacier . . . [T]here was no use in protesting. He had made up his mind to look after us and that was that. We thanked him warmly and trekked off up the valley, mindful that he had not also tried to arrange wives for us.

This incident remained in my mind for many seasons. Indeed, I could hardly forget for I returned to his encampment on many occasions and tried my best to repay the hospitality. My position had materially improved in his eyes. Now I appeared with larger groups, complete with cooks and assistants and abundant food supplies. We had horses to carry the gear, and most of the groups included at least a few young ladies which, even with assurances to the contrary, Red Beard eyed as potential suitors for my single status.

Whether Red Beard appreciates my attraction to trekking through his territory is something I cannot tell, for his migratory life remains essentially unchanged, as does his hospitality. Reason enough for me to undertake the simple delight of trekking in Kashmir each season.

Garry Weare is a leading authority on Kashmir and author of *Trekking in the Indian Himalaya*, (Lonely Planet, 1986). He is currently Director of Overseas Operations for World Expeditions.

The Vale of Kashmir The Kashmir Valley, or 'Vale of Kashmir' as it is known, is approximately 150 km long by 50 km (93 x 31 miles) wide and is completely ringed by mountains of the Pir Panjal range. The Vale is extremely fertile and in summer the weather is pleasant because of the altitude (1585 to 2743 m; 5199 to 8997 ft). Apple orchards, fields of rice, *tongas* (horse-drawn carts) and untouched villages await the traveller willing to venture beyond the realm of the main cities of the Valley.

Srinagar The ancient city of Srinagar, the summer capital of Kashmir, is situated on a complex of waterways, lakes and the Jhelum River. The old city of Srinagar is a maze of medieval buildings and narrow overhung streets. Said to date back to the 3rd century BC, Srinagar was supposedly built at the behest of the great Buddhist King, Ashoka. *Sri* means beauty or wealth of knowledge, and *nagar* means city. Srinagar is a centre of the arts and learning and has always had a university.

One of the five great rivers of the Punjab, the Jhelum winds through the city and is crisscrossed by numerous bridges. Sometimes called the 'Venice of India' because of its famous houseboats and *shikaras* (water-taxis similar to gondolas), Srinagar is a very popular holiday destination for Indians escaping the monsoon season and foreigners coming to explore Kashmir's valleys and mountains. Srinagar is accordingly geared for travellers.

There is little in the way of good trekking gear to be bought in Srinagar and, compared with Kathmandu, only a limited number of experienced agencies that can organise ponies, cooks and guides. There are, however, numerous interesting places to explore and trek to. Several old hill resorts are starting-points for some of the more popular treks and most are worth a visit in their own right. All the hill stations can be reached by local buses from Srinagar and in season the more popular places are serviced daily by tourist coaches. Taxis are an alternative, especially if the cost can be shared by several passengers. The usual tourist accommodation in Srinagar is unique.

Houseboats The British Raj, following the mogul tradition of escaping from the plains in summer, were denied permission to purchase land for their summer houses by the local kings who still maintained sovereignty. Not to be outmanoeuvred, the British developed the idea of houseboats with all the comforts of home. Contemporary deluxe houseboats are up to 25 m (82 ft) long and have bathrooms, dining rooms, sundecks, lounges with chandeliers, carpets and woodcarvings in the style of English drawing-rooms and, when the power is working, cold drinks.

Today the two main lakes of Srinagar — Nagin and Dal — are ringed by houseboats that function as mini floating hotels. Most never leave the banks where they are moored side by side. One family or company may own up to three or four houseboats each, with names such as Maharajah's Palace, Empress of India, or Jewel in the Crown. The boats have no means of propulsion and most are built in situ. Nagin Lake is regarded as the most beautiful and peaceful, even though it is only separated by a causeway from Dal Lake. The water is deeper and in Nagin Lake less polluted but even so, swimming is not advised as the houseboats' effluent drains straight into the lake.

The more remote luxury houseboats of Nagin Lake prove a welcome haven from the dust and bustle of Srinagar.

Competition for houseboat custom is fierce, and at both the airport and the Government Tourist Office Reception Centre in Srinagar travellers will be besieged by aggressive touts. Once you board your houseboat, most of the cares of the city are behind you except for the waterborne merchants and curio sellers who are among the most persistent salesmen in the world. At appointed times

Today houseboats on the lakes and waterways of Srinagar operate as small hotels. They owe their origin to the British Raj who were denied permission to own summer houses by the local kings.

Kashmir is renowned for its arts and crafts. Fine handmade silk and woollen carpets abound, pashmina goat's wool shawls, brightly painted papier-mâché boxes, ashtrays, ornaments and decorations, as well as finely carved walnut furniture and figures are sold wherever one goes throughout the city streets and waterways of Srinagar.

WATER TREKKING

A relaxing excursion is to go by shikara into the city or around the Dal or Nagin Lakes. It is possible to venture even further afield to the Mansabal or Wolar Lake upstream on the Jhelum River, on a multi-day journey by water, camping along the way on the riverbanks.

Trekking Kashmir Style

Trekking in Kashmir differs markedly from trekking in Nepal, mostly because of the different landscapes and land-use patterns. Kashmir has pine-clad slopes and alpine meadows in contrast to the semi-tropical forest and rugged slopes often found in Nepal. It also has fewer permanent settlements in the mountains, which results in fewer crowds and less population pressure in alpine zones; the mountains are used in spring and summer for grazing. In broad terms the mountains in Kashmir are smaller but it is likely that you will see more of them on trek and cross more passes.

Porters are seldom used in Kashmir. Loads are predominantly carried by mules or ponies. In some places ponies are ridden as well but usually only on gentle terrain. On the trail each ponyman may look after two or three animals, which involves loading and unloading them at the beginning and end of the day and shepherding them across difficult terrain or through swollen streams. The ponies can sometimes get out of control or, worse still, run off with their loads. At night they are hobbled, but even so they can travel considerable distances unless carefully

through the day and night the amplified wails of the muezzin calling devout Muslims to prayer drift across the water.

Everything happens on the lake. Other visitors include flower-sellers, who come by twice a day, and money changers, chocolate-sellers and barbers. For early risers a shikara ride to the vegetable market is well worth the effort. Here farmers with shikaras laden with produce, trade boat to boat with merchants.

watched. If you are using the services of a ponyman and his beasts of burden, be careful how your gear is packed into kitbags and loaded onto the animals as it invariably gets a very rough ride. Using ponies can be expensive on private treks unless you establish a rate beforehand.

Wherever you trek in Kashmir's high meadows during the summer you're bound at some stage to come across the nomadic herders, the Gujars, who usually tend herds of horses, water buffalo and cattle while the Bakarwals mostly look after sheep and goats. Both groups speak their own language which is not generally understood by the Kashmiris.

Gulmarg Gulmarg, ('meadow of flowers'), a famous hill-station just 50 km (31 miles) from Srinagar, is a popular day or overnight trip. Its reputation stems partly from an 18-hole golf course, the highest in the world (2730 m; 8954 ft), and the excellent views. There are numerous reminders of the days of the Raj, from the stone church in the middle of the meadow, to the lodges and famous hotels such as Highland Park dotted around a broad grassy bowl. In summer there is fly fishing and one can take short treks through alpine meadows or a climb to Khilanmarg, the main hill behind the resort. From its crest on a clear day Nanga Parbat, 'the lord of the mountains', is visible to the north and the twin (7100 m; 23,288 ft) peaks of Nun and Kun can be seen to the west. Pony trekking is also available in summer.

SKIING In winter the Gulmarg becomes India's major alpine ski resort. Foreigners have been visiting the area to ski since the late 1960s. By Western standards the lift facilities are limited but they are being upgraded. Cross-country skiing is growing and heli-skiing is now available.

Yusmarg In the Pir Panjal hills 40 km (25 miles) south of Srinagar is the meadow of Yusmarg. Far less developed than

Gulmarg, it is popular for its carpets of wildflowers in spring. This hill-station is also the starting-point for several shorter treks. Most of the extended treks in Kashmir, however, are to the east of Srinagar.

Sonamarg – Sind Valley Sonamarg, another small hill-station, is the last main town on the road through the Sind Valley to Ladakh before the Zoji La Pass, 20 km (12 miles) further on. Sonamarg means 'meadow of gold'. This centre is also the staging-post for treks to Lakes Gangobal, Vishansar, and Krishansar and some of the most beautiful meadows of alpine flowers in Kashmir. A popular circuit is a week's journey via the Nichinai Pass to the lakes, then down the Wangat Valley. From Gangobal Lake you are in striking distance of one of the three summits of Haramurkh, which is 4876 m (15, 993 ft), and the highest peak in the area.

Phalgam – Lidder Valley At the junction of the Aru (the West Lidder) and the Sheshnag (the East Lidder) Rivers is the hill resort of Phalgam (Pahalgam), 95 km (59 miles) from Srinagar. This, the most popular resort in the Kashmir Valley, is

The Pir Panjal Range, which lies to the south of the main Himalaya range, separates the Kashmir Valley from the Warvan Valley and rises to an average elevation of 5000 m (16,400 ft). This is the first barrier to the monsoons.

(Right) The people of Kashmir are predominantly Muslim and speak Urdu. In the villages, however, Kashmiri is the main language. The locals wear a woollen smock known as a *ferun*. Hidden beneath the garment is a *kangri* — a clay pot held by a wicker cradle which is full of hot coals (this is how Kashmiris keep warm in winter).

(Previous pages) Traditional agriculture is still practised the length of the Himalaya. In a remote Kashmir valley the entire family threshes and winnows the grain by hand in the face of a storm that will soon cover fields with the first of the winter snows.

the main staging-point for pilgrimages to the Amarnath Cave, four days' walk to the east, and treks to the Kolahoi Glacier via the Lidder Valley. Phalgam is popular with Indian holidaymakers. Travellers organising their own treks can buy provisions and hire ponies and ponymen here, though at the height of the season these can be expensive.

AMARNATH PILGRIMAGE: The *yatra*, or pilgrimage, to Amarnath to see the sacred *lingam*, an ice stalactite in a grotto, is a holy quest for Hindus. The giant icicle, believed to be a manifestation of Shiva's phallus, is largest from mid-June to mid-July and this is probably the best time to make the journey. The trail is very crowded in the lead-up to the Sawan, the full moon in July or August, when up to 30,000 pilgrims, or *yatris* as they are known, make their way to the cave to offer food, sweets and flowers. By this time the icicle may well have melted to only a foot high in the warmer air. The yatra is highly regulated and joining the procession will be a colourful time. This is a moderate trek and crowds at the peak time could well be more of an ordeal than the walking.

Kolahoi Glacier The trek up the Lidder Valley, from Phalgam to the Kolahoi Glacier and Mt Kolahoi and back, takes about six days and is relatively easy going. Mt Kolahoi is one of the most popular destinations in Kashmir because of the beautiful but moderate terrain and the ease of making trekking arrangements in Phalgam. The route goes via Aru and Lidderwat and reaches an altitude of 3795 m (12,448 ft). The trek can be extended to the Sindh Valley by crossing the Yemhar Pass. The main trail meets the road to Sonamarg at Kulan but there are other options for reaching Sonamarg.

Kashmir to Ladakh The main route across country on foot from Kashmir to Ladakh used to be by way of the Zoji La, but since 1960, when the road was completed, trekkers now favour the Boktal Pass to cross the Great Himalaya Range.

It is possible to begin such a trek at Phalgam, proceed up the East Lidder Valley, then cross either the Guloi Gail Pass into the Warvan, or Wadvan Valley as it is also known. The route then passes by way of Humpet to Kanital and then over the Boktol or Lonvilad Pass. At this point the greenery of Kashmir is quickly left behind and the severe Zanskar desert landscapes predominate. The 4268 m (14,000 ft) Boktol Pass involves crossing glacier ice which earlier in the season may still carry fresh snow concealing crevasses. This can make the crossing more dangerous unless ropes are used.

On the other side of the pass the trail leads down to Panniker in the Suru Valley. From here a jeep road heads down the Suru Valley to Kargil, the halfway point on the Srinagar–Leh road. The people of this region practise the Shiite Muslim faith and are culturally Baltistanis, more akin to Pakistan than Kashmir.

Warvan Valley Another popular route over the same pass commences to the south of Phalgam at Lehinvan and crosses the 4000 m (13,120 ft) Margan Pass into the Warvan Valley. The route then heads upstream to rejoin the main trail across the Boktol Pass at the village of Skunni.

The Warvan Valley is one of the few mountain valleys in Kashmir to be completely isolated throughout the winter because of snow. A road is gradually being built over the Margan Pass.

From either starting-point, Phalgam or Lehivan, the route to Panniker takes about a week to trek in good conditions. Early or late in the season (May or September) the Boktol Pass may be closed to pack animals by snow.

Kishtwar Further to the south again from the Warvan Valley is the remote region of Kishtwar, the only notable trekking area of Jammu. From Kishtwar it is possible to trek across the Himalayan Range to Padum, the main town of the Zanskar region, by way of the Pardar La, as the people from Kishtwar know it, or the Umasi La, as it is called by the Zanskaris. The route from Kishtwar is up the Chenab Valley, then up the Pardar Valley.

Zanskar Zanskar lies south-east of Leh and has only had road access since 1978 by way of a jeep track from Kargil to Padum via the villages of Panniker, Parachik and Rangdum. For climbers, Parachik is the best northern access to the twin peaks of Nun and Kun.

Zanskar is extremely remote and can receive bitterly cold weather, so any trekking through this region requires careful planning and preparation. The landscapes, however, are as spectacular as anywhere in the Himalaya.

Ladakh The contrast in the landscapes between Kashmir and Ladakh — between green meadows and harsh deserts — mirrors the cultural contrast between the predominantly Muslim Kashmir and Ladakh with its mix of Tibetan Buddhism and ancient animism (the worship of gods in animate objects, springs, trees and mountain passes).

More Tibetan in character and landscape than the rest of the Indian Himalaya, Ladakh is renowned as a stark, mountainous desert landscape. The Buddhist influence here adds to the colour and interest for travellers, as throughout the region there are numerous monasteries perched high on hillsides.

Prior to the coming of Buddhism in AD 600, the indigenous people were an Indo-European race, the Mons. Tibetan kings gradually expanded their influence building forts and palaces. The most famous of these kings, Senge Namgyal, was responsible for building the palace at Leh and three large monasteries. Ladakh possesses over twenty monasteries or *gompas* as they are known locally. The name means 'lonely place', and several days can easily be spent visiting the more significant and accessible monasteries.

The Himalayan mountains to the south block the monsoon weather and this results in a rain shadow on the northern side. Though Ladakh receives only a few millimetres of rain a year, rivers such as the Indus and Zanskar, which have their source in far away glaciers, support most of the major settlements in the region. Apart from these oases, the hills and valleys are almost completely devoid of vegetation.

While known as 'Little Tibet', Ladakh has been politically part of India since the

One of the many routes from Kashmir to Ladakh crosses the Pir Panjal Range via the Margan Pass into the Warvan Valley. Cut off from the rest of Kashmir by snowfall for four months of the year, the Warvan Valley itself is a good trekking area.

middle of the 19th century. Ladakh is, however, geographically part of the Tibetan Plateau and the people look to Tibet as the home of their religion and culture. The disputed borders, to the north with Pakistan and to the east with China, meant that until 1974 the region was completely closed to tourists. The Chinese annexation of Aksai Chin in 1962 provoked the Indian Government into securing the remaining part of Ladakh by establishing highways from Srinagar to Leh and Manali to Leh. The 'Beacon Highway' and the Manali–Leh road are open to tourist traffic.

India now maintains a sizeable and high-profile military force in Ladakh. There are army camps up and down the Indus Valley and it is said there is one soldier for every native Ladakhi.

Leh The capital of Ladakh, Leh nestles at the foot of barren ranges that form the edge of the Indus Valley. Those arriving at Leh by plane will need to take it easy for the first few days in order to let their bodies acclimatise to the altitude (3514 m; 11,526 ft).

A visit to Leh gives a fascinating window on the past. On a rocky ridge directly above and overlooking the city is the old palace. This eight-storey mud-brick edifice was built in the 16th century by King Namgyal, but has been long abandoned so it is now rapidly deteriorating. Visitors to the palace should be cautious as the floors are very dangerous. Even higher again above the palace is the Leh Gompa. A steep zigzag path leads up to this eyrie which has a commanding view of Leh and the Indus Valley beyond.

Ladakh is in a rain shadow and the harsh desert mountains are sparsely settled. Prospective self-organised trekkers and climbers should be completely self-sufficient as, away from the main centres, there is little in the way of accommodation or supplies.

(Previous pages) The distinctive Gompa of Chemre is just one of more than twenty to be found in the Indus Valley. Some 300 monks are bound to this monastery which is itself a dependency of the nearby Hemis Gompa, the largest and most important in Ladakh.

Leh, a city of 20,000 people, has a bustling market with hundreds of street stalls and every afternoon Ladakhi women sell vegetables in the main street. Many of the souvenir shops selling Tibetan artifacts and jewellery are owned by Kashmiri businessmen while the street stalls are run by Tibetans. Just outside Leh at Choglamsar is a Tibetan refugee camp where handicrafts are produced and there is an SOS (European aid organisation) children's village and boarding school.

GETTING THERE It is possible to fly with Indian Airlines to Leh each day of the week either from Delhi or Srinagar or both. More detail is covered earlier in the section on the Western Himalaya. Because of the altitude, the weather and the mountain setting of Leh, flights are often cancelled and it is advisable to have confirmed bookings into and out of Leh .

The tortuous road, Beacon Highway, from Kashmir to Ladakh, over the 3500 m (11,480 ft) Zoji La, is open only during the summer, usually from May to November. The 434 km (270 miles) journey takes at least two tiring days.

The narrowness of the road over the Zoji La itself constricts traffic to a one-way system. In the morning the Srinagar-bound traffic departs from Drass at 8 a.m. while at 2 p.m. the Leh-bound vehicles start from Sonomarg.

In season, buses, taxis and jeeps all ply the Beacon Highway. The road varies greatly in condition and traverses extremely harsh terrain. Early in the season the way may be just a narrow cutting through snowbanks but most of the way it snakes over barren mountains. The journey offers some of the most spectacular sights in the Himalaya and though an arduous trip, travelling overland either to or from Leh is to be recommended.

Monasteries and Palaces The Tibetan character of Ladakh is manifested throughout the region in the magnificent gompas that rise up all over the valley.

Their striking whitewashed walls and lofty positions make them highly visible from a distance and no visit to Ladakh is complete without seeing at least one of these. For those with limited time the most accessible and interesting monastery to visit is Tikse.

TIKSE This multi-level structure overlooks the Indus from a rocky ridge 17 km (11 miles) from Leh. A new wing of the monastery proper houses a giant seated statue of the Maitreya, the 'coming' Buddha. In the main prayer hall, as in most similar rooms in the other monasteries, religious *thanka* (thangka) paintings hang around the walls and yak butter candles are kept burning all the time.

HEMIS This is the largest monastery in the Indus Valley and administers many other monasteries. Hemis is some 50 km (31 miles) by road from Leh and tucked away in an isolated side valley above the Indus. Each June Hemis has a three-day festival that attracts large crowds. Several days can be profitably spent visiting these and other monasteries such as Alchi, Spitok, Chemre, Shey and the palace at Stock.

STOCK PALACE This is the only royal residence that has been maintained and is still lived in, though only twelve of its eighty rooms are habitable. The Rani of Stock has set up a museum with a priceless collection of thankas and the royal family's jewellery on display.

The old town has countless narrow alleyways and tiny street stalls crowded into a walled area at the base of the hill below the palace. Today the city sprawls towards the Indus with new hotels and buildings cheek-by-jowl with army installations. Ancient mani walls, traditionally built at the entrance to towns, are now surrounded by houses and by the roadsides are clusters of giant stupas and chortans. Traditional Ladakhi dress is still worn by the older men and women. The most colourful worn by the women is the *perak*, a headdress decorated with turquoise and coral beads.

Traditional Ladakhi women still wear decorated headdresses known as the *perak* (left). The more lines of turquoise, the higher the status of its owner. When the woman dies the *perak* is passed on to her eldest daughter. Tibetan tradition is also still very much alive in the Gompas of Ladakh which are adorned with religious paintings known as *tankas* (Above)

Kargil Kargil, 203 km (126 miles) from Srinagar, is notable as the most common overnight stop on the road to Leh. It is also the second-largest town in Ladakh. Here the road forks and the southerly route eventually winds its way to Padum, the main centre in Zanskar.

The orthodox (Shiite) Muslim faith is very strong in Kargil and women are seldom seen in public. Kargil is also the main centre of what is known as 'Little Baltistan' which encompasses the Suru, Drass, Wakka and Bodkarbu Valleys. Today this name refers mostly to the region's ethnic unity, the people having more in common with those along the Indus River in Pakistan than the neighbouring Kashmiris or Ladakhs.

For trekkers heading in to Zanskar, Kargil is the last place to stock up on provisions, although it is better to come prepared from Srinagar than to rely on the Kargil Bazaar.

Lamayuru The other main town of interest, just off the road from Srinagar to Leh, is Lamayuru. There the remains of the oldest gompa in Ladakh still stand in the precinct of what is still one of the more important monasteries in the Indus Valley.

Lamayuru also marks the start and finish for many treks heading into Zanskar. From Lamayuru there is a six-day route to Rangdum via the Kanji La pass but there is an alternative starting-point at Khalse, another village along the road and closer to Leh. From Lamayuru two other possible treks run west roughly parallel to the Indus River. The shorter is a four-day trek to Alchi, the site of monasteries with some of the oldest wall paintings in Ladakh. The longer route branches off on the second day and eventually ends up at Stock, just across the river from Leh.

Ladakh Trekking As a place to trek, Ladakh contrasts starkly with other parts of the Western Himalaya. The high altitude and sparsely populated desert landscape make it more challenging for a self-sufficient group treks are less troubled by such limitations. The best times to visit Ladakh for walking or climbing are July, August and September. Early in the season, around May and June, rivers can be swollen by the spring thaw, while early snowfalls in October can block higher passes.

Trekking in Ladakh, like the rest of the Western Himalaya, does not require a permit but the area one mile to the north of the Zojila to Kargil–Leh Road, one mile east of the Leh–Uphshi road and one mile west of the Uphshi–Mandi Road, is restricted to foreigners. There are a few trekking operations based in Ladakh, most of them in Leh. Arrangements can also be made in Srinagar. If you wish to backpack, you must be experienced and completely self-sufficient with food and accommodation .

Most treks in the Ladakh–Zanskar region take between seven and ten days but there are several worthwhile shorter ones. The most popular ones are: Leh to Kargil via the Suru Valley; Kargil to Zanskar then to Manali; and Leh–Markha Valley to Zanskar.

MARKHA VALLEY The trek from Stock to Hemis by the Markha Valley has become one of the most popular in Ladakh because of its convenience, accessibility and beauty. The usual starting-point for this eight-day route is Stock, the village directly across the Indus from Leh. An alternative start is the village of Spitok further downstream. Both are readily accessible from Leh by bus or taxi. The better part of the route runs parallel to the Indus Valley and, depending on the starting-point, crosses one or two passes.

Padum (Padam) Padum is the focus of trekking in the Zanskar region, with popular routes starting here and going north to Lamayuru. It is also possible to trek over several passes to the east and eventually reach the Markha Valley and so to Leh. The jeep track to Padum from Kargil is over the Pensi La Pass which is only open from July until October because of snow. Padum then becomes a destination itself or a route mark rather than a starting-point. If you are heading south from Padum there are two alternative ten-day treks to get to Manali. One way, over the Shingo Pass, ends at Darcha while the other takes the Surichun Pass and joins the Leh–Manali road at Sarai Kilang.

In summer the Rhotang Pass road is open back to Manali, the main staging-point for trekking in the Kulu Valley of Himachal Pradesh.

HIMACHAL PRADESH

> Days spent in the Kulu Valley are . . . the most stunning things to do in India. Serious trekking is uncomfortable, unsexy, sordid and shakes some people rigid. The food is crummy. You don't change clothes for ten days, but there is no other experience so glorious.
>
> **LONDON CITY**
> **BUSINESSMAN'S VIEW**
> *Luxury in India,* 1987

The mountainous region now called Himachal (literally 'Himalaya state') Pradesh was once known as the Punjab Himalaya but with the partition of the then Punjab district into Punjab and Haryana in 1966, a new region, Himachal, came into being. Three roughly parallel ranges run across Himachal Pradesh. The northernmost is the Zanskar Range, the next most southern is the Pir Panjal and the lowest is the Dhauladhar Range.

Four distinct areas form the major part of Himachal Pradesh — Chamba, Kulu, Lahoul and Spiti — which are drained respectively by the Ravi, Beas, Chenab and Spiti rivers. The southern areas of Kulu and Chamba experience the monsoon rains and are consequently more heavily vegetated than the drier northern areas of Lahoul and Spiti. These latter two regions, adjacent to Zanskar, are inhabited by people of Tibetan origin, while the people of Kulu and Chamba are mostly Hindu. Chamba and Kulu were independent Himalayan kingdoms until the mid-1840s when the British defeated Gulab Singh.

For trekkers and climbers, the peaks, hills and valleys of Himachal Pradesh are less frequented but no less interesting or challenging. A prime focus for both activities is the Kulu Valley, with the town of Manali as its main staging-point, but Simla is the main administrative centre of the region.

Simla (Shimla) The capital of Himachal Pradesh, Simla became the summer capital of India in the days of the British Viceroys. Even today, forty years after independence, Simla has a distinctly British feel, mainly in the style of the buildings. Being the summer capital of India for so many years meant that the hills and forests around Simla were explored by the very first trekkers. Situated at 2100 m (6,888 ft) above sea level, the town itself meanders 12 km (7 miles) along a ridge. The surrounding slopes are covered with pine, rhododendron, fir and Himalayan oak which change in appearance with the seasons.

Spring and autumn are the best seasons to visit Simla. While it is not in the heart of the Himalaya, there are numerous day walks. The Jalori Pass, although a 'bussable' route, is a worthwhile trek and takes up to five days.

Dharamsala The Kangra Valley at the foot of the Dhauladhar Range is considered one of the most beautiful in the Himalaya. The main town of the region, Dharamsala, is important as the home of the Dalai Lama, Tibet's spiritual and worldly leader. The region has become a focus for Tibetan refugees who have a settlement at nearby McLeod Ganja. Here there are several *ashrams* and Tibetan hotels to cater for the faithful who come from all over the world.

The lush Kulu Valley, feted in tourist brochures as 'the valley of the gods', is drained by the Beas River. Manali, a traditional Indian holiday resort at the head of the valley, is gaining in popularity as a base for climbing and trekking in the mountains of Himachal Pradesh.

Kulu The Kulu Valley is one of the main attractions of Himachal Pradesh and in summer it is extremely popular with Indian holidaymakers. The valley is also gaining a reputation with foreign travellers, though the trekking and climbing support businesses are less developed than in Kashmir. When the Leh to Manali road is open to foreigners, there is certain to be some growth in such services.

The fertile Kulu Valley, widely known as the 'Valley of the Gods', is 80 km (50 miles) long and is a main fruit-growing area, producing apples and apricots. Drained by the Beas River, the valley begins to the north in the Pir Panjal Range. The main towns of the valley are Kulu and Manali. Just 10 km (6 miles) below Kulu is Bhuntar, and the airport for the region.

The town of Kulu, the headquarters of the district, meanders along the banks of the Beas River. As well as being the starting-point for treks, Kulu is famous for the Duserra festival that takes place over eight days in October each year. While Dussera is celebrated all over India, in Kulu it has very special significance. The entire region takes on a festive spirit and the town of Kulu becomes the scene of a giant market. Cattle, produce and clothing abound but for foreigners the main handcraft of the district, the Kulu shawl, is a popular purchase.

Manali Forty km (25 miles) beyond Kulu, the town of Manali, at 1829 m (5999 ft), is the main focus of trekking in Himachal Pradesh. This is also a popular holiday destination for Indians and many Indian

The Hampta Pass has been crossed on skis in winter but in summer when clear of snow it is a popular trekking route from Manali to Lahul. At 4200 m (13,800 ft) the pass should not be attempted without a gradual ascent over several days to properly acclimatise.

Prime Ministers have retreated to Manali to escape the pressures of high office. There is a full range of hotels and a busy bazaar where most expedition and trekking food requirements can be purchased. However, trekking and climbing equipment is not available to buy or hire, so you should come self-sufficient.

Manali is a good place to recuperate after the bustle of Delhi or even Kashmir. While not a luxury class of spa, the Vasisht Baths and hot springs provide a place to relax and refresh. The Hadimba Temple, built in 1553, has a four-tiered pagoda roof worth seeing, and Manali also has a thriving Tibetan gompa that is the focus for Tibetan refugees.

Sometimes references are made to Manali as the 'Chamonix of India'. While this is perhaps a little overstated, there is plenty of scope for excellent alpine climbing within several days from the town. The Himachal Pradesh Mountaineering Institute just outside Manali provides training in basic and advanced climbing for Indian nationals and foreigners. It also hires some equipment.

Worthwhile climbs in the region are: Indrasan at 6221 m (20,405 ft); Deo Tiba at 5925 m (19, 435 ft); Ali Ratna Tiba at 5470 m (17,942 ft); Papsura at 6451 m (21,159 ft); and White Sail at 6445m (21,140 ft). Indrasan, Deo Tiba and Ali Ratna Tiba are at the head of the Malana Valley. White Sail and Papsura are in the vicinity of the Malana, Tos and Bara Sligri Glaciers. Permits are required.

Trekking from Manali There is excellent trekking in the Kulu region. A popular route from Manali takes you to Beas Kund beneath Hanuman Tibba. This can be made into a longer circuit by crossing the Solang Pass and returning to the Kulu Valley via the Manali Pass.

Another route via the Parvatti and Malana Valleys can also be combined to make a worthwhile trek. The start is at Nagar, two hours by bus from Manali on the Kulu–Manali road. Nagar was made the capital of the then Kulu State in 1660. Today, points of interest are the Nagar Castle perched on an overhanging cliff, and the Roerich Art Gallery, which houses painting and sculptures of this avant-garde Russian painter who settled here in the 1930s. From Nagar you proceed in stages to Manikaran. It is possible to take a bus back to Kulu or Manali.

Rhotang Pass The Rhotang Pass, at 4122 m (13,520 ft) — 'the Pass of Bones' — can be crossed by vehicle from June to September. This is the only present access to the Lahaul Valley but a planned tunnel through the range will give year-round access. Out of season the pass can be crossed on foot and local traffic and pack animals struggle back and forth in all weathers.

In winter the Rhotang Pass is also the site of some modest winter sports, particularly downhill skiing and tobogganing. Attempts are also being made to introduce heli-skiing to the Kulu region which, according to accomplished skiers, has plenty of potential for this.

The Rhotang Pass is also the gateway to treks to Zanskar. Darcha, in the Bhaga Valley on the road to Leh, is the start of the week-long walk to Padum. The route then crosses the main Himalaya Range at the Shingo La at 5300 m (17,384 ft) and proceeds up the Lunak Valley. A side trip to the 15th century Phugtal Monastery is highly recommended. Other worthwhile trekking possibilities are those between the Baralacha La Pass and Chandratal.

Hampta Pass In spring, summer or autumn a five to seven-day circuit from Manali can be made by crossing the Rhotang Pass and returning via the Hampta Pass. When the Rhotang is open a bus or jeep can usually take you as far as Chatru. In winter the circuit can also be traversed on nordic skis.

Lahaul and Spiti North of the Kulu Valley by some 100 km (62 miles), the twin valleys of Lahaul and Spiti were first opened to tourists in 1977. They are beyond the influence of the monsoon. Despite its rather barren landscape, Lahaul is famous for its potatoes. This valley marks the southern limit of the Tibetan art and culture. The Hampta Pass is sometimes crossed from the opposite direction as part of a trek that leads into Lahaul, but the main access is over the Rhotang Pass, 51 km (32 miles) from Manali. Keylong, the capital of Lahaul, is an oasis of greenery on the banks of the Bhaga River. Nearby monasteries rate among the main sights of the region.

While Himachal Pradesh is not a major focus for organised treks there is much scope for self-organised treks and small-scale climbing expeditions to interesting objectives. There are many who prefer the Kulu region as a place to get away from the beaten tracks and crowds of Kashmir. To the south and east of the Himachal Pradesh the Himalaya reaches its most dramatic heights of the Western Himalaya in the state of Uttar Pradesh.

UTTAR PRADESH

I arrived in time to see the summit of Nanda Devi through a hole in the clouds, rising above the sacred ground of her Sanctuary, surrounded by a legend of inaccessibility. Far below us, the slender thread of the Rishi led our eyes back towards the mountain. It was a fleeting glimpse. Soon the mists closed all mountains from us.

I was feeling quite tired, but was soon entranced by the thousands of flowers that littered the slopes. The sky was grey and it was the earth that drew my eyes to it. No wonder the Garhwal is called the Garden of the Himalayas. The droplets of water that hung from the petals brought a freshness and immediacy. They were of all colours, and gave a gentler beauty to the fierce landscape on which they were scattered.

PETER BOARDMAN
The Shining Mountain, 1980

Only the north-western portion of the state of Uttar Pradesh includes part of the Himalaya. Despite its relatively small area there are many places and peaks that are very holy. Long before mountaineers and trekkers discovered the delights of the region, millions of Hindu devotees were making annual visits to the shrines sacred to the worshippers of Shiva, Krishna and Vishnu at Yamuntori, Gangotri, Kedarnarth and Bardinarth. The traditional pilgrimage or yatra visits these shrines in order from west to east.

Garhwal

The Garhwal, as it is usually known to climbers and trekkers, is the most impressive region of mountains in the Indian Himalaya. Often referred to as the Kumon Himalaya by geographers (which it is technically adjacent to), for the sake of this book, the Garhwal extends from Sutlej River in the west to the Nepalese border in the east. The region was all but closed to foreigners from 1960 to 1972 following border problems with China. In 1974 the 'Inner Line' was moved, reopening the headwaters of the Ganges to trekkers and climbers.

CLIMBING The Garhwal was the focus of most of the climbing activity in the Himalaya in the 1920s and 1930s, with the likes of Kamet being climbed in 1931. Trisuli, at 7120 m (23,354 ft), was in 1907 the very first 7000 m peak to be ascended (see history of climbing, page 32).

In recent times the mountains of the Garhwal have become the focus of numerous lightweight climbing expeditions. The biggest prize, the Nanda Devi Sanctuary, was declared a national park in 1983 but is now closed to expeditions, trekkers and shepherds to protect its delicate ecology. This is not a complete setback for climbers, however, as there are more than 100 peaks above 6000 m (19,680 ft), including more notable ones such as Chagabang at 6896 m (22,619 ft); Dunagiri at 7066 m (23,176 ft); Kedarnath at 6968 m (22,855 ft); and Shivling at 6543 m (21,461 ft).

NANDA DEVI The most important peak of the region, Nanda Devi (the Goddess Nanda) at 7817 m (25,640 ft), was first climbed in 1936 by Noel Odell and the redoubtable Bill Tilman. The access to this beautiful mountain sanctuary is via the Rishi Gorge. The starting-point for this trek (when open) is from Joshimath which is also the main centre closest to the start of the Valley of Flowers trek.

TREKKING Only a few commercial trekking companies venture into the Garhwal. The most popular route is to the Valley of Flowers. Generally speaking there is little accommodation away from the pilgrim routes and even on these yatra trails the standards are such that it is as well to be self-sufficient. Two of the main staging-points for trekking in the Garhwal are Rishikesh and Mussoorie.

The main temple at Gangotri, in the Garhwal, is dedicated to the goddess Ganga. This is on the path to the most holy source of the Ganges which, because of glacier retreat, is now beyond Gaumukh. Many pilgrims visit the temple which is open from May until October.

Rishikesh Rishikesh, the starting-point for treks to Badrinath, is an overnight bus or train ride from Delhi. The nearest airport, Dehra Dun, is 20 km (12 miles) away and is serviced by Vayudoot, India's third-level airline. Rishikesh is a wooded hill retreat set on the Ganges. It is the site of many *ashrams* and yoga centres and, like Hardwar, a focus for pilgrims.

Mussoorie Once described by the colonial British as 'queen of the hill-stations', the town of Mussoorie is another staging-point, particularly for treks to Gangotri and Yamuntori Valleys. Overlooking the Doon Valley at 2000 m (6560 ft) it has views of the mountains to the north-west. Mussoorie is the site of Sir George Everest's house — Sir George was once head of the Indian Survey and Mount Everest was named after him.

The Valley of Flowers The Bhyuntar Valley, immortalised in the 1930s by English mountaineer Frank Smyth as the Valley of Flowers, has been a popular destination for trekkers. Since grazing has been stopped the blooms are said to be choked by weeds. The trek to Lake Hemkund, a side trip from Gangria, is a sacred pilgrimage for Sikhs. The Valley of Flowers is now a National Park, entry is regulated and camping is not permitted. Rupkund trek is now becoming popular.

Yamuntori (Yamunotri) From the roadhead it is only a 14 km (9 mile) trek to Yamunotri following the most direct pilgrim route. This is well-served by tea stalls and lodges.

Gangotri Reaching the headwaters of the Ganges is one of the holiest pilgrimages a Hindu can make. The actual source of the river is at Gaumukh, a day's walk from Gangotri. There are numerous ways of extending this route to other destinations, such as the Gangotri Glacier and Kedertal. The trek to Kedarnath along the old pilgrim route begins from Malla, 73 km (45 miles) before Gangotri.

Kedarnath Panch-Kedar are five temples which represent five different forms of Shiva and are found in five different valleys. A fourteen-day trek includes all the temples and several unique views of the Garhwal. The shrine at Kedarnath itself, dedicated to Shiva, is a day's walk from the roadhead at Gaurikund.

Badrinath For trekking from Badrinath, the traditional resting-place of Vishnu, it is usual to arrange matters at Joshimath 44 km (27 miles) further back. The main treks in this region are the Valley of Flowers and Hempkund. Nanda Devi Sanctuary is closed, but it is possible to take a longer trek around the outer rim.

The Corbett National Park Established in 1936, the Corbett National Park is now named after hunter, conservationist and author Jim Corbett. India's first National Park, it is renowned for its wildlife.

Eastern Himalaya

The main entry point for visitors to the Eastern Himalaya is Calcutta. See also Bhutan, page 194.

CALCUTTA

Calcutta, the fourth largest city in the world, is home to 10 million people. It was founded in 1690 on the banks of the Hooghly River by Job Chamock at the behest of the East India Company.

Calcutta is the capital of West Bengal and the focus of culture in India. It is the hub of a thriving film industry, and houses the largest library in India (9 million books) and the Indian Museum.

From Calcutta most trekkers and climbers fly north to Bagdogra to reach Bhutan, Sikkim or Darjeeling. The railway stations nearest to Gangtok (the capital of Sikkim) are Siliguri and Jalpaigura, both about 100 km (62 miles) distant, and trains to and from Delhi and Calcutta can be caught from them. Gangtok is connected by road to Darjeeling and Siliguri.

SIKKIM

Once an independent Himalayan kingdom like Bhutan, then a British protectorate, Sikkim is now part of the Republic of India. The name Sikkim means 'new house or place' in Nepalese while its Sanskrit meaning is 'crested'. Sikkim is wedged between Nepal and Bhutan and its climate and mountain geography are similar to those of its neighbours.

Sikkim is heavily forested and abounds with wildlife, rhododendrons and hundreds of varieties of orchids and wildflowers. The best time to experience the blooms are April to June and October to early December.

The world's third highest mountain and most easterly of the 8000 m peaks, Kanchenjunga (Kangchenjungen) at 8586 m (28,162 ft) straddles the border with Nepal to the east.

Gangtok The administrative capital of Sikkim, Gangtok lies on a steep hillside in the central western part of the country at an altitude of 1800 m (5904 ft). It is not a particularly interesting town as the older temples and buildings have been overshadowed by the sprawling new areas.

The indigenous people of Sikkim are known as Lepchas but there has been an influx of Sherpas, Newars, Tamangs, Gurangs and Rais from Nepal. Like Bhutan, Sikkim is predominantly a Buddhist state. Most of the historical and cultural sights are monasteries. Pemayangtse, the second oldest and most important monastery, is in West Sikkim; Tashiding, a few kilometres away, is famous for its artistic decorations. Thousands of Buddhist pilgrims trek to Tashiding each spring to participate in a special festival.

The closest airport to Sikkim is Bagdogra in North Bengal. From there it is a train journey to Siliguri and, finally, 60 km (37 miles) by road to Gangtok or 124 km (77 miles) from Bagdogra.

Because of the sensitive state of the Chinese border to the north, a special permit is required to visit Sikkim. This is available from the Ministry of Home Affairs in Delhi or from Indian consulates. All applications must be forwarded to Delhi, so allow at least three months for the wheels to turn. Permits are usually only for seven days and extend only for Gangtok and several monasteries. Trekking groups can, by all accounts, get a special permit for ten days to trek in the Dzongri area, provided they are accompanied by a government-approved guide. The situation regarding permits and open and closed areas is subject to change, so check with the nearest Indian consulate or in Delhi for the latest regulation before making firm plans to trek in Sikkim.

Trekking in Sikkim The most popular trekking route is from Gangtok to Pemayangtse via Rumtek, then on to Yaksum, Bakkhim and Dzorgri, which is on the ridge towards Kanchenjunga. Trekkers in Sikkim should be self-sufficient but it may be possible to stay in villages. As in Bhutan, trekking in Sikkim is in its infancy and many of the routes are through areas that seldom see foreigners.

DARJEELING

Darjeeling is one of the main destinations for anyone visiting the eastern portion of the Indian Himalaya. It is usually combined with a trip to Sikkim.

Darjeeling, at 2127 m (6977 ft), owes its popularity to having been one of the hill-station resorts to which the British Raj retired each summer. Its continued reputation is due to the excellent views the area offers of Kanchenjunga, at 8586 m (28,162 ft), and the associated peaks from Observatory Hill, or Tiger Hill at 2555 m (8380 ft); 11 km (7 miles) to the south. Watching the sun rise over Mount Everest from Tiger Hill is a traditional attraction for sightseers.

Darjeeling is home to the Himalayan Mountaineering Institute, once directed by Tensing Norgay who, with Hillary, was the first to climb Mount Everest.

Kangchenjunga, the most easterly of the 8000 m peaks and the third highest in the world, lies on the border of Nepal and Sikkim. Access for climbing however, is only via the Nepalese side (above) but distant views of the peak from Darjeeling are popular with sightseers.

If you go overland to Darjeeling, a special permit is usually required. This is available from the Foreigners' Registration Office in Calcutta, Delhi or Indian consulates abroad. The permit is for seven days but can usually be extended for a further seven. No permit is required if you enter and exit via Bagdogra Airport and stay no more than fifteen days. Bagdogra Airport is 96 km (60 miles) from Darjeeling with regular bus services.

Trekking permits are free of charge at the Foreigners' Registration Office in Darjeeling. Treks from Darjeeling are best taken in April to May and October to November. In April and May the rhododendrons and magnolias are in full bloom. The most popular route is from Darjeeling to Sandakphu to Phalut and back to Darjeeling in four to six days. There are several different possibilities for the return, either via Rimbek-Bijanbori or Rimbek-Manebhanjang. Another variation is to start from Manebhanjang but still trek to Sandakphu.

If you are on your own, there are trekking agents in Darjeeling, and equipment can be hired from the Darjeeling Youth Hostel, a useful source of maps and information. Porters can be found in Manebhanjang and Dhotray and there are some teashops en route to Sandakphu.

ARUNACHAL PRADESH

The union territory of Arunachal Pradesh, the far eastern end of the Indian Himalaya, is virtually untapped as far as trekking and climbing are concerned, as it is seldom open to foreigners, let alone tourists. The Tsangpo (Brahmaputra) River breaks southward through the great Himalayan divide in the eastern half of the territory.

Arunachal Pradesh is politically very sensitive as it shares its international border with Bhutan, China and Burma, and the Indian Government has a strict policy of protecting the tribal people from outside influence. It is unlikely that this policy will change in the foreseeable future.

The architecture of Darjeeling is a strong reminder of the British Raj, as is the Toy Train ride on a 2 ft (0.6 m) gauge railway from New Talpaiguri to Darjeeling itself. The British were also responsible for introducing tea plantations to Darjeeling in the 1840s. Darjeeling tea has made this place a household name throughout the world. There are guided tours of the Happy Valley tea estate.

Though not major centres for trekking or climbing, Darjeeling and Sikkim offer interesting alternatives for those who have already been to the other main places in the Indian Himalaya.

NEPAL

The great white peaks filed past — Dhaulagiri, Annapurna, Himalchuli; symbolical names that spoke to the soul rather than referred, as in some countries, to historical events or the memories of famous men. Dhaulagiri means 'Mountain of Storms' and Annapurna, 'Giver of Life'. . . They towered above all other things. Nobody owned them — they belonged to all. Over thousands of years they had been accessible to people of all races and creeds — through prayer. All Indian and Tibetan mythology praised these mountains as the home of the greatest gods.

PETER BOARDMAN
Sacred Summits, 1982

The name Nepal is closely associated with trekking and climbing. Bounded by land on all sides, it is only 800 km (497 miles) long by 200 km (124 miles) wide. The giant nations of China to the north and India to the south may overshadow Nepal in many ways, but for geographic diversity and cultural heritage it stands apart. The towering peaks of the Himalaya run the length of Nepal's northern border, the greatest concentration of high mountains in the world.

As the birthplace of modern commercial trekking, Nepal offers the greatest scope for walking and climbing of anywhere in the Himalaya. It is also possible to travel in all manner of styles, whether self-organised, in fully-catered trekking groups, or on full-scale expeditions.

There are three main regions where trekking is permitted: the western areas dominated by the Annapurna ranges; the Langtang Valley and Helambu; and the Khumbu region in the east. Each of these areas has countless different trails but the most popular are well catered for by lodges. These are obviously the most suitable for teahouse trekking but many of these trails suffer from overpopularity and the villages can be very commercialised. The more offbeat trails are where you can find the real Nepal.

Wherever you go in Nepal, or what you plan to do, you will inevitably enter the country via Kathmandu, or go there to organise the details of your trek or climb.

There are only two main staging-points in Nepal: Kathmandu and Pokhara. Pokhara is discussed in the section on regions while Kathmandu will be examined on the following pages.

Nepal is essentially a land of small villages due to its rugged terrain. Kathmandu and Pokhara are the exceptions, both occupying large fertile valleys and now supporting rapidly expanding populations. The middle hills and valleys are home to a major percentage of Nepal's 17.5 million people.

Kathmandu

Much of the charm of this part of the world lies beyond the cities in the more remote regions, where traditional arts and crafts, agriculture and village life have changed little over the centuries. In the cities traditional goods still take their place alongside the trappings of the West in humble street stalls.

Kathmandu is the gateway to and capital of Nepal. The airport is serviced daily by ten major international airlines, while the national carrier, Royal Nepal Airlines, provides extensive external and internal air services.

Within the precincts of the city, buses, taxis and rickshaws are all available, but bicycles are a popular means of travel for sightseeing. Kathmandu now has many modern airconditioned hotels, and a full range of accommodation is available including backpackers' dormitory-style hotels for a few dollars a night. Most accommodation is in the Thamel district.

The first sight of Kathmandu from the air brings to mind visions of Lilliput, the

NEPAL AT A GLANCE

Area
145,400 sq. km (56,124 sq. miles).

Population
17.5 million, growth rate 2.2%.

Government
Monarchy. His Majesty Birendra Bir Bikram Shah Dev heads a partyless Panchayat system.

Capital
Kathmandu (Kantipu), population 360,000.

Flag
Two red triangles, one above the other with blue fringe. White moon upper triangle, white sun in lower.

People
29 ethnic groups (Kathmandu Newar and Brahmin-Chetri dominate the cultural landscape).

Language
Nepali 58% (national language); Newari 3%; Indian dialects 20%.

Religion
Buddhist and Hindu, but officially Hindu.

Highest and lowest points
70 m to 8848 m (230 ft to 29,021 ft) – Nepal's terrain is mountainous. 14% is cultivated, 13% pasture and 32% forested.

Currency
Nepalese rupee – 21 rupees = approx. US$1.00.

Time
Nepalese time is 5 hours and 45 minutes ahead of GMT and 15 minutes ahead of Indian time.

Portion in Himalaya
Nepal lies wholly in the Himalaya.

Best time
April and May – pre-monsoon; September and October – post-monsoon.

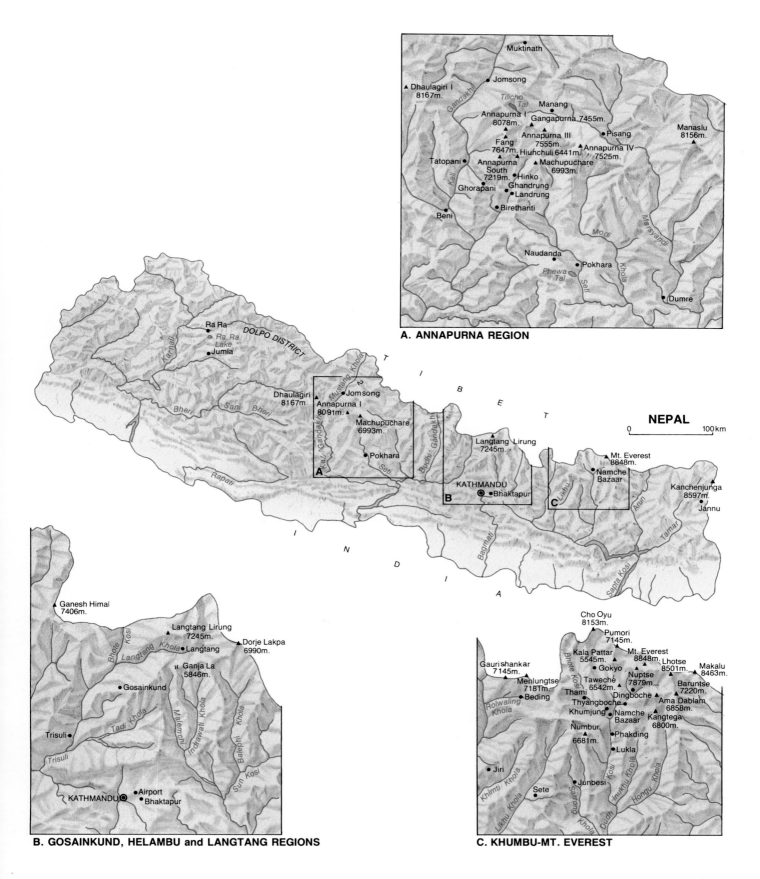

A. ANNAPURNA REGION

Muktinath

Jomsong

Dhaulagiri I
8167m.

Tilicho Tal

Manang

Annapurna I
8078m.

Gangapurna 7455m.

Pisang

Manaslu
8156m.

Annapurna III
7555m.

Fang
7647m.

Annapurna IV
7525m.

Hiunchuli 6441m.

Machupuchare
6993m.

Tatopani

Annapurna
South
7219m.

Hinko

Ghandrung

Ghorapani

Landrung

Beni

Birethanti

Naudanda

Pokhara

Phewa Tal

Dumre

Gandaki

Kali

Seti

Modi

Marsyandi Khola

NEPAL

0   100 km

Ra Ra

Ra Ra
Lake

Jumla

DOLPO DISTRICT

Karnali

Bheri

Sani Bheri

Dhaulagiri
8167m.

Jomsong

Annapurna I
8091m.

Machupuchare
6993m.

Pokhara

Mustang Khola

Budhi Gandaki

T   I   B   E   T

A

B

Langtang Lirung
7245m.

KATHMANDU
Bhaktapur

C

Mt. Everest
8848m.

Namche
Bazaar

Kanchenjunga
8597m.

Jannu

Bagmati

Likhu

Arun

Tamar

Rapati

Seti

I   N   D   I   A

Sapta Kosi

B. GOSAINKUND, HELAMBU and LANGTANG REGIONS

Ganesh Himal
7406m.

Langtang Lirung
7245m.

Langtang

Dorje Lakpa
6990m.

Bhote Kosi

Langtang Khola

Ganja La
5846m.

Gosainkund

Trisuli

Tadi Khola

Malemchi Khola

Indrawati Khola

Balephi Khola

Trisuli

Sun Kosi

KATHMANDU

Airport

Bhaktapur

C. KHUMBU-MT. EVEREST

Cho Oyu
8153m.

Pumori
7145m.

Kala Pattar
5545m.

Mt. Everest
8848m.

Gaurishankar
7145m.

Gokyo

Lhotse
8501m.

Makalu
8463m.

Menlungtse
7181m.

Beding

Taweche
6542m.

Nuptse
7879m.

Baruntse
7220m.

Thami

Dingboche

Ama Dablam
6858m.

Thyangboche

Khumjung

Namche
Bazaar

Kangtega
6800m.

Numbur
6681m.

Phakding

Bhote Kosi

Rolwaling Kholi

Lukla

Jiri

Khimti Khola

Sete

Junbesi

Likhu Khola

Sarrong Khola

Dudh Kosi

Imukhu Khola

Hongu Khola

legendary island of *Gulliver's Travels*. Terraced hills of green and mud-brick houses dotted throughout give one the feeling of stepping back in time, but Nepal is making rapid progress in catering to needs of Western travellers.

Entry details

Trekkers and climbers arriving by air will rarely have any problem with customs clearance with accompanied baggage, but clearance of unaccompanied baggage can take days. The import and export of Nepalese rupees is forbidden but when you leave the country the bank will refund only 15% of the amount you can prove you legally exchanged. Special per-

mits are required for 16 mm novice cameras and you are allowed to take into the country only one pair of binoculars, one still camera and one video camera.

Organisation and Permits

All the organisational and bureaucratic aspects of trekking and climbing in Nepal have to be arranged in Kathmandu. Anyone trekking or rafting in Nepal must obtain an appropriate permit from the Ministry of Home Affairs' Central Immigration Office in Kathmandu. One working day is all that is usually required to obtain a trekking permit, provided all the necessary information is furnished. Two passport photos must accompany your appli-

Days can be spent sightseeing in the crowded streets of the old parts of Kathmandu. An early riser will find plenty of activity in the daily vegetable market in the main square.

(Previous pages) The pagoda style of temple architecture originated in Nepal. Durbar Square in Patan, one of the three cities of the Kathmandu Valley on the southern outskirts of Kathmandu, has some of the finest examples.

cation. The price of the permit will range from 60 to 80 rupees depending on whether you are rafting or trekking, and it may take a day to obtain. On the application form it is necessary to specify the region, route and timing of the proposed trek. Once out trekking it is not possible to change details or extend the time, so make sure you apply for the most distant destination and the maximum amount of time in the first place. On the more popular trails there are various checkpoints where you may have to present your permit and passport, so keep them with you at all times.

Certain areas are also restricted and so it's best to acquaint yourself with the limits of your planned region if you are organising your own itinerary and trek. If you are part of an organised group or working through a Nepalese trekking agency, all these concerns will usually be taken care of.

If you are looking after these matters yourself, a week may well be necessary before you can head for the hills. On organised treks at least one or two days are usually spent in Kathmandu prior to setting out. This time can be well spent sightseeing.

Sightseeing

Nepal has three religions, Buddhism, Hinduism and Tourism.

ANON

The ancient cities of Kathmandu, Patan and Bhaktapur all lie in proximity and offer a window to the past, with parts having seen little change in thousands of years. Sometimes called the Florence of Asia, the Kathmandu Valley has a wealth of historic and artistic attractions. In each town the *durbar* or palace square is surrounded by fine buildings, with carved windows, stone sculptures and art works.

Bhaktapur, the most medieval of the valley towns, is known as 'the city of devotees'. Its many pagoda-style temples date back to the 17th century. Patan, founded in AD 250, is said to have the strongest Buddhist influence. Its artists have become famous through the centuries for sculpture — statues, metalwork and woodcarving. Today, Tibetan refugees carry on the artistic traditions, producing fine woollen goods, carpets and religious paintings for Western travellers.

While Nepal is predominantly Hindu, Buddhism is so much part of the culture that these two religions often share the same deities and temples. Lumbini (Lhumbini), in the western part of the Terai, was the birthplace of the great Buddha. This and other sacred places in Nepal are the focus of many pilgrimages for devotees from East and West. The architecture of the cities testifies to the peaceful co-existence of these religions. Swayambhunath, with the watchful eyes of Buddha on the four sides of the central Stupa, has a commanding site overlooking the valley. Two Indian temples also grace this complex. It is said to be the oldest Buddhist shrine in the valley.

Kathmandu Valley

The Kathmandu Valley was not linked to India by road until the 1950s. In the high hills everything must be carried by man or beast. A network of roads now connects major centres in India and China and foreign aid is helping to construct more.

Kathmandu Valley treks

There are several short treks around the rim of the Kathmandu Valley which can help give the flavour of the Nepalese countryside without the problems of altitude, uncertain aircraft schedules or spending days on buses or bumpy roads.

The village of Nargakot situated on a hill to the west of Bhaktapur is the starting-point for several moderate treks. This village is also renowned for its views

Though Nepal is a very poor country, the dignity and friendliness of its people is unparalleled in the region. The older hill people show the effects of a very hard life but through catering to trekkers and climbers the next generation stand to reap the benefits.

of the Himalaya. The alternative favoured by some is to leave Kathmandu very early (at least two hours before sun-up) and take a taxi to Nargakot. The treks from here head north-east to Sanklu, east to Choangu Naaraaya (temple) or south to Banepaa which is on the road to the Chinese border.

Regions

The hills of Nepal are criss-crossed with trails and tracks that link villages together, follow water courses and cross mountain ranges. Many of these are used all the time by the local people. Routes that have become popular as treks usually have some spectacular mountain or view as their destination but there are always side trips or variations you can take. Fifteen main treks are mentioned here, but it is only possible to cover a fraction of the potential combinations. If you are after more detailed information, Bezruchka's *A Guide to Trekking in Nepal* or Armington's *Trekking in the Nepal Himalaya* are recommended.

There are some forty-three remote airstrips in Nepal, many of which are starting-points for trekking or jungle excursions. Mountain sightseeing flights are also available to whisk one to the roof of the world, with close views of Everest and other Himalayan giants. Seen from the air, the difficulties of land communications in Nepal become apparent. Some of the more popular remote airstrips for trekkers are at Lukla in the Khumbu, Jomsong at the head of the Kali Gandakhi Valley, and Julma in the far west of Nepal. From these points and the many other roadheads scattered throughout the hills, most trekking routes commence.

It is useful to examine some of the more popular paths in more detail to help you evaluate what would suit your needs. The Nepal Himalaya geographic divisions are (from east to west) the Karnali section, the Gandaki section and the Kosi Section which are named after the major rivers that drain these sections. From a trekking and climbing perspective, however, it is more convenient to look at the western, central and eastern sections. Some guidebooks look at the specific Himals and regions. In all there are about fifteen main trekking routes with another dozen or so regular variations or side trips. On virtually every trek you will come across mountains that require permits. The main 'trekking peaks' are in the Khumbu and Annapurna regions.

Western Nepal

Western Nepal is rarely visited, but as more and more people are returning to Nepal for their third or fourth trek, out-of-the-way routes are beginning to appeal.

Large portions of the far western region of Nepal, however, are restricted to trekkers. The Dolpo, made famous by Peter Matthiessen's *Snow Leopard*, is one such area that is off-limits, as is the Mustang region to the north of Jomsong. There are nevertheless so many accessible places that such limitations are of little concern to the first-time trekker.

One route open to trekkers is from Jumla to Ra Ra Lake. Jumla is usually reached by plane from Kathmandu.

The Dhaulagiri Circuit

This strenuous three-week trek commences from Pokhara and makes a circuit of the Dhaulagiri massif. Nominally a restricted route, some companies offer it in their brochures. The usual path goes via Beni or the Kali Gandakhi, then follows the Myagdi Khola on the trading route towards Dhorpatan before turning north up the Gotti Kohla. The trail traverses the length of the Chhonbordan Glacier to reach Dhaulagiri Base Camp. Dhaulagiri I, at 8167 m (26,788 ft), is the highest of six peaks that all bear this name and was not climbed until 1960. A Swiss expedition, including Kurt Diemberger and Norman Dyhrenfurth, eventually made the summit.

The continuation of this circuit takes you over French Pass at 5360 m (17,581 ft) — the curse of the trek — then Dambush (Thapa) Pass and down to the villages of Tukche or Morpha in the upper Kali Gandakhi. The return to Pokhara is the same as for the Jomsong Trek.

Jumla to Ra Ra Lake

Ra Ra Lake, the largest in Nepal, became a National Park in 1975. A circuit of the lake is 13 km (8 miles) and a day's trekking is highly recommended. The remoteness of the region means the natural vegetation and wildlife thrive almost undisturbed. The lakeside villages are now deserted because the locals were relocated when the National Park was declared.

The trek from Jumla to the lake and back can be done as a circuit in eight days but the walking is strenuous. There are no teahouses or lodges en route so you need to go with an organised group or else be completely self-sufficient. The route to and from Ra Ra Lake can involve some long days and in places the trail is not particularly clear. It would be prudent to obtain the services of a local guide. This trek is well worthwhile for those interested in getting off the beaten path and experiencing Himalayan wilderness.

Central Nepal

The principal treks in the west all begin or end at Pokhara and at one or more points take in the spectacular peaks of the Annapurna region. *Trekking North of Pokhara*, by John Hayes, gives details of the following treks.

Pokhara

One hundred miles (161 km) west of Kathmandu lies Pokhara, Nepal's second largest city. It can be reached by bus in seven to eight hours and there are daily flights from Kathmandu.

Limited accommodation is available in Pokhara, you will find Western-style hotels such as Fishtale Lodge and New Crystal Lodge and cheaper Tibetan hotels near the airport. Few of the hotels are of the standard of the better Kathmandu hotels. One of the preferred places to stay is on the shores of the Phewa Tal lake. This first became popular in the 1960s with hippies and travellers looking for an idyllic place to 'hang out'. Pokhara is still a place you can rest and relax in but most westerners who visit are more intent on heading into the hills which seem to be right on the city's doorstep. The mountains of Annapurna, Dhaulagiri and Machupuchare ('fishtail peak') are visible in clear weather.

Many treks begin from Pokhara but a host of villages and sights within several hours' journey make this also a popular base for those who do not wish to trek. Views of the mountains are at their best from October through to May, but visitors interested in sightseeing find the climate acceptable all year round. The monsoon in June and July is accompanied by daily rain, but outside this period the middle hills are pleasant all the time.

Seeing the sunrise on the Annapurnas from Poon Hill above Ghorapani, is one of the classic trekking experiences of the Himalaya. The resulting spread of teahouses and villages catering to the large influx of trekkers however have placed great pressures on the natural environment.

Treks in this region can be of any duration — from just a few days to a month or more — and still be very worthwhile. For the less adventurous, less fit or those who have time limitations but still wish to sample trekking for one to three days, there are several popular areas relatively near Pokhara. One route, known as the Royal Trek (because it was taken by Prince Charles on his visit to Nepal), is offered by several companies — the highlight is the spectacular views of the sacred mountain of Machupuchare.

There are four popular longer treks in the Annapurna region that cover the full range of possibilities: the easy circuit to Ghorapani (Ghorepani) in the Annapurna foothills; the moderate Jomsong-Muktinath trek; the strenuous Annapurna sanctuary trek; and the Annapurna Circuit, a strenuous trek that also goes to high altitudes.

Annapurna Foothills

The most popular shorter routes focus on the spectacular views to be seen from Poon Hill above Ghorapani. The Annapurna foothills trek takes you in a circuit through the villages of Naudanda via Landrung and Ghandrung to Ghorapani. Poon Hill, above this village, has an excellent view of Annapurna South, Annapurna II and the intervening foothills. This trek has become so popular over the years that teahouses and lodges have blossomed in every village, putting heavy pressure on the surrounding forests. This area is also now one of the least secure because of its proximity to Pokhara and the heavy traffic. Everyone, but particularly lone trekkers, should be careful with their belongings and safety.

Jomsong (Jomosom)

The northern part of what is now the Annapurna circuit was a restricted area for many years. In 1977 the region around Manang was declared open, making the circuit possible. Up until that time all trekking had been concentrated in the Kali Gandakhi Valley, reputedly the deepest in the world with the riverbed at 2590 m (8495 ft), while the mountains Annapurna I in the east and Dhaulagiri in the west reach over 8000 m (26,240 ft).

This trek from Pokhara to Jomsong, or even up to Muktinath, is one of the classic teahouse treks of the Himalaya. The character of the country changes dramatically as you head up the gorge. In the lower reaches there are two possible routes to get to the Kali Gandakhi Valley from Pokhara. One way is over the Deorali Pass at 2743 m (8997 ft) and Ghorapani Pass via Ghandrung and Lapdrung, and the other goes via the villages of Naudanda and Birethanti on the banks of the Modi Khola.

After the Deorali Pass, the route moves into country inhabited by the Thakali people who are very shrewd traders and business people. They have built lodges up and down the Kali Gandakhi to cater for trekkers. The most well-known village is Tatopani, where weary trekkers can relax in hot springs. Beyond Tatopani the countryside becomes increasingly arid until at Jomsong it is extremely dry.

Jomsong has an airstrip which is serviced daily (weather permitting) by Twin Otters aircraft from either Kathmandu or Pokhara. Some trekkers elect to fly back to one of these cities but the irregularity of the flights can mean frustrating delays. Jomsong is not a particularly comfortable place to wait. At an altitude of 2240 m (7347 ft), it is often cold and usually windy after 11 a.m. Duststorms are also frequent. It is usually better to walk back to Pokhara than to plan on flying out.

Jomsong is well inside the southern extent of the Buddhist-influenced region which extends as far as Ghasa. It is also the administrative headquarters, where there are government officials, merchants and a police checkpost where trekking permits must be shown. The trail from Jomsong ascends to Kagbeni, then to Muktinath at 3710 m (12,169 ft), which is the destination for many pilgrims, both Hindu and Buddhist.

TEAHOUSE TREKKING TO JOMSONG

CHRISTINE GEE

Like many pioneers of commercial trekking, Christine Gee started out trekking from lodge to lodge.

Mr Cruickshank pointed to a map and said: ' . . . Everest is here on the border of Nepal and India . . . ' I was momentarily distracted [by] gazing at the dot of egg yolk on his home-made green jumper. That was in 1964, when I was aged nine, and in grade five at Beechworth High School in north-eastern Victoria.

I didn't hear much about Nepal again until I needed a place to live when I was a student in Canberra in 1975. A friend told me about a house that had a room to let. The man who answered the door wore a blue denim shirt and 'bushwalking type boots'. Within minutes, talk of the room to let had changed to an animated conversation about the three months he had just spent trekking in the Everest region of Nepal. His face was awash with joy as he tried to explain the friendliness of the people, how unreserved and funny they were, and how magnetic and huge the peaks were. I felt his excitement at the revelation that in Nepal it was possible to walk three to four to five weeks without seeing a road, a car, and where the sound of a telephone would never be heard. His name was Goronwy Price.

In 1975 we formed Australian Himalayan Expeditions, as a way for us to keep travelling back to Nepal.

Porters with their dokos are the only way of moving supplies in much of Nepal.

The company grew to be the largest trekking company in the world and, now trading as World Expeditions, it takes more people trekking to Nepal than any other foreign trekking organisation.

I recall arriving in Nepal for the first time on January 26, 1976. I felt excited beyond words to be visiting the place which had been so central to my relationship with Goronwy, and to the beginnings of our trekking organisation.

There were no mountain views this time to prepare me for what was to come. Finally we broke through the clouds, and the Kathmandu Valley came into view. We landed, and stepped out in the warm sun. All around glistening white peaks said 'hello', and it all seemed so relaxed, so rural and rather chaotic! Being raised in the country I felt immediately at home, and even enjoyed the cacophony of battling through Kathmandu Airport. Goronwy was there, beaming and holding onto bright orange garlands of flowers.

Slender Nepalis in white stovepipe pants, grey jackets, and cotton hats beavered away at sorting out the luggage, which was piled into old-style cars that looked kind of "stuck together".

Lurching down untarred roads we passed by women in saris, clutching children adorned with gold earrings and with black makeup around their eyes. Cows stood in the middle of the road, with not the slightest intention of shifting. We cautiously negotiated them, as cows are sacred in this tiny Himalayan kingdom.

Bottles of water with marble stoppers looked so old-fashioned, but soon the wooden temples of Kathmandu left me gasping.

We pulled up at the Hotel Nook, a tiny little hotel on Kantipath, not far from the well-known Annapurna Hotel. Creaking stairs led to a room with hard beds and lights that didn't work, but their vegetarian spring rolls were fantastic.

The following day we awoke in the dark, and Goronwy and I and one of our first groups loaded up a mini-bus and set off to Pokhara in West Nepal to begin a well-known trek from Pokhara to Jomsong.

I will always remember seeing my first teahouses en route. Ladies with wadding around their tummies, squatting beside tiny open clay ovens stirring *dhal bhat*, a vegetable curry and lentil soup, which I was soon to discover a passion for. This was fortunate, as we ate it three times a day for the next two weeks!

Pokhara is quite a sizeable town beside a beautiful lake. We arrived in the evening feeling rather frazzled by the fumes, roaring engines and endless stopping and starting en route by our bus. The clouds had come in so we camped in a school ground. 'Tea Mensab' stirred me the following morning. I snuggled deeper into the soft down of my sleeping-bag, and searched in vain for the possibility of another half-hour in bed. Goronwy said he had a surprise for me.

Before me bathed in soft pink light were the Annapurnas. The sherpas smiled and giggled as they watched my face swoon in wonder at the beauty before me. Machupuchare (the fishtail mountain) was pointed out, and I felt touched by the power and the magic of being in such beautiful surrounds with local people who were so very warm, so relaxed and so much fun to be with. I came to know, even then, that people often go to Nepal to see big mountains and come home raving about the warmth of the locals.

The dreamlike feel of the morning soon gave way to savage battles with my lack of fitness as I tackled the first hill. Goronwy had warned me ' . . . you go up perhaps two thousand feet [610 metres], and then down three thousand feet [915 metres] winding along mountain trails that link mountain villages . . . most people think they prefer the downhill but that can play hell on your knees. Believe it or not you will eventually prefer the uphill . . .' At that point I didn't have that perspective on the problem, and eventually made it up the first hill by recalling the entire score of *Peer Gynt*, which I had played on the clarinet in the local orchestra when I was a child!

Lunchtime became the focal point after that, and my initial wariness at the hygiene of the local teashops dissolved into a ravenous gorging of two steaming plates of dhal bhat, spinach, some boiled eggs and four cups of dusty tea.

The passing traffic along the trail was a great distraction. Everything is carried into the mountains on people's backs, and I could not at first believe the weights being carried in wicker baskets called *dokos*. From sofas, to tree trunks, to the sick going to hospital a week's walk away, to a hundred balls of feathers destined for a chicken curry in a Kathmandu restaurant.

We stopped for the night at a village called Birantanti. Sleeping-bags were rolled onto dusty floors, and we fell asleep amid the smoky insides of a local house.

Tatopani further along the trail gave us a wondrous treat of steaming hot pools to bathe in, although decorum with a whole village of children come to watch proved challenging.

Getting married in the villages of Nepal became real to us one day when we saw a young teenage girl being carried, to the raucous strains of a local band, to the ceremony in her village. Clad in a bright red sari she looked expressionless and accepting of a tradition that had probably been in place for centuries. Certainly for the village it was a great occasion, and we could see that the celebration was a great change from the hard work these villagers put into their daily lives.

The feeling of isolation from modern supports and communications was a relief and I felt such a sense of clarity about life at home. Walking along a trail you are freed from everyday tensions and responsibilities. The only important question seems to be 'How long to the next village? . . . When will we stop for lunch? . . . What peak is that?' and so on. I did notice, though, an unending discussion amongst our group of food and favourite restaurants back home! Trekking certainly builds up your appetite.

That passion for oral satisfaction was soon satisfied by much gorging back in Kathmandu.

This fourteen-day trek took us from lush rice-terraced hillsides clinging to precipitous gorges, up through pine forests perfumed with tree-high daphne bushes, and finally up to the windswept, arid Tibetan plateau near Jomsong, the clear ice spire of Dhaulagiri being the final highlight of the trek. Having arrived at Jomsong we turned round and came all the way back! At that time in Nepal it was not possible to do what is now known as the Annapurna Circuit, where you travel beyond Jomsong, over the high Thorong Pass and into the Manang Valley which takes you back to the road end and to Kathmandu.

Nepal offers a sacred quality that is difficult to describe, but which is repeatedly talked about, is photographed, is the reason why you go back again and again and again . . . and again.

I wonder if Mr Cruickshank ever made it there too?

Christine Gee is co-founder of World Expeditions and the Royal Nepalese Consulate General (Hon.) of NSW.

The Annapurna Circuit

The circuit of the entire Annapurna Himal takes at least twenty days and is regarded as one of the classic treks of the Himalaya. It is recommended to travel anti-clockwise, beginning at the village of Dumre on the Kathmandu–Pokhara road. Other possible starting-points are Sisuwa (closer to Pokhara) or Gorkha (closer to Kathmandu). As with many of the trekking routes, the starting-points vary over time as tracks become roads, and the start of the Annapurna Circuit is no exception. A road being built to Besi Shar (Lamjung) will cut several days from the journey. The existing track is hot and dusty and many trekking companies seek alternative routes to the first part of the journey.

This direction is better for gradual acclimatisation and the grades up to the high point, Thorong La at 5416 m (17,764 ft), are gentler. If the reverse direction is taken, you are forced to make a 1300 m (4264 ft) ascent and a 900 m (2952 ft) descent in a day. For most of the way up to the pass from Dumre the route follows the Marsyandi Khola River. The early days of the trek are through cultivated terraced farmland and villages inhabited by Brahmins, Chetris and Gurungs. In the Gurung villages it is not uncommon to meet Gurkha soldiers who speak excellent English.

After five days the trail passes into the Manang district which is Tibetan in character. The village of Manang at 3737 m (11,600 ft) is a tight complex of multi-storey mud-brick houses on the side of a hill. The Manang *bhotis* are Buddhist and the village is decorated with prayer flags and *chortans*.

Though the Manang region has only been open to trekkers since 1977, it quickly gained a reputation for its spectacular views of the north side of the Annapurnas and particularly for a large icefall that tumbles into a lake.

It is possible to get to Manang from Dumre all year round but the Thorong La is often deep in snow during the winter months. Storms, however, can occur at any time of the year. Before you cross the Thorong La it is prudent to spend one or two days acclimatising at Manang. Villages and accommodation in this region are sparse so it is best to be self-sufficient or cross with an organised group.

Once over the pass the descent to Muktinath is extremely steep. Muktinath is the end of the trail for pilgrims and trekkers coming from the opposite direction up the Kali Gandakhi. The rest of the Annapurna circuit retraces the Jomsong trek outlined on page 175.

Annapurna Sanctuary

This trek goes to the hub of the Annapurna massif by following the Modi Khola River to its source. In 1956 Col. Jimmy Roberts became the first foreigner to enter the sanctuary. The spectacular basin is surrounded by a ring of snow-peaks: the 'fishtail', Machupuchare, at 6993 m (22,937 ft); Annapurna III at 7555 m (24,780 ft); Ganga-Puna at 7455 m (24,452 ft); Glacier Dome at 7193 m (23,593 ft); Annapurna I at 8091 m (26,538 ft); Annapurna South at 7219 m (23,678 ft); and Hiunchuli at 6441 m (21,126 ft).

The trek can be a rushed fourteen day or a relaxed fifteen to sixteen day round trip. For about half of the route you return over the same ground, but this does not seem to deter many trekkers from following in the footsteps of the famous mountaineering expeditions who have used this same route to reach their base camps (e.g. Bonington's Annapurna south-west face expedition.)

The trek begins at Pokhara and heads for Dhampus, Landrung and Ghandrung as if making for the Kali Gandakhi. At Ghandrung the route turns to the north and passes the village of Chomro on the way up the Modi Khola. After Chomro the route winds through thick bamboo forest for a day. The trail here is often slippery and wet due to the heavy rainfall this part of the Himalaya receives. Just above Hinko, where there is a large overhanging

(Previous pages) Himalayan cultures have many ways that western visitors should be aware of in order not to offend. A Nepalese man dressed in all white should not be touched as he has had a death in his family and is considered contaminated.

The temple at Muktinath in Nepal is a sacred shrine and pilgrimage site for both Buddhists and Hindus. The main religious festival at the time of the August/September full moon attracts thousands of pilgrims.

rock that is sometimes referred to as a cave, the trail is subject to avalanches if there has been a heavy snowfall. It is then necessary to wait several days for the snow to ablate or pack down before proceeding. Trekkers have been buried by avalanches, so extreme caution should be exercised. If storms occur, commercial treks usually divert up the Kali Gandakhi.

Today there are teahouses and lodges all the way into the sanctuary but some of them are rather primitive. Mud floors, a bamboo thatch roof and a warming fire, however, can seem very appealing after a day trekking in the rain, although fires are leading to serious deforestation.

The first good views inside the basin are at Machupuchare (Machhapuchhare) Base Camp from where the full majesty of

Machupuchare, Annapurna III, Fang and Annapurna South can be seen. A further two hours up brings you to Annapurna Base Camp at 3960 m (12,989 ft) where you can enjoy a 360-degree panorama from Annapurna I's awesome, nearly vertical south face, first climbed by the British in 1970 (see climbing historical section on page 32), round to Machupuchare, which has only seen one expedition on its flanks in 1957. This was also a British expedition, led by Jimmy Roberts, but the team stopped short of the summit in deference to the locals, to whom the mountain is sacred.

Annapurna I was the first 8000 m peak to be climbed (see page 35). 'Annapurna', in Sanskrit means, 'the provider'. Five peaks share this name.

The Sanctuary region has three trekking peaks: Tent Peak at 5500 m (18,040 ft); Fluted Peak at 6390 m (20,959 ft); and Hiunchuli at 6441 m (21,126 ft). These, however, do not receive as many ascents as the trekking peaks of Pisang or Chulu to the north. For lovers of mountains, the Annapurna Sanctuary trek is recommended, though its difficulty should not be underestimated.

Langtang, Helambu and Gosainkund

Due north of Kathmandu are some of the most accessible treks in Nepal. The three main regions are the Langtang Valley, Gosainkund, and the Helambu region. There are many possible variations to see some or a combination of these places depending on the time available.

Treks to the Langtang Glacier and Gosainkund commence from Dhunche. This can be reached by a four-hour bus ride from Kathmandu. The third possibility is to start from Panchkhal, about two hours by bus west of Kathmandu, to Lomosangu and the Chinese border.

The Langtang Valley runs roughly south-west from the Tibetan border below the highest peak in the region — Langtang Lirung at 7245 m (23,764 ft) — which straddles the boundary. H.W. Tilman was the first westerner to discover the delights of the area in 1949. He was followed by two Swiss — Tony Hagen and, later, Womer Schulthess. The latter set up a Swiss cheese factory at Kyangjin. In Tibetan, *lang* means 'yak' and *tang* means 'to follow'. The name is tied up with a legend about how a lama followed his lost yak into the valley. The beast supposedly died and was skinned at Langsisa, hence the red rocks.

Langtang National Park Nepal's largest National Park is 1710 sq. km (660 sq. miles), occupies much of the upper Langtang region, and is home to Himalayan thar and musk deer. The best times to trek in the park are March to early May, October and November. There are sixteen villages in the park but most people live in the village of Langtang.

Helambu is 75 km (47 miles) north of Kathmandu and easily reached in a seven- or eight-day trek. It can also be part of a two-week circuit of the Langtang and Helambu combined. The path across the Ganja La pass, 5122 m (16,800 ft) above Kyamjin Gompa in the upper Langtang, is the link between the two valleys. In winter, the pass can close, and it should not be attempted unless you have a guide or mountaineering experience and the proper equipment. The Helambu is home to sherpas who are quite different again to those of the Khumbu. Tarke Gyang, the main village, has many wealthy families who conduct a thriving business in so-called antiques. From Tarke Gyang the trail forks. To the north is the Ganja La and to the west are the passes of Thaerpati and Laurebina.

Gosainkund These lakes are the focus each July or August for Hindu pilgrimage. The God Shiva is said to reside in one of the lakes as a rock jutting above the surface.

The 'necklace' of lakes, of which Gosainkund is the main one, is at an altitude of 4380 m (14,366 ft), just below a pass from the Trisuli Khola to Malemchi village. A circuit is possible from Trisuli Bazaar back to Kathmandu via Sudorijal or the Malemchi Khola Valley.

Rowaling Valley

Though not very popular today, the Rowaling–Himal trek explores the region just to the west of the Khumbu and passes under Gavrishankar, at 7145 m (23,436 ft). Currently a restricted route, it is possible to go into Rowaling with a trekking peak permit from Ramdung. The trek begins from Charikot, which can be reached by van from Lomosangu, which is in turn connected to Kathmandu by bus. An alternative start is the town of Barabise, further north than Lomosangu, on the road to Lhasa. The Rowaling region has no inns or lodges so on this two-week trek

A sub peak of Gaurishanker, which is a very holy mountain for the Sherpa people, can be seen just above the village of Beding in the Rowaling Valley.

Namche Bazaar takes about four days. This is a potentially very serious undertaking for trekkers because of the altitude and the danger from bad weather, cold, rockfalls and the usual problems associated with glacier travel. You need to be well acclimatised and have ropes, crampons and ice-axes. The assistance of a Rowaling sherpa guide who has made the crossing before will help to minimise the danger.

The route on the other side descends to the valley of the Thami or Thengpo Khola and passes through the village of Thami (Thame) which is famous for its monastery built into the hillside. Thami is one of the main religious centres in the Khumbu and each June is host to the Mani Rimdu festival which attracts sherpa participants and Western visitors.

It is possible to trek from Thami down to Namche Bazaar in a day. In the reverse direction. The route over the Tesi Lapcha is sometimes used as a way to bypass Lukla by people escaping from the Khumbu region.

Eastern Nepal

The Khumbu

Jiri to Everest

One of the most rewarding approaches to Everest involves walking all the way from the roadhead at Jiri. Local buses depart very early each morning from Kathmandu for Jiri, on a 188 km (117 miles) journey which takes six bone-jarring hours. The trek to Everest via this start usually takes at least fifteen days. On the return there is the option of flying part of the way back from Lukla, which can make the round trip — Kathmandu to Kathmandu — take about three weeks.

The advantage of walking in from Jiri is that it allows for proper acclimatisation to altitude and gives one a chance to experience more of rural Nepal. The walk in is also steeped in history as it was used by

you need to be self-sufficient. The main village near the head of the trek is Beding, which has a small monastery. A side trip offers good views of Menlungtse (Jobo Garu), at 7181 m (23,554 ft) the highest peak in the Rowaling Himal.

For those with climbing skills it is also possible to cross from the Rowaling into the Khumbu via the Tesi Lapcha Pass at 5755 m (18,876 ft). From Beding to

As we watched, the rims of Everest and Lhotse were gilded by the morning sun and a narrow beam of sunlight coming through the South Col lit the surface of the Ice Fall. To the rocks around me it was but one of a million moments of eternity — to me it was a special time, and one that I would savour years afterwards. It was hard to believe I was really there.

PADDY PALLIN
Never Truly Lost, 1987

the Everest expeditions of the 1950s and 1960s, rather than flying to Lukla, although the exact route is not followed today. This vicinity is known as Solu-Khumbu and is to the south of the Khumbu itself.

The early stages of this route entail day after day of up and down as the trail cuts across the grain of the country. Two passes have to be negotiated before reaching the Dudh Kosi ('milk river'). The main one is the 3530 m (11,578 ft) Lamjura Pass on day three, which takes you higher than Namche Bazaar, but despite the altitude there are no views to speak of. From the pass the trail drops down to the Junbesi Khola River. On top of the next ridge is Tragsindho (Trakshindo), where there is a cheese factory and an excellent view if the skies are clear. The next descent is to the Dudh Kosi Valley. The trail then climbs up and down to Khari Khola and continues to Chaurikankar, where you pass beneath the village of Lukla. You can fly there to start the walk and reduce the journey by seven or eight days.

The trail to Everest above Lukla is one of the most developed in the Himalaya. There are numerous teahouses and lodges and many individuals make the journey on their own or at least organise it themselves. The main route continues to follow the Dudh Kosi along well-made and often busy trails. It is not unusual to pass a trekking party every hour or so as well as many locals and porters. From Lukla it is a two-day trip to Namche Bazaar with the entrance to Sagamatha National Park at Jorsale about halfway. An entrance fee is payable, and park rules and regulations should be observed.

Sagamatha National Park

Sagamatha National Park covers an area of 1200 sq. km (3109 sq. miles), all of which is above 3000 m (9840 ft). It was set up with assistance from the New Zealand Government in 1976. In 1979 Sagamatha was declared a world heritage site in recognition of the cultural significance of the Sherpa people, its flora and fauna, and the presence of the world's highest mountain.

The Sagamatha National Park has been regarded as only a partial success because it was conceived as an effort to reduce deforestation in the region. Yet a growing number of teahouses and lodges, some of them run by the park, burn timber day and night in inefficient stoves for heating and cooking. Timber is also burnt to provide hot showers for some of the 10,000 trekkers who pass through the park annually. While the park has not lived up to many people's hopes, it is at least helping to draw people's attention to the problems of conservation and overuse. Detailed information about all aspects of the Sagamatha National Park are in Margaret Jefferies's book *The Story of the Mount Everest National Park*.

Namche Bazaar

Namche Bazaar, at 3440 m (11,283 ft) is at the crossroads of several main trails and can be likened to Chamonix in the French Alps. To the sherpas it is the focal point of their culture. It is the administrative centre for the Khumbu region and the main village catering to trekkers and climbers. There are many lodges and houses that offer food and accommodation. Namche is an ideal place to spend several days acclimatising as there is plenty to see, as well as many shops and stalls selling jewellery, trinkets, clothing and trekking gear.

The trail to Namche Bazaar above Lukla follows the course of the Dudh Kosi for much of its length. The sherpas of the region are able to grow maize and potatoes in the summer and wheat cabbage, turnips and cauliflower in the winter.

(Previous pages) The spectacular mountains of Nepal's Khumbu region are among the most accessible in the Himalaya because of the airstrip at Lukla. If flying into such altitudes, however, a day or so should be spent acclimatising before you proceed higher.

Khumjung

Above Namche is the village of Khumjung which is bigger than Namche but not so commercialised. This is worth a visit on its own even if you are not going on to Gokyo. The Hillary School at Khumjung, built by the Himalayan Trust, has catered to primary and secondary students since 1983. On the hill opposite is the Everest View Hotel, now being refurbished after years of neglect. This Japanese-owned establishment is serviced by the Shyangboche airstrip, although only Pilatus Porter planes land.

Above Khumjung is the village of Khunde which contains the only hospital in the Khumbu region. This was also built by the Himalayan Trust. At the Khumjung Gompa there is reputed to be a yeti's scalp. A donation to the lama will help unlock the key to its storage box. Tests conducted in the West suggest it is possibly from a serow (a type of deer) but biologist A. J. Cronin questioned this.

Everest View Hotel

The Japanese hotel at Shyangboche, known as the Everest View (five rooms) is being reopened in 1989. The owners plan to build a pressurised room that can hold seven or eight people. It costs US$140 a night, $20 of which goes to the conservation fund, and $240 for the round plane trip in a Pilatus Porter.

Thyangboche

Thyangboche, at 3870 m (12,694 ft), is a day's walk from Namche Bazaar. The most direct route involves a long traverse, a descent to the Dudh Khosi, then a long climb up through pine forest. Thyangboche has a very special location, nestling as it does on a saddle in a clearing surrounded by pine trees. Its Buddhist monastery was founded in 1923. Thyangboche has one of the most outstanding views in the world. From the monastery you can see a 360-degree panorama of mountains up and down the valley. At the head of the valley the top of

Just above Namche is a police checkpost where trekkers should sign in and higher again, on the top of a hill, is the Sagamatha Park headquarters. This includes a museum where an hour or two can be fruitfully spent learning about the region and taking in the magnificient views all around.

Each Saturday Namche comes alive with a market that draws people from all over the Khumbu to buy and sell. Several hundred people congregate on terraces near the entrance to Namche and for much of the day there is a frenzy of activity. Market day is an excellent opportunity to enjoy the trading and photograph the people and events.

Mount Everest (Sagamatha, Qomolangma) can sometimes be seen just above the Lhotse–Nuptse Ridge. The summit pyramid is often bathed in cloud borne by the ferocious jetstream winds that lash the mountain for much of the time. The most impressive peak seen from here is Ama Dablam ('mother's charm box') named for an upper-face bulge of ice that resembles the charm boxes worn around the necks of many sherpa women. Closest to Thyangboche itself are the beautiful peaks of Kangtega and Thamserku. Further down the valley Khumbiyula, the sacred peak above Namche Bazaar, continues the panorama.

Thyangboche is the destination of many shorter commercial treks within the Khumbu. Thre are several lodges there and some trekking companies have their own establishments. The monastery there is the setting for the November-December performance of **Mani Rimdu**, a Sherpa celebration of Buddhism's victory over the Bon religion. Mani Rimdu is also usually performed at the Thami monastery in May.

Pheriche

Pheriche (4240 m; 13,907 ft) is an ideal place to spend an extra night acclimatising on the way to base camp. This is the site of the Trekkers Aid Post run by the Himalayan Rescue Association. During the pre-monsoon and post-monsoon trekking seasons, it is usually manned by a volunteer Western doctor who can be consulted if you have any problems with altitude. Pheriche was once only a summer yak herding settlement but now, it is occupied year-round.

Kala Pattar (Black Rock)

The high point on the Everest Base Camp trek is a hill above Gorak Shep known as Kala Pattar. The best views of Mount Everest, the Khumbu Icefall, Nuptse and Pumori are to be seen from here. Everest Base Camp itself is further on again across the ever-shifting moraine and glacier ice at the foot of the Khumbu Icefall. In the pre-monsoon, post-monsoon and winter climbing seasons there are usually always one or more expeditions in residence at the base camp.

Thyangboche Monastery (left), located in a spectacular setting atop a ridge with views all around, was founded in 1916 by Lama Chatang Chotar. An earthquake destroyed the main temple in 1934 then in January 1989 a fire destroyed the entire monastery and most of the richly decorated murals, decorations and artifacts (right). It is hoped to rebuild the monastery through an international fund-raising campaign.

Trekkers should not expect hospitality here and anyone planning to stay should be completely self-sufficient for extreme conditions. Expeditions have limited resources and are not in a position to cater to the many visitors wandering through their camp. If you are particularly interested in how expeditions operate, you can occasionally join a support trek to the Base Camp. For this, you make a financial contribution to the climb and you are usually given special treatment. In the Khumbu, as in most areas, there are numerous side trips or variations to a particular route. The trip up to Gokyo is well worth considering, as is venturing up the Imja Khola to Island Peak.

Gokyo

The side trip up to Gokyo begins from Namche or you can branch off after several hours on the main route to Thyangboche. The trek up to the Gokyo lakes should be taken in stages. Two or three days is recommended. The hill above the Gokyo lakes affords one of the best views of Everest. Some say it is better than Kala Pattar (Kala Pathar) above Gorak Shep 25 km (16 miles) away, as Everest stands taller than its neighbours from this point.

The longest glacier in Nepal, the Ngozumpa lies further in the valley below. At its head is Cho Oyu at 8153 m (26,742 ft), the sixth-highest mountain in the world. Good views of Gyachung Kang, Lhotse, Makalu, Cholatse and Tawachee are also to be had. For some, the trek to Gokyo is a preferred alternative to the more crowded base camp route.

Imja Valley — Island Peak

At Pheriche the trail divides to head up to Dingboche at the mouth of the Imja Valley, or to continue towards Everest Base Camp. This side trip up the Imja offers a tremendous mountain panorama of the south face of Lhotse–Nuptse, the east face of Ama Dablam and Amphu Lhabtsa (a high pass that leads into the Hungu Valley). From the summer grazing village of Chukung at 4700 m (15,416 ft), proceeding further up the valley on the moraine brings you to Island Peak, 6189 m (20,300 ft), one of the most popular trekking peaks in Nepal. Island Peak is not a very technical climb but a permit is required and if you are inexperienced, a guide is essential. It is also one of the main peaks guided by trekking agencies, so it is possible to join a group which will provide equipment and experience.

This side trip to Chukung and back can be done from Pheriche in a day, which is an ideal opportunity for acclimatisation. Another popular variation on the trek from Jiri to Everest is to fly in to Lukla.

Lukla

Landing at Lukla is like parking your car in a garage at 80 mph.

ANONYMOUS

The short take-off and landing (STOL) airstrip at Lukla was built to help bring in building materials for the construction of Khunde Hospital in 1965 by a team led by Sir Edmund Hillary. Expanded in 1977, a control tower was built in 1983.

The flight from Kathmandu takes thirty-five minutes aboard a nineteen-seater De Havilland Twin Otter. Weight restriction on the flight is strictly observed. Seldom more than fourteen passengers are carried and your hand luggage as well as checked bags are weighed. Anyone who has ever flown into Lukla has no quibble with such precautions. The 'runway' is on a hillside that ends in a steep rockface. The uphill grade helps to slow the planes on landing and accelerate them on take-off. The flight is certainly one of the more exciting scheduled routes in the world. Window seats on the left-hand side of the aircraft on the way to Lukla and right-side seats on the way back give you the most spectacular views of the Himalaya.

Flights to and from Lukla are also subject to vagaries of weather and often there are insufficient aircraft or pilots. Many days can be wasted waiting for a flight into or out of the Everest region. Planning to walk at least one way helps to minimise such disruption to your plans and gives you more of the true mountain experience.

Many trekking companies offer a 'panorama trek' which flies into Lukla and goes as far as Thyangboche, the site of the famous Buddhist monastery, and then returns to Lukla to fly back to Kathmandu. Relying on flying in both directions is an added risk but the demand is strong.

Flying into Lukla at 2840 m (9315 ft) is a sudden and considerable altitude gain. On arriving you should take it easy and perhaps spend a day or two there to give your body time to adjust. (See altitude sickness page 66 ff).

Makalu Base Camp/Arun Valley

The Makalu Base Camp and Arun Valley treks both begin from the village of Hille which is also the starting-point for the Kanchenjunga trek. Hille is the usual roadhead for the region to the north and home to a large population of Tibetans. The closest main centre is Dharan Bazaar, an eleven-hour bus ride from Kathmandu.

The Makalu Base Camp trek is not particularly hard but it is long — the round trip takes twenty-four days. It can be shortened by about ten days by flying into or out of Tumlingtar. From Hille the trek route crosses the Mahabarat Range and descends into the subtropical Arun Valley. The course of the river is followed by a well-used trading route as far as Tumlingtar. The route then climbs up to the adjacent ridge to the last market town of Khandbari, before dropping back down, crossing the Arun River again, and then ascending the Kasuwa Khola. The Barun Pass at 4312 m (14,143 ft) is crossed before descending into the rugged Barun Valley. Travelling alongside the lower Barun Glacier brings you to Makalu Base Camp at 4800 m (15,744 ft) and the imposing sight of Makalu's 2440 m (8003 ft) granite south face.

Makalu, at 8463 m (27,759 ft), lies on the Tibet/Nepal border and is the fifth-highest mountain in the world. The Tibetan translation of the name probably means 'the great black one'. It was first climbed by a French team in 1955.

The Arun Valley trek is often used as an alternative and more exotic way for commercial groups to arrive at the Khumbu region. There is no reason why experienced and well-equipped self-organised trekkers should not pass this way as well. However, the route is long, less well-known and not well-served with lodges. Starting at Hille, the same trail as the Makalu Base Camp trek takes you as far as the Dingla on the Arun River, before crossing (via Phedi) the Salapa Pass at 3475 m (11,398 ft) into the Hongu Valley. You then proceed via the Surkie La into the Dudh Kosi Valley below Lukla. These treks often continue up to Thyangboche and Everest before flying out of Lukla.

Kanchenjunga

The Kanchenjunga region in the far east of Nepal is the most recent area to be opened to the organised trekking groups. Expeditions have long visited the region to attempt Kanchenjunga and Jannu. The main centre for the region is Dharan Bazaar. The trekking can begin at Hille, the start for treks to Makalu Base Camp.

The early days of the trek are through the foothills until the village of Taplejung is reached. The route then diverges, either to the north face base camp via the village of Gunsa, or to the southern base camp at the Yalung Glacier with its views of Jannu (7710 m; 25,289 ft). On the return trip many choose to fly from the airstrip at Taplejung, but the schedules are unreliable and the local traffic usually has preference. The walking on both routes is more green and lush than anywhere else in Nepal and there is plenty of wildlife and natural forests. Kanchenjunga lies

Snow storms, rain, high winds and cloud are just some of the reasons why flying into and out of Lukla in the Khumbu is fraught with delays. Hundreds of people have on occasion waited for a week at a time. It is often better to plan to walk all the way than to try and fly.

Expeditionary raft and kayak descents of Nepal's more remote rivers have been made by foreign teams and local rafting guides, usually for the challenge and adventure of being the first to explore a particular section of water. Once they have been done they seem to lose their appeal.

Chitwan National Park

A fertile jungle-covered plain lies to the south. Known as the Terai, these lowlands are within sight of the snowcapped peaks. Once the domain of the tiger and rhinoceros, today these forests are fast being cleared and settled. With the eradication of the malarial mosquito, the plain is now the ricebowl of Nepal. A great central trough of foothills and valleys lies between the mountains and the plain.

Once the Rana's exclusive hunting reserve, the Royal Chitwan National Park is now the largest remaining natural forest. Set up by the Rana in 1970, it is a refuge for many jungle animals facing extinction with the settlement of the Terai. Tiger Tops Jungle Lodge, Macchan Jungle Lodge, Temple Tiger Tented Camp, Narayani Safari Lodge, Guida and Elephant Camp all offer opportunities to experience the tiger, one-horned Asian rhinoceros and deer in the wild. Valuable conservation work is being carried out through studies on the ecology of tigers and establishment of a crocodile hatchery.

Nepal is probably most famous for natural wonders that occur high in the Himalaya. From March through to May whole hillsides are ablaze with giant red rhododendron trees. Many small blooms and delicate orchids are less arresting but none the less beautiful. Photographers and naturalists find a feast of spectacular sights within the mountains, rivers and jungles of this tiny kingdom. A myriad of terraces cling to the hillsides like giant staircases. Their sweeping curves, often bathed in lush crops, are tilled by time-honoured methods.

astride the Indian (Sikkim) Nepalese border so it is not possible to make a circuit of the mountain. The name Kanchenjunga means 'treasures of the snows'.

River Rafting

Commercial rafting in Nepal is concentrated on the Trisuli, the Seti and the Narayani, though occasionally other trips are offered on the Sun Kosi and Tamur rivers. The length of the trips can vary from one or two days to over a week. Most people prefer to include a shorter rafting trip on a trekking or sightseeing tour rather than spend their complete holiday rafting. No special skills or experience are required to join a commercial rafting trip.

FROM MR BALL IN PERSONNEL TO EVEREST

MICK CHAPMAN

Sherpa guides and hoteliers are adept at taking inexperienced travellers in hand from the moment they arrive in Nepal. Mick Chapman's first encounter with the Everest trek was no exception.

Grant and I both held esteemed deskbound positions in the British Civil Service, our futures were secure and rosy. Yet a little too predictable. We needed a challenge in life, one that we could look back on in later years and say, we did it. During extended lunch-hours and tea-breaks, we became armchair explorers. Books by Bonnington, Hillary and Tilman fired us into action. It was now or never. We were going to go to the Himalaya, destination Everest Base Camp. Our resignations signalled counselling by Mr Ball from Personnel, who kindly informed us that this sort of thing was not done. Worse still, if we were reaccepted by the Civil Service then we would, in a year's leave of absence, lose two-and-a-half contribution points towards our pension. As this was forty-four years away, we thanked Mr Ball, promised to return after one, then headed into the city and bought our tickets to Kathmandu.

The difficult part was over. 8 December 1974 would see us in Kathmandu. Being young, adventurous and not paying a great deal of attention to detail, where we would stay had not even crossed our minds.

Sherpa guides and hoteliers are renowned for their friendly disposition.

Finding a hotel was the least of our problems. As the door of the airport customs hall opened a sea of bodies lurched forward. Our rucksacks disappeared and we were manhandled into the back of a tired-looking vehicle (presumably a taxi). Our new-found friend, Ram, introduced us to the delights of the Asia Hotel.

'Most conveniently located hotel, friendly atmosphere, hot shower available, good foodings and twenty-four hours electricity, budgetly priced. You stay my hotel then taxi free.'

''Ugh!' agreed Grant.

We were two minutes into Nepal, and Ram was obviously in control. We

lurched off leaving a trail of black smoke surrounding two young boys, professional 'bump starters'.

Once established in residence, the quest for a sherpa crew became our next priority. Juju Bhai, the hotel manager, assured us that Pemba Sherpa was the man for us.

'He is cousin to *the* Tenzing sherpa. He has guided foreigners all over Nepal, many times trekking, five times to Everest, expert cook, fluent in English, German, French and also reasonable cost. Many peoples from my hotel use Mr Pemba. He is good man.'

The following day a lunchtime meeting was arranged and Pemba duly arrived on time. He was a short stocky character, in his mid-thirties, exuding a quiet but confident air. He looked like a mountain guide, dressed in woollen breeches, longjohns, down jacket and boots. We talked all afternoon. Everything he assured us was 'no problem'. He would arrange an assistant and some porters, buy all the necessary food, hire the tents, arrange permits, etc. We were obviously in good hands, even if he denied knowledge of being Tenzing Sherpa's cousin.

The bus to Lomosangu was all that we imagined, chugging along in a cloud of diesel fumes, extremely overloaded and very uncomfortable. The journey lasted some six hours. Pemba was out the window in a flash, up onto the roof retrieving our baggage from underneath a tarpaulin. Porters were quickly recruited and were led off by Dorje, Pemba's assistant.

The climb out of the valley towards Perku was a mere [1524 m] 5000 ft pull. Grant and I staggered upwards bearing 15 kg [33 lb] loads. Pemba followed closely behind, all his possessions for our month's expedition in a shoulder-bag.

Even though it was the winter season, the heat of the afternoon soon took its toll. That night Pemba and Dorje entered into a lengthy conversation with one of the locals, Bir Bahadur. A packet of cigarettes, 20 rupees and an amicable wobble of heads signalled he was our man. If we were to carry on and enjoy it then a shedding of a few kilos from our rucksacks was necessary.

The first two weeks of our trek were a series of ups and downs as we crossed the grain of the country. Once we had established the pattern of the trekking day and learnt the art of pacing oneself uphill, life became altogether very pleasant. Our crew could not do enough for us, always attentive, the food excellent, the scenery absolutely stunning. The Himalayan giants Gaurishanker, Menlungtse and Numbur dominated the northern skyline.

It was with great excitement that we approached Namche Bazaar, the capital of Sherpa country. Nestling in a natural basin, the small town is surrounded by majestic peaks. Though by Himalayan standards not monsters, their haunting beauty reflected the sherpa belief that their summits housed the local gods.

Namche boasted the best-stocked shops we had seen on the trail. Items for sale included dried yak meat, 'ancient Tibetan artifacts', chocolate bars, expedition equipment and clothing. Amidst the stack of tinned pumpernickel bread Grant spotted a tin of prawn cocktail. That night we dined in style. Chips, baked beans and our seafood delicacy.

Pemba assured us that the hardest part of the trek was over. The trekking days would now be shorter and a little less strenuous as it was necessary to restrict our daily height gain to ensure we did not suffer from altitude sickness.

Above Namche our first prominent view of Everest reared above the peaks of Nuptse and Lhotse. To the right of the valley a smaller but far more spectacular peak, Ama Dablam, stood alone, partially obscured in cloud.

From Namche we moved into Thyangboche, where we camped in the monastery grounds, possibly the most spectacular camp-site on our trek. From here we moved on to Pheriche and then a steady climb through the terminal moraines led us to our final campsite at Lobuche.

Everest was climbed by the likes of Bonnington. Our goal was to get as near as possible. Our destination was Kala Pattar, an [5488 m] 18,000 ft 'hillock', climbed not because it is there, but because *it* is over there. Mount Everest, at [8850 m] 29,028 ft the highest mountain in the world, is best viewed from this vantage-point.

I could hear the crunch of footsteps in the snow approaching our tent.

'Morning. Tea.'

Having gone to sleep the previous night at 8 p.m., I had been lying awake for the last three hours awaiting this call. Wrestling out of my sleeping bag, I crawled slug-like to open the tent zip. Dorje thrust in steaming mugs of tea for Grant and myself.

'Morning Mr Mick, Mr Grant, today very good weather. No problem.'

At [4878 m] 16,000 ft both Grant and I had woken with slight headaches. A light breakfast and a few more cups of tea later, we set out as dawn began to break. The walking was easy, until we reached the sandflats at Gorak Shep. From here the trail climbed steeply onto the hill of Kala Pattar. As we climbed my head began to pound away in rhythm with my heart. The initial 200 m [656 ft] or so was a steep pull. I was having difficulty pacing myself at this altitude.

'Mick, look behind you, there she is,' Grant said excitedly.

'There's who?'

'Everest.'

Grant was obviously in better shape than myself. I began to fear that I would not make it. How come Grant was feeling so flash? Behind me Pemba was approaching at a speed that gave me even less confidence of reaching the top.

'No problem Mr Mick, only ten more minutes.'

Cruising past, he joined Grant who was busy getting shots of Everest before it went out of fashion.

'Mick, we'll see you on the top in ten!' shouted Grant, eager to push on.

It was probably more like twenty before I staggered onto the boulders at the top of Kala Pattar. The view was incredible, not just of Everest, but the whole panorama. I felt the need to express myself, yet I was unable to utter a word. Photos could not begin to capture the moment. How could one begin to describe this experience to friends back home? I had this feeling that I would not see Mr Ball again.

Mick Chapman, an Englishman, has been based in Nepal for ten years and has led close to 100 treks throughout the country. He has pioneered many alternative trekking routes for Peregrine Expeditions which he manages in Nepal.

BHUTAN

> The King (of Bhutan) once told the world bank experts he was not so interested in the GNP (Gross National Product) as the Gross National Happiness of his people.
>
> **DOUG SCOTT**
> *A Summary of Climbing and the Anglo-Indian Ascent of Jitchu Drake, 1988,*

Known to the locals as Druk Yul ('land of the thunder dragon'), the name Bhutan holds the greatest mystery of any place in the Himalaya. See also Eastern Himalaya, page 163.

The isolated, oval mountain kingdom 160 km (100 miles) by 322 km (200 miles) has been independent for more than 2000 years. It is only since the 1974 coronation of the present King, Jigme Singye Wanchuk, that Bhutan has been open to the outside world. In that year only 287 visitors were allowed in. Fifteen years later the quota of tourists stands at 2500 people a year, but not all places are taken because of the high costs imposed by the Bhutan Tourism Corporation. These range from $US85 to $US200 a day, depending on whether you are part of a mountaineering expedition or a 'cultural' visitor. The main attractions of the country are its unspoilt landscapes and traditional culture.

The Buddhist religion plays a pivotal role in the lives of the Bhutanese and the priesthood is very strong. When Bhutanese become monks they do so for life.

The Bhutanese people are a strong, stocky, Mongolian race and wear their hair closely cropped. Men and women all dress in woven kimono-like robes called *baku* and *kira* respectively.

The head of the state religion (Tantric Buddhism) belongs to the Drukpa sect and he and their religious rites play an important role in the festive life of the country. The entire population becomes involved with religious celebrations which involve processions and masked temple dances call *cham*. The colourful ceremonies are performed by professional dancers, monks and villagers wearing elaborate costumes.

Against the very strong cultural tradition there are equally strong, age-old practices for agricultural management. Fortunately very little of Bhutan is cultivated compared with Nepal. Two-thirds of the country is heavily forested and the timber is put to good use in well-made Swiss chalet homes.

Most of the population live in small settlements in the valleys of the middle region. Nepalese settlers (Duors) have mainly occupied the country adjacent to the southern border. Grazing and agriculture form the basis of the economy.

One of the unique features of Bhutan is the *dzong*, a cross between a monastery and a fort. The first one to be constructed, the Simtokha Dzong, was built in 1627 at the entrance to the Thimphu Valley. Dzongs are traditionally constructed without any plans or nails. In 1970 the very large Tashichodzong (Tashichodzan) was built to house the government offices in Thimphu. It is also the seat of religious power in the country. Though dzongs are normally built in valleys, the most spectacular example, Tongsa Dzong, is perched on a hillside above the Tongsa River in a series of storeys. The most famous and spectacular dzong is Taktseng Monastery (tiger's lair or nest) on a ledge near a cliff of 800 m (2624 ft).

Despite being a steep walk up through oak forests, the Taktseng, in the Poro Chu Valley, is a must for any visitor to Bhutan. The monastery is a shrine to the Guru Rimpochi (Padma Sambhava) who supposedly introduced Buddhism to Bhutan and Tibet in the 8th century astride a tiger. This, like most of the other occupied monasteries in Bhutan, is no longer open to tourists. The monks and lamas rightly fear the disruption of camera-wielding visitors to their monastic existence.

BHUTAN AT A GLANCE

Area
7,000 sq. km (18,142 sq. miles).

Population
1.3 million.

Government
Constitutional monarchy led by His Majesty Jigme Singye Wangchuk.

Capital
Thimphu – altitude 2400 m (7872 ft).

Population
20,000.

Flag
Diagonal yellow and red background, central white Thunder Dragon.

People
Charchops – eastern Bhutan. Ngalops – central and western Bhutan. Nepalese.

Language
National language is Dzongkha, spoken in western Bhutan; Bumlhargkla in central Bhutan; Scharchopka in the east and Nepalese.

Religion
Mahayana Buddhism, and Hinduism.

Highest and lowest point
From Duars Plains, less than 100 m (328 ft) to Kula Kangri at 7553 m (24,774 ft).

Currency
Bhutanese Ngultrum, equivalent to the Indian Rupee.

Time
Indian.

Portion in Himalaya
Entire country is within the Himalaya.

Best times
March, April, May, October, November.

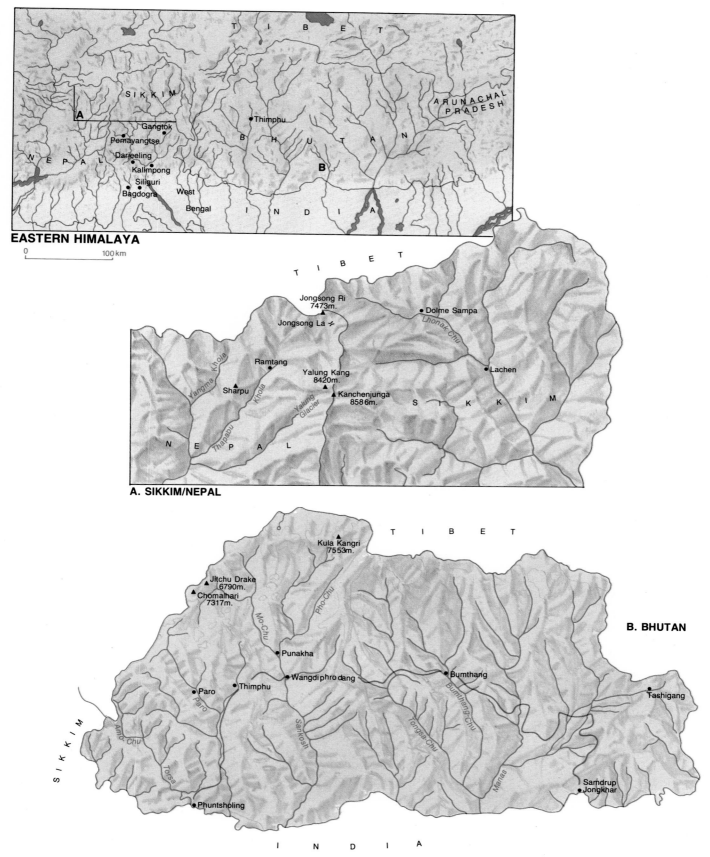

EASTERN HIMALAYA

0   100 km

T I B E T

S I K K I M

Gangtok

Pemayangtse

Thimphu

A R U N A C H A L
P R A D E S H

Darjeeling
Kalimpong
Siliguri
Bagdogra

N E P A L

West
Bengal

B H U T A N

I N D I A

A. SIKKIM/NEPAL

T I B E T

Jongsong Ri
7473m.

Jongsong La

Dolme Sampa

Lhonak Chu

Ramtang

Sharpu

Yangma Khola

Thapabu Khola

Yalung Kang
8420m.

Kanchenjunga
8586m.

Yalung Glacier

Lachen

S I K K I M

N E P A L

B. BHUTAN

T I B E T

Kula Kangri
7553m.

Jitchu Drake
6790m.
Chomalhari
7317m.

Mo-Chu

Pho-Chu

Punakha

Wangdiphrodang

Bumthang

Paro

Thimphu

Tashigang

Paro

Amo-Chu

Santosh

Tongsa-Chu

Bumthang-Chu

Maras

S I K K I M

Torsa

Phuntsholing

Samdrup
Jongkhar

I N D I A

195

Bhutan is anxious to preserve its ways which is why the number of tourists is limited. There is no tipping in the country and strong anti-smoking sentiments are held. There are even signs to discourage motorists from blaring their car-horns in an effort to preserve the peacefulness of the place. The concern with preserving tradition comes through even in the way traditional hunting skills have been integrated with the culture.

Archery is the national sport of Bhutan and is practised all year round. Range tables, as the shooting greens are known, are found in most villages and the contests are held over 150 m (492 ft). Very large bows, some taller than the shooters, are often used. Tournaments are accompanied by celebration and dancing.

Though Bhutan has survived unconquered through natural defences, today it is in a very different geopolitical position. Since Bhutan is wedged between China to the north and India to the south, east and west, it is not surprising that India has played a powerful role in its economy. India has built all-weather roads and trains the Bhutanese army, which helps it to monitor China's military movements on the northern border. China itself has designs on the region as it disputes the border on the adjacent Indian province of Arunachal Pradesh.

Thimphu (Thimpu)

Thimphu, the capital of Bhutan, lies in broad fertile Wangchu Valley at 2400 m (7872 ft). Up until 1955 it was only the summer capital but it has grown rapidly in the last ten years. Apart from the rebuilt Tashichodzong fortress which faithfully followed the architectural style of the old building, the main building of Thimphu is a large chorten constructed in 1974 in memory of the third king, Kigme Dorje Wangchuk.

One of the sites worth seeing in Thimphu is the Sunday market. On this bustling occasion you can sample the

local foodstuffs, purchase souvenirs or just take in the colourful mix of religious and secular life for which Bhutan is renowned.

Road access to Bhutan from India was not established till 1964 via Phuntsholing on the border. From there it is a six-hour journey on a winding 180 km (112 mile) road to Thimphu. The only airport is at Paro, ninety minutes west of Thimphu by road. Druk-Air, Bhutan's national carrier, now operates services from Kathmandu and Bangkok as well as Calcutta, which has been the main transfer point for flying to Bhutan. The closest airport outside Bhutan is Bagdogra, in India, serviced from Calcutta. From there it is a three-hour drive to Phuntsholing on the border.

Trekking

It is virtually impossible to trek or climb on your own in Bhutan as everything has to be done in an organised group through the Bhutan Tourism Corporation (BTC). Tourists or trekkers may enter the country only if they are part of a group of at least six people.

Ponies or yaks transport expedition or trekking loads in Bhutan. A guide, a cook

Masked male monks regularly perform religious dances, known as the *cham*, to the sound of drums and cymbals in Thimphu the capital of Bhutan.

(Right) Taktseng, 'the tigers lair or nest' is the most famous dzong in Bhutan. It nestles on a granite cliff ledge 800 m (2 624 ft) above the valley. Entry for tourists to this, and other occupied monasteries in Bhutan, is restricted.

(Page 198) Paro Valley from Paro Dzong looking towards Chomalhari, is part of the most popular extended trekking route in Bhutan.

and helper are assigned to each group by the BTS, which needs to be advised well in advance of a trip.

There are some twenty possible treks in Bhutan ranging in length from three to twenty days. The longer routes are quite strenuous but there are greater potential rewards. In the remote high valleys near the border there are said to be musk deer, blue sheep and snow leopards, but these are rarely sighted. Trekkers to these areas are more likely to come across nomadic sheep and yak herders with their flocks. The mountain views of the northern ridge line that forms the border with Tibet are often obscured by cloud in afternoon storms, which makes climbing difficult, if not impossible, and trekking often very wet underfoot.

Adventure travel companies usually offer just one option in Bhutan, the two-week Chomalhori trek which travels to the base of Chomalhori at 7315 m (23,993 ft), the westernmost peak in the country on the border with Tibet.

At the time of the first ascent of this mountain by Spencer Chapman and Pasang Dawa in 1937, it was thought to be the highest in Bhutan. Chomalhori (which means 'goddess of the holy mountain') is one of the most sacred in the region. After an ill-fated expedition in 1970 in which two Indian mountaineers disappeared near the summit, a complete ban was placed on climbing the peak. Villagers complained that their cattle had suffered from the climb. However, this has not prevented trekkers from visiting.

The Mount Chomalhari trek in the north-west begins at Paro Dzong and in twelve days ascends the Paro Valley. Then, via two passes, the highest being Nachu La at 4932 m (16,177 ft), it reaches the base of Chomalhari. The return trip to Thimphu is via the Mo Ch, 'the Mother River'. There is a shorter three-day trek from Thimphu to Paro which is known as the Druk Path. This takes in the Paro Valley again, then crosses over a forested pass to the Phajoding monastery.

The 'snowman trek', a combination of the Lunara trek and the Chomalhori trek, is the most challenging in Bhutan. It covers a distance of 362 km (225 miles) and crosses eleven passes, three over 5000 m (16,400 ft). The route winds through the wild north of Bhutan, believed to be the home of the abominable snowman.

Climbing

Climbing expeditions to Bhutan are, like trekking, permitted but not encouraged if the local environment or people are likely to suffer. There have been only one or two expeditions a year in recent years, partly due to the great cost imposed by the Bhutanese Government. Expeditions are usually required to have a minimum seven members but there seems to be a degree of flexibility in the regulations.

The Bhutanese began to open their mountains in 1983 in a limited fashion, but some mountains that were open earlier have since been restricted. The peaks in Bhutan are serious propositions and have already resisted some very powerful climbing parties.

Jitchu Drake at 6790 m (22,271 ft), while not the highest peak in Bhutan, is the only one currently open to climbers. Jitchu Drake means 'the angry swallow' and there have been several attempts on the peak since it was first opened in 1983. The south summit of the mountain was first reached in 1984 by a Japanese expedition. The true summit was eventually climbed in May 1988 by Doug Scott, Victor Saunders, and Sharu Prabhu (see page 37 for account), in a lull in what seems to be typically bad weather for the region.

The highest mountain in Bhutan is Kankar Punzum, at 7541 m (24,734 ft). At the time of writing, it has not yet been climbed, despite numerous attempts by powerful teams. An American, two Japanese and a British team have all been defeated by poor weather and bad snow conditions and now the mountain has been taken off the list of peaks available.

'BHUTAN. GOOD PLACE?'

BOB ASHFORD

Bob Ashford is one of only a few people who have had more than one opportunity to visit Bhutan.

To be honest I wasn't that excited about Bhutan.

It was the 28th of October, 1980, the daytime temperature was still 32°C [90°F] and we were very tired. We had left Kathmandu at 8 a.m. the day before, driven for twenty-four hours with only a few stops to stretch our legs and eat, and had just arrived at Bagdogra in India.

Bagdogra's only claim to fame is that it is a huge military cantonment and an important airfield for the fighter jets that patrol India's northern Himalayan border with China. In 1980 this was the access point to Bhutan. Now you can also fly with Bhutan's tiny airline, Druk Air, direct from Calcutta to Paro in the next valley to Thimpu.

But we had to drive and the wear and tear of the journey was beginning to tell. Even more depressing was the fact that there were another tedious five hours to go before we reached the untidy border town of Phuntsholing. Phuntsholing is squeezed between the eastern banks of the Ammo Chhu River and the first precipitous ranges of the Bhutanese Himalaya. Nowhere else in the Himalaya do the mountains sweep so abruptly skywards from the hot and dusty Indian plains as they do in Bhutan. Phuntsholing gave me the im-

A betel nut chewing fieldworker at Wangdiphrodang's weekly market in Bhutan.

pression that it was hanging on by the skin of its teeth.

Mr Rinchen Lama, my companion, was Bhutanese. But he had fled the country fifteen years previously following 'some changes in the government'. I thought he put it rather well – but then, he had been high in political ranks and he obviously had a way with words!

'This is my first trip since 1964,' Rinchen told me as he stared out of the window.

'How do you feel now you are so close?' I asked him carefully.

'Well, I'm very excited' – a long pause as he continued to stare out of the window – 'and very nervous. Bhutan is a very traditional country.

Changes take place slowly. Even tourists have only been allowed to visit for a few years.'

Rinchen's status had improved only less than a year ago. When he had been invited back for a visit he, in turn, had invited me. At the time I was excited. Now his nervousness was affecting me too.

It was my experience with adventure tourism in Nepal that had prompted Rinchen to invite me. 'Maybe we can do something in Bhutan?'

Phuntsholing was like any other Indian town in my opinion and I was disappointed. I told Rinchen, as he returned from the tiny immigration post, 'If it wasn't for the *baku* (the traditional male dress, rather like a dressing gown) those guys are wearing, I'd swear we were still in India!' As we drove off, leaving the crowds behind, dusk settled fast and we started the twisting hairpin climb to our hotel.

On a sweep of the headlights on one of the bends we caught eight spotted deer scrambling for cover. Hardly two minutes later we trapped a magnificent jungle cat in the dazzle. *Now* I was getting excited and Rinchen, aware of my fanatical interest in wildlife, particularly birds, turned to me with a big grin and said, 'Well, Mr Bob! Now we are in Bhutan. Did I not tell you it was a good place?'

The following morning, long before breakfast, I was up, binoculars in hand, to explore the forest. Because these southern mountains get the first and greatest drenching from the monsoon rains, the forests are exceptional. Too steep to log or farm they are havens for wildlife.

Shouting to myself in an excited whisper, 'They're green magpies!' I spotted a pair of large, long-tailed birds. They were brilliantly green and only a few feet away. Their wings flashed amber-bronze and their bills glowed coral-red. I had never seen this species before and I just knew this was going to be a great day. I rushed back to Rinchen who was tucking into his breakfast. 'Listen, mate. I've decided. Bhutan *is* a good place!'

The long, spectacular climb over the mountains to the tiny town of Thimphu kept me entranced all day. Only a million people live in Bhutan, most of them in the fertile valleys between [2134 to 2744 m] 7000 to 9000 ft. It was so different from Nepal. Quieter, more serene and beautiful. Through it all threaded a narrow twisting road. It was the road that Rinchen had built.

'When the monsoon was finished I would bring the Nepalese coolies up from the plains and we would start again. It took us four years to build.' As he talked I admired the long crashing waterfalls and the delightfully decorated three-storey houses. The Bhutanese seemed to be well off in comparison to other parts of the Himalaya. We got to talking about Bhutanese politics and Royalty. Rinchen told me about King Jigme Singye Wangchuk who came to the throne in 1972 at the age of 18.

'. . . I would ride my horse up and down, marking out where we were to go. Then I would take tea on a ridge so I could look down on the plains.' They were [2744 m] 9000 ft below, almost directly. The views were inspiring, the road breathtaking. 'I am proud of my road, Mr Bob.'

I was to make many trips to Bhutan. I explored her jungles, her rivers, her extraordinary monasteries, and trekked amongst her magnificent mountains. Of all the Himalayan regions I have explored, Bhutan is still my favourite. It's because it is still intact. The sheer pressure of tourism has not been allowed to desecrate the forests, the wildlife, those unique dzongs or the values that set Bhutan apart from every other region of the Himalaya. In particular the hospitality of the Bhutanese is warm and genuine. There is not the slightest hint of jaundiced weariness towards the visitor. Rinchen was overwhelmed by his welcome.

We spent the evening in the home of Nado Rinchen, a close family friend of Rinchen's and Director of Education. He spoke English perfectly. They all did. Nado was very enthusiastic about his country and urged me to explore.

'Bob, you must go and see Bhutan. Take some yaks and trek in the mountains. There are tribes up there even we do not know about.'

As the evening settled into a warm, boozy, nostalgic haze, I turned to Rinchen and said 'Mr Lama! If you want my opinion, Bhutan is a very good place.'

Eight days later Rinchen and I were having breakfast below Chomalhari, Bhutan's highest and holiest peak.

'Chomalhari is [7317 m] 24,000 ft high. We are at [4573 m] 15,000 ft. It is through this valley the Tibetans would come. But they never conquered Bhutan.' But I had been distracted. Strange, flute-like calls were coming from two large birds with long down-curved bills. I recognised them instantly as ibisbill, rare birds of the higher altitudes and dramatically plumaged in black, white and grey.

'They must have young, Rinchen. They're going bananas about us.'

'We are Buddhist,' replied Rinchen.

'All birds and animals are safe in Bhutan.'

I noted the 'we' and smiled. Rinchen had been away fifteen years and this was a very emotional pilgrimage for him. There hadn't been a chorten, a prayer wall, a flapping prayer flag he didn't stop at.'

An icy wind numbed the end of my nose and set the prayer flags flapping and clattering against their posts. Between these sounds wove the haunting calls of the ibisbill. It was a wonderful place for breakfast.

Then out of the mess tent came Dawa, our cook. He had been trained with absolute correctness by Swiss chefs in Thimphu.

Across the loose scree and moraine he stumbled. Grasped tightly between his hands was a silver platter. On the platter were two fried egs. Every now and then, as the wind tried to blow them away, Dawa would clamp a hand down firmly on top of them. We watched in awe!

Miraculously he and both eggs arrived. Grinning wildly at his success, he produced with a great flourish from his back pocket two knives which he slid under each egg and proudly served us. Rinchen and I, without a word and respectfully impressed . . . took a mouthful. Not a trace of heat remained. They were ghastly!

Dawa grinned. 'Bhutan. Good place?' Rinchen and I roared with laughter. 'Yes, Dawa. A bloody good place!' and finished our eggs.

Bob Ashford is one of Australia's more experienced adventure travel company operators. For two years he lived in Nepal pursuing his interest in birdwatching, which led him to co-author *Himalayan Kingdoms, Nepal, Sikkim and Bhutan*. Bob currently manages a trekking company, The Adventure Club.

TIBET/CHINA

> In recent years an uneasy peace on both sides of the Himalayan border has done little to diminish Tibet's extraordinary isolation. Even with the arrival of satellite photography it remains to this day the least known, least explored country on earth, rich in mysteries, still beckoning us with its secrets and still denying us the answer – a vacuum at the centre of the world.
>
> **CHARLES ALLEN**
> *A Mountain in Tibet, 1986*

For much of its length, the crest of the Himalaya forms the border between China and Tibet to the north and Bhutan, Nepal, India and Pakistan to the south.

The western end of the greater Himalaya, particularly the Karakoram, butts up against Xinjiang (Sinkiang) province in China. The remainder of the northern extent lies wholly within Tibet. The Himalaya is the reason for the vast areas of desert in the north. Most of the windswept Tibetan plateau is above 4500 m (14,760 ft).

Numerous other mountainous areas in China (Anna Machin Range, Minya Konka, Kongur and Mustagh Ata) have been the focus of climbing expeditions and occasional trekking parties but these are beyond the realm of the Himalaya and so outside the scope of this book.

Tibet

Until 1951 Tibet was ruled by Buddhist monks headed by the Dalai Lama. Up till this time, life was probably not much different than it had been for the previous 300 years. The monasteries were centres of great wealth, power and control over large tracts of land, and some 20 per cent of the male population became monks.

The People's Liberation Army (PLA) first moved into Tibet in 1951 with the approval of the Dalai Lama and for the next eight years there was an agreement whereby the Chinese authorities did not interfere with the local, political, social or cultural systems or freedoms. On 19 March 1959 this peaceful co-existence broke down and the PLA began to suppress the rebellious Tibetans with force. Some 10,000 people were reported killed and about 80,000 Tibetans, including the Dalai Lama and his family, fled to India and Nepal.

Since then, Tibet has been firmly under the control of the Chinese communists. During the 1960s and 1970s, the monasteries were closed or demolished and the monks forced to return to civilian life. During the cultural revolution the Red Guard destroyed much of the heritage of Tibet. In 1979 a more liberal policy allowed for greater religious freedom and for the gradual opening up of the region to foreigners. The Chinese would like the Dalai Lama to return to Tibet to legitimise their occupation of the country, but he refuses to do so until the Chinese live up to their promises.

The suppression of Buddhist culture extends throughout Tibet. Here the children of Gyantse, once the third most important city of Tibet, which lies on the main route from India and Nepal to Lhasa, conduct a communist flag-waving parade instead of observing a traditional festival.

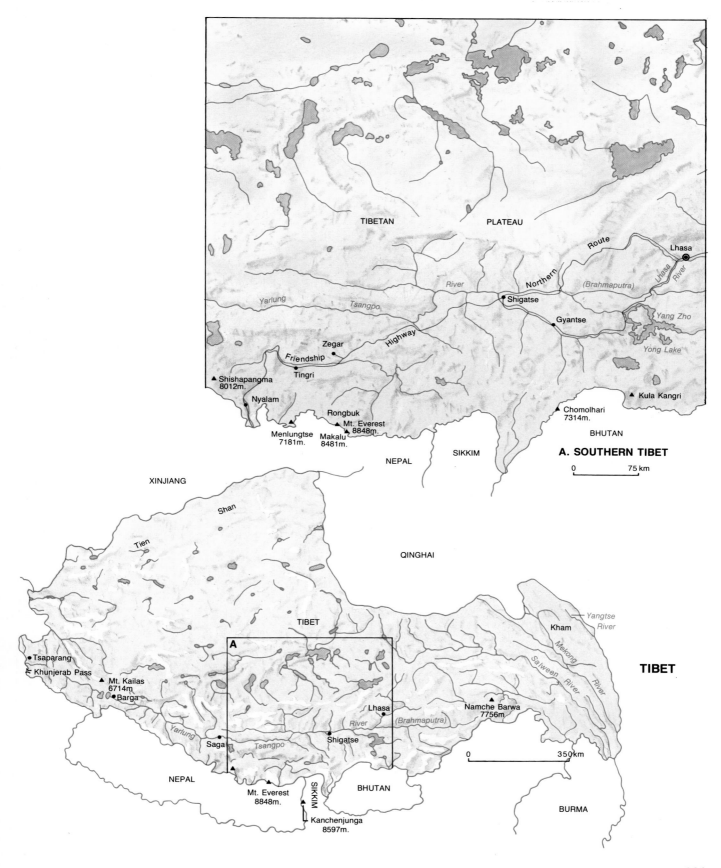

A. SOUTHERN TIBET

TIBETAN PLATEAU

Lhasa

Yarlung — Tsangpo — River — Northern — Route — (Brahmaputra) — Lhasa River

● Shigatse

● Gyantse

Yang Zho

Zegar ● — Highway

Friendship

● Tingri

Yong Lake

▲ Shishapangma 8012m.

● Nyalam

● Rongbuk

▲ Menlungtse 7181m.

Makalu 8481m.

▲ Mt. Everest 8848m.

▲ Chomolhari 7314m.

● Kula Kangri

BHUTAN

NEPAL

SIKKIM

0   75 km

TIBET

XINJIANG

Shan

Tien

QINGHAI

Yangtse River

TIBET

Kham

● Tsaparang

Mekong River

Salween River

〆 Khunjerab Pass

▲ Mt. Kailas 6714m

Lhasa

● Barga

● Shigatse

River — (Brahmaputra)

▲ Namche Barwa 7756m

Yarlung

Tsangpo

● Saga

NEPAL

SIKKIM

BHUTAN

0   350km

▲ Mt. Everest 8848m.

⊥ Kanchenjunga 8597m.

BURMA

203

Lhasa

The city of Lhasa, at 3683 m (12,080 ft), is dominated by the thousand-room Potola Palace. It was once the centre of the traditional government and the winter residence of the Dalai Lama. Lhasa is still Tibet's administrative and trading centre.

There are many other distinctive sites in Lhasa, including Drepung, the world's largest monastery, and Jokhang Temple, the most holy shrine in Tibet. Since the seventh century this temple has been the destination of millions of pilgrims from remote villages all over Tibet, mostly because of its sacred statues and shrines. The courtyard and porch of the temple are usually crowded with pilgrims.

Other Lhasa attractions are Borkar Bazaar; Dragon King Park; Norbulinka (the Dalai Lama's summer palace); Sera Monastery (founded in 1419 by the Yellow Hat monks); and Drepung Monastery, which once housed 8000 monks.

The most common way of reaching Tibet is to fly from the west via Chendu, the capital of the Sichuan province, to Gonggar, Lhasa's airport. From here it takes one-and-a-half hours by bus to Lhasa, 90 km (56 miles) to the north. Because of the high altitude of Lhasa, visitors who travel by plane should not exert themselves unduly for several days. (See page 66 ff on altitude sickness.)

Climbing

Most of the world's highest unclimbed mountains lie in China and the north sides of many 8000 m peaks, or those that lie wholly in Tibet and China, are much in demand by leading mountaineers. It is very expensive to mount any expedition in China or Tibet, however – often two to three times the cost of an expedition on a similar scale in Nepal, India or Pakistan. Long approach marches can push the costs up even more and a Chinese cook, liaison officer and interpreter have to be employed.

Each expedition has to negotiate separately with the Chinese Mountaineering Association (CMA), which necessitates a trip to Beijing in advance to arrange the protocol. Because the Chinese see expeditions as a way of earning foreign exchange, like most Himalayan countries, they favour large parties. Applications for peaks, however, are dealt with on a first come, first served basis. The peak fees in China are very expensive.

Trekking

There are only a few popular treks on the north side of the Himalaya (and one or two regular commercial itineraries), mostly because the access is very limited and the terrain so inhospitable. Less than 254 mm (10 inches) of rain a year fall on much of the Tibetan Plateau and the roads are exceedingly few.

Commercial trekking in Tibet began in 1981. The recognised treks to date are Qomolangma Base Camp, Everest

Tashilhunpo Monastery, the seat of the Panchen Lama, is in Shigatse, the second most important city of Tibet.

(Right) Pilgrims come from all over Tibet to prostrate themselves in the courtyard of the Jokhang Temple, the most holy shrine in the country and the focus of Buddhist religious life.

Kangshung Face, Makalu Base Camp, Xixabangma (Shishapangma) Base Camp, and Namche Barwa. Brief details of these are included in the Lonely Planet guide, *Tibet: A Travel Survival Kit*, by Michael Buckley and Rob Strauss.

Trekking in Tibet (China) comes under the auspices of the mountaineering regulations which are administered by the Chinese Mountaineering Association (CMA). Trekking on your own is not advisable and usually not practical in most parts of Tibet because of the high altitude, lack of facilities and potentially troublesome political situation. This is not to say that it is impossible – see Sorrel Wilby's account (on page 212 ff).

Tibet can be conveniently divided into east and west.

Eastern Tibet (Kham)

East Tibet, geographically and culturally very different from the western part of Tibet, is home to the Khampas people. The men are distinguished by the red yarn braided into their hair and Khampas guerilla forces have been fighting the Chinese army for many decades.

The Mekong, Yangtse and Salween rivers rise in East Tibet and are influenced in part by the monsoon. This results in luxuriant vegetation which can be seen on the treks in the vicinity of Namche Barwa and Kula Kangri.

NAMCHE BARWA (NAMCHA BARWA)

Mount Namche Barwa, at 7756 m (25,440 ft), is the highest unclimbed peak in the world and is regarded as the eastern limit of the Himalaya. While foreign climbers are not permitted to attempt the mountain, it is possible to trek in this botanically rich area.

KULA KANGRI

This peak range at 7538 m (24,725 ft) forms part of Tibet's border with Bhutan almost due south from Lhasa. A ten-day trek to the remote valleys at the foot of the north side of the Bhutanese Himalaya is now offered by some companies.

RONGBUK VALLEY

The Rongbuk Valley (the 'valley of the precipices') trek to the north face of Qomolangma (Everest) is the most popular commercial trek in Tibet. The starting-point is Lhasa. From there it takes many dusty days by bus or truck to Rongbuk at 5030 m (16,498 ft) via the Yamdrok Tso lake, the fortress trading towns of Gyantse (Gyantze) and Shigatse (the second largest town in Tibet), and Zegar.

These towns are focal points of Tibetan Buddhism. In 1904 Gyantse was seized by the British, under Sir Francis Younghusband, in their push to open Lhasa for trading and buffer the threat to the British Raj from Russia and China. The early British attempt on Everest also came along this route, having pushed north from Darjeeling in India, and the earliest records and photos of the region are from these exploits. (See climbing history on page 32 ff).

TIBET AT A GLANCE

Area
Over 1 million sq. km (386,000 sq. miles). Less than 10″ (25 cm) rain annually.

Population
Estimated at over 2 million.

Government
Part of People's Republic of China.

Capital
Lhasa – altitude 3607 m (11,830 ft). Population 150,000.

Flag
(Chinese) – Red background with one large golden star and four smaller in front, in top left-hand corner.

People
Tibetan.

Language
Tibetan; Han Chinese.

Religion
Lamist (Tibetan Buddhist).

Highest and lowest points
Chomolungma (Mount Everest) 8850 m (29,028 ft).

Currency
FEC (Foreign Exchange Certificates) for all goods and services outside of Lhasa – these are not widely used. Renminbi ('people's currency') RMB. Unit of money is Yan, one of which equals 100 Fen or 10 Miao. FEC can be changed on the black market in big cities for a better rate than at the banks.

Time
Same as Beijing time.

Portion in Himalaya
Southern border lies astride the crest of the Himalaya with only a narrow strip of mountains in Tibet.

Best time
June to November (spring to late autumn).

(Left) The north side of Everest (Qomolangma) from Pang La, a 5200 m (17,056 ft) pass above Xegar on the road to Rongbuk and Everest Base Camp.

Skirting a stream on the Rongbuk Glacier above the (Tibetan) Everest Base Camp, trekkers pass through a maze of ice towers known as *seracs*.

(Previous pages) The massive Potala Palace towers above Lhasa. Begun in the seventh century, it was once the centre of power in Tibet and the Dalai Lama's winter residence. With its 1000 rooms extending up thirteen storeys on the escarpments of Red Hill, it rises more than 300 m (984 ft) above the valley floor. Today the Potala is a state museum.

Rongbuk monastery, beneath the north face of Everest, was once home to many monks and nuns but it was wrecked by villagers under the influence of the cultural revolution's political re-education programme. The monastery is now being gradually repaired.

The Rongbuk Valley is a sanctuary with a strict ban on killing animals. Domestic animals have to be slaughtered outside the valley.

QOMOLANGMA (MT EVEREST) BASE CAMP

In contrast to the difficult approach on the Nepalese side of Everest, it is possible to drive to the base camp from the northern side. The road was built by the Chinese when they climbed the mountain in 1960.

The base camp is 7 km (4 miles) beyond the Rongbuk monastery.

On the trek to the northern base camp of Mount Everest it may be possible to reach camp III at 6500 m (21,300 ft) without ropes or technical climbing experience, but you should be experienced with glacier travel. The last part of the journey (between 5500–6200 m; 18,040–20,336 ft) is on moraine and glacier ice through a maze of seracs, towers of ice the size of church steeples. Extreme caution should be exercised because of the altitude (see pages 66–68).

XIXABANGMA (SHISHAPANGMA)

Xixabangma base camp trek, begins from Nyalam on the Friendship Highway. It is possible to drive the 25 km (16 miles) to

The people and culture of Kasgar in Xinjiang (Sinkinag) province of Western China were previously little known to modern travellers. With the opening of the Karakoram Highway it is now possible to reach this remote city from Pakistan.

(Left) The ruins of Xegar (Shegar) Dzong (fort) at Xegar in Tibet. The 'Shining Crystal' Monastery once housed 400 monks.

base camp at 5000 m (16,400 ft) but if walking it takes two or three days. There is beautiful trekking around the northern slopes of the peak and fantastic views of the Himalaya, but access from the Highway takes longer than from the south.

Shishapangma, at 8046 m (26,391 ft), is the only 8000 m peak wholly in Tibet. It wasn't climbed until 1964 when a 200-strong Chinese expedition succeeded in putting a ten-person team on the summit. Shishapangma means 'crest above the grassy plains'.

FRIENDSHIP HIGHWAY

The route from Lhasa to Kathmandu was opened to foreign travellers in 1986. The road, however, was completed twenty years earlier by the Chinese, supposedly to encourage trade, but the strategic importance cannot be under-estimated.

Providing transport is available, the journey from Lhasa to Kathmandu can be accomplished in three days but vehicles are seldom available from Shigatse. It is better to have transport sorted out in Lhasa where it is possible to hire jeeps, but this can be expensive. Beyond Shigatse, public transport to the Nepalese border is infrequent but there may be the occasional truckload of pilgrims returning south.

There are two routes to Shigatse from Lhasa. The northerly way is the most direct but the southern route is more interesting culturally.

The road along the border of Nepal and Tibet is not continuous, because of landslides. There is a descent for about an hour from the Chinese checkpoint to the Nepalese checkpoint, but there are porters to carry your gear. On the Nepal side after the Friendship Bridge there are buses twice a day and taxis to take you to Kathmandu.

Most of the traffic flows from China to Nepal around Christmas because the 5488 m (18,000 ft) passes become blocked by snow. Extreme caution should be taken by travellers because of the remoteness of the route. Even if you take public transport, you need to be self-sufficient in food, clothing and shelter against the possibility of being stranded.

Western Tibet (Xinjiang)

The ruins of the ancient kingdom of Guage lie near the village of Tasaparang. This site and Mount Kailas are the main points of interest for sightseers in Western Tibet.

MOUNT KAILAS (KAILASH)

Mount Kailas, at 6740 m (22,107 ft), has been sacred to Hindus, Buddhists and worshippers of the Bon religion for thousands of years. To the Hindus, Kailas is the mountain home of Lord Shiva and his consort Parvati. For Tibetan Buddhists, Kailas is the centre of the universe and the home of the god Bemchoy. To Hindu and Buddhist pilgrims from India and Nepal and to the locals, the 52 km (32 miles) trek around the mountain is one of the holiest devotions it is possible to make. One circuit is supposed to remove a lifetime of sin and it takes 108 circuits to achieve Nirvana. Mount Kailas is an imposing peak with its symmetrical shape and the rock striations that have given it the name 'swastika mountain'.

Around Lake Manasarower to the south of Kailas is also an important pilgrimage.

K2

Organised trekking groups and expeditions sometimes approach K2 from the north but access depends on the river levels. This trek, like most Tibetan treks, is a strenuous undertaking. The nearest main centre is Shache. Camels are used to carry luggage and supplies.

SILK ROUTE

The road from Islamabad to Kasgar quickly leaves the Himalayan region once it crosses the Khunjerab Pass (see Pakistan, page 124). From there it passes by the Tien Shan Mountains. This road follows one of the ancient silk routes.

MY JOURNEY THROUGH TIBET

SORREL WILBY

Excerpts from Sorrel Wilby's account of her solo trek across Tibet illustrate that there are still great personal adventures to be had in the realm of the Himalaya.

At Barga's no-star, one-storey hotel I met some pilgrims returning from the holy peak, Mount Kailas. They offered me some Tibetan tea, and I managed to drink three cups of the traditional beverage. Tibetan tea is made with salt and yak butter, and it isn't the easiest drink to get used to. But it was time I started liking it. If I wanted to understand Tibetans, I had to try behaving like one and, if possible, even attempt to sound like one. I fumbled through my pack and found *Tibetan for Beginners and Travellers*. Dr Melvin Goldstein had compiled it with the average tourist in mind, but my circumstances were slightly different.

'Chu tsha-bo du gay?' (Is there any hot water?), I began. That raised a few eyebrows. 'N-gay kang miy-giy di-mi ka ba to? (Where is the key to my room?) That wasn't too helpful – my 'room' didn't even have a door on it! 'San-ju ka ba to?' Someone pointed to the plains behind me and laughed. The whole world is a toilet. Go anywhere!

Leaving Barga, I joined a throng of Indian and Tibetan pilgrims, monks, nomads, and their flocks of sheep, yaks and horses, all circumambulating Mount Kailas, revered by Buddhists and Hindus alike.

My companions on the trek seemed dumbfounded at my presence – a westerner, apparently walking all the way from Mount Kailas to Lhasa. With a mixture of sign language and a small but growing Tibetan vocabulary, I managed to communicate with my fellow pilgrims. Some asked about my family, my crops, my sheep, – who would tend to them while I struggled to attain spiritual purification? To avoid explanation I simply replied by chanting the devotional Tibetan phrase 'Om mani padme hum' (Hail the jewel in the lotus).

By the time I had completed the circuit of Mount Kailas I was so weary and worn that the phrase had transformed itself in my mind to: 'Oh-mummy-take-me-home.' The phrase gained added appeal a week later when I was attacked by three guard dogs at a small military outpost. Their energetic greeting left me with gaping wounds on my right leg, heel and arm. A military doctor in the compound stitched me up after plying me with swigs of Chinese fire-water in lieu of anaesthetic. The treatment failed to ease the pain and my screams echoed through the compound. But I felt even worse the next morning: in addition to the pain, I had a massive hangover.

Hard luck struck beyond Moncier, when I lost all my gear – pack, tent, sleeping bag, everything. Tired of the strain of a 65 lb [30 kg] pack, I had put my belongings on a passing truck and asked the driver, a Tibetan named Tsering, to leave it at the next nomad camp a day's trek ahead. Unfortunately, he didn't understand my beginner's Tibetan and took the pack all the way to Ali, a good five days' travel on foot. It was at the end of those five days that I miscalculated badly and very nearly froze to death on the nightmare 40-mile [64 km] hike.

Ali is an ugly place – a scar on the western cheek of Tibet. My second morning there I ventured into the streets.

The mandatory morning broadcast stirred Ali into action. Truckers rose from their cabins near the river, cranking their bodies and the engines of their vehicles into life.

I finally located the truck driver with my belongings. Retrieving my Swiss army knife from the pack, I removed the stitches from the dog-bites in my leg and arm. I smiled farewell to Ali.

There was a hint of early winter in the air. It was September 14 and I was headed for the town of Shongba, about a hundred miles away down the Sirchuan-He River Valley.

As the valley and I grew comparatively narrower, the mountains on either side assumed characteristics of remembered food from home. Honeycomb-weathered cliffs waited to be dipped in the chocolate shade of afternoon. A bend in one rockwall became a row of exotic artichoke hearts. On the left side of the river, Turkishdelight-coloured hills glistened temptingly in the sunlight. Behind them, dark Christmas pudding mountains lightly dusted with sugar icing completed my imaginary banquet. I stopped frequently to slake my thirst at the bubbling river ... ahhh, champagne!

At Gargai the town headman, or goti, gave me permits and letters to other goti ahead, asking them to help me on my way.

At the five-house 'town' of Shongba I learned that the goti was away and his deputy – unable to read my permits and passes – clamped me under house arrest. I was so depressed, I ate a whole bar of Toblerone.

Freedom finally came after eight long days. The goti returned and apologised, then introduced me to Yarbo, a guide who was destined to become one of my dashing knights-in-fur-armour. With snow fast on our heels, Yarbo and I crossed the edge of a dry salt pan and headed into central Tibet, the most challenging phase of my journey. Here was an area totally devoid of foot roads or trails.

Along with the challenge came beauty. On the second day we reached a river. A hundred wild Tibetan donkeys were standing on the far bank. The reflection of the sun on the water dappled their underbellies.

After some days Yarbo turned back, entrusting me to another volunteer guide, who in turn passed me to another, and so on. The journey was a blend of fatigue and fascination. Finally I reached Yagra, the last village before the forbidding Gandise Ranges, the great snowclad barrier across the route to Payang.

My arrival in Yagra was timely. Nomads from all directions had ridden or walked to the isolated village for the great yearly regional horse-racing festival. Nomad riders on deceptively

Taking a nap in Shigatse, the second most important city of Tibet.

scraggly mounts competed for three days, drank for three days, danced and laughed for three days.

I broke the last [966 km] 600 miles of my journey into five sections: three days to the town of Drongba; five more to Saga; seven or so from Saga to Lhatse; four or five from Lhatse to Xigatse. From there, Lhasa was only ten days away. The entire route lay along the great southern roadway across western Tibet.

Just before the town of Lhatse I came to a lake and stopped for a time. The distant, purple-tinged mountains and the white, cotton-candy clouds floating above them were reflected in the lake's mirror-smooth surface. I strolled around a bend in the embankment and surprised several hundred water geese and ducks, bobbing up and down like floating lilies on the gentle ebb of the vast pond. As one, the birds took off in fright – a thunderous cloud of flapping wings, a cyclone of sound and energy. They circled a few feet above the lake, then landed.

It was a day for splendour, for rare and simple gifts. Just hours after leaving the lake I reached a farming commune and stopped in my tracks. Before me there was a tree! It didn't have any leaves on it, but it was still a tree, the first I had seen in months.

On November 25 I reached the holy city — [2898 km] 1800 miles and four months behind me. A single tear fell from my eye. It was not for pride, not for myself. I suddenly realised the magnitude of what I had gained, not lost, on my journey through Tibet.

Sorrel Wilby's account of her adventures was published in: *Tibet: A Woman's Lone Trek Across a Mysterious Land* (Macmillan, 1988). Sorrel is an accomplished photo-journalist. One of her recent assignments was to document the Australian Bicentennial Everest Expedition.

Appendices

PHOTOGRAPHY

Photography is an extremely rewarding pastime to combine with travelling in the Himalaya. Whether it is through looking for better angles, getting up early to capture the dawn light, or seeking permission to photograph an interesting person, the circumstances that can arise through taking memorable photographs will enrich your holiday immeasurably.

Be Prepared

If you want to take pictures while you are away but are not already a photographer, it is worth the effort to buy or borrow a camera well before your trip. You should expose several films to familiarise yourself with the equipment and the results you can get from various situations. Better to have disasters at home than risk your record of a never to be repeated holiday. If you are keen, enrolling in a photography class could be worthwhile.

Whatever type of film you decide to use, be it slides or transparencies, colour or black and white, take plenty from home as you can't count on buying any while you are away. If you can buy film in a major Himalayan town, there is no guarantee that it will have been stored correctly. Even if the film is within the use-by-date, it may have spent days in the sun in transit and so be suspect.

Cameras and Lenses

For almost all travel photography the 35 mm format is unsurpassed. The type of camera you use is a matter of personal preference. No matter what the brand, it should be rugged, reliable and easy to operate. A model that enables you to take wide angle, close up and telephoto images is preferable. No longer are Single Lens Reflex (SLR) cameras (where the viewfinder shows what will appear on the film) with interchangeable or zoom lenses, the only type capable of such variations. Most brands now also have a compact autofocus model with a mid-range zoom lens. Whilst such a camera may be preferable to one with only a fixed focal-length lens, an SLR with a mid-range zoom, is the most versatile choice.

If only one lens is to be carried, a zoom with a range from wide angle, 35 mm to medium telephoto, 105 mm or 135 mm, is the best option. If a second lens is to be carried then a 28 mm (wide angle) lens is best suited to Himalayan landscapes. If you prefer two fixed focal length lenses rather than a zoom, then a 100 mm lens for portraits, as well as the 28 mm, is ideal.

Accessories and Filters

Any lens you use should have a skylight or UV filter to protect the front element from getting scratched. If your filters are scratched already, replace them with new ones. These filters help to cut down the haze. A polarising filter is also worth using in certain circumstances. It is most effective for cutting down water reflections and giving more saturated colours in blue skies where there are some clouds. Do not leave a polarising filter on the lens all the time, however, as it cuts down the amount of light reaching the film by at least a stop. It is also advisable to avoid stacking filters (screwing one on top of another).

A small but sturdy tripod is the next most useful item for longer telephoto shots, when shooting in low light or when trying to get the maximum depth of field. A cable release should also be part of your kit, however, the self-timer release can be used to trip the shutter if one is not available.

Film

How much to take? A 36 exposure roll per day is a good average for serious photographers, but most will find several rolls per week more than adequate. Compared to the cost of the airfares and accommodation, however, the extra expense of taking several additional rolls above the maximum you think you will need, is always a good policy.

Prints or Slides

Think carefully about what you ultimately want to do with your photos before deciding on whether to shoot colour print or slide film. Trying to use both is awkward unless you have two cameras. Colour print film is ideal if all you want is an album to browse through at a later time. This is the most convenient form of personal record of your adventure. If you wish to try and publish images or give slide shows then you should use transparency film. Colour prints can also be made from slides but they are more expensive than having prints from colour print film. If you wish to produce fine art prints, or would like to sell photos to a newspaper, then black and white film is ideal.

It is most important to use a brand film you know and like. If you are starting out then the following suggestions are a reliable starting point, but they are by no means the only possibilities. For transparency film, Kodachrome 64 is still the best option for general shooting, but where there is plenty of light, or if you are prepared to use a tripod, then Kodachrome 25 ASA will give sharper images with more detail in the shadows. If a faster slide film is needed, then Kodachrome 200 is excellent. Many professional photographers as a matter of course, set the film speed adjustment, the ASA (or Din) on their cameras, a little higher than the film specification suggestion. 64 ASA, for example, would be set to 80 ASA. This results in more saturated colours as the image is then slightly under exposed.

For colour prints, Kodak Gold 100 ASA or 200 ASA is a reliable choice but the new Ektar range of print films 25, 125 and 1000, present exciting possibilities. For black and white films, depending on your needs, either Iford FP4, Kodak Tri X, or T Max100 or 400, are all satisfactory.

Processing

It is best not to have film processed in any Himalayan country as the quality control standards are likely to be less than what you are used to. This can be frustrating if you are in the habit of seeing your results soon after shooting. Spending a month on a trek and exposing twenty rolls of film without any idea as to whether your camera is still functioning correctly can be nerve-racking, but there is usually little choice. This is all the more reason to have your gear checked out thoroughly before you leave and be very careful with your film and camera on the trail.

Equipment Care

Travelling in the Himalaya is liable to test your camera in every conceivable way. Heat, cold, dust, moisture and physical abuse are all possible in an average trekking or climbing day. Most cases sold with cameras provide little weather proofing or protection. There are now many excellent waterproof padded nylon pouches, bags and waist-belts available to protect your cameras from rough handling and inclement conditions.

Looking after your film begins as soon as you leave home. Avoid repeated exposure to X-ray machines at airport security checks as the effect is cumulative. Once you are in the hills, keep your film cool and expose it as soon as you return home. Too low a temperature is more often the problem than too much heat in the Himalaya.

Cold Weather

Cold bedevils cameras, film and, not least of all, photographers, but the best pictures usually require considerable time out in the elements and the most atmospheric shots are often taken in the worst weather. In extreme cold, when you frame and focus, be careful that your cheeks and eyelids don't get frozen to the camera's metal parts. A rubber eye-cap and some cloth tape on the camera back will help to solve this problem. Such difficulties rarely arise until temperatures plummet to minus 10° C.

To reduce the problems of battery drain caused by the cold, keep your camera warm until you begin shooting. Once the camera has cooled to the outside temperature, taking it back into a warmer environment results in condensation forming on the cold surfaces. This moisture will eventually evaporate, but if you want to shoot straight away then you will have to dry the lens. Photographic tissues are best but make sure the lens has a protective skylight or UV filter. This way any amount of cleaning will not scratch the lens or damage the delicate coating.

Keeping the camera dry in a blizzard or preventing snow on the lens is a challenge. Steady rain is similarly a problem. Lens hoods and lens caps will help but ultimately there is little one can do but carry a pocket full of tissues. For additional waterproofing of the camera body, tape over the terminals, hinges, battery covers and seldom used switches with insulation or 'gaffer' tape.

Some compact 35 mm cameras and the Nikon underwater cameras, Nikonos, are completely waterproof. Looking through the viewfinder on these models, however, does not show whether the lens is covered by water or flakes of snow. Always double check the lens just before shooting.

Photography in cold dry air has its own problems. Using a motor drive, or even winding on too vigorously, can result in static discharges that appear as clear blue specks or streaks on an exposed transparency. This can be minimised by winding on and rewinding slowly. There is an additional reason for extreme caution with the camera's film transport mechanism. At low temperatures the film base becomes brittle and is easily broken. Sometimes just the sprocket holes are torn out. All need not be lost under such circumstances. First, try rewinding the film. If this does not work then you will have to open the camera back in a black bag or, as a last resort, try tunneling head-first into a sleeping bag to rescue the broken film.

Camera Batteries

Camera batteries last only a few hours under very cold conditions. Start out with fresh batteries and carry spare sets with you inside your jacket: the warmer they are, the longer they will last. For extended bouts of photography in cold weather some manufacturers sell an external battery pack that gives a more powerful battery supply that can be kept warm inside your jacket. These are connected to the camera by a metre of cable.

Most modern single lens reflex (SLR) cameras are fully electronic with through the lens (TTL) metering and a battery-powered shutter mechanism. Some of these models have a mechanically operated back up shutter speed in case your batteries do expire and you do not have spares. When using the camera in this mode you will have to guess the exposure, take note of the speed and choose an appropriate aperture. A hand-held lightmeter is invaluable in these circumstances as are cameras with fully mechanical shutters.

Exposure Compensation

While the Himalaya offers some of the most exciting photography opportunities in the world, there are also many pitfalls. Shooting snow scenes without compensating for the bright conditions, will leave you with underexposed film. This is most frustrating when shooting transparency film as you do not usually have any way of compensating later on. With print film, compensation can be made up to a point, when the prints are being exposed.

Dark (under exposed) slides result when using the camera on automatic in the snow. Washed out (overexposed) snow scenes are less pleasing than shots with slightly more saturated colours and some detail or texture in the snow itself. Light meters are designed to expose a scene as if the subject were a mid-grey. Snow reflects much more light than, for example, a ploughed field. Your light meter reads the white snow as grey and instructs the camera to expose accordingly. For correct exposure in any scene where there is a lot of snow you will have to set the camera on manual and open up one or two more f stops . With automatic cameras that have no manual mode this adjustment can also be achieved by shifting the film speed (Din or ASA) dial. Some cameras have special compensation steps marked on the same dial. Turning this to the +1 position will compensate the meter reading by one f stop (doubling the amount of light), and properly handle scenes where a white background occupies half the viewing area. Remember to return the dial to the original setting when no longer shooting snow scenes.

A hand-held light meter that can also record incident light (light falling on the subject rather than reflected by it) will give a more accurate overall exposure. A camera meter reading off the back of one's hand or glove will more closely approximate the correct exposure in most instances. Bracket exposures around this reading (that is, take additional shots half a stop more and less) to ensure you don't miss the shot.

When to Photograph

In winter the sun has a much lower angle throughout the day and so there are always shadows to give added interest to your shots. If the weather is overcast, try avoiding landscape shots that include too much grey sky. This is ideal weather for portraits. On sunny days avoid shooting out of doors in the middle of the day, as the light is very harsh and contrast is heavy. Dawn and dusk are ideal times to catch the best light.

While these are only a few pointers for shooting in the Himalaya, there is no substitute for being very familiar with your camera before you go and for taking plenty of shots while you are away. With the right equipment, a little experience and plenty of enthusiasm, you too could become hooked on the delights of photography in the clear crisp light of the Himalaya.

Photography Checklist

Camera
Lens
Additional lenses
Second camera body or camera
Filters (skylight, polarising)
Tripod
Flash gun
Cable release

Carrying pouch or waist bag
Shoulder bag
Photographer's vest
Blower brush
Lens tissues
Chamois leather
Spare batteries X 2 sets
Plastic Bags
Jeweller's screwdriver
Gaffer tape

ADDRESSES

There are many cultural, geographical and national friendship societies and associations around the world that are a source of contact with people who have knowledge and, in many cases, first-hand experience of the Himalaya. There are also countless specialist trekking, guiding and adventure travel companies who are likewise a source of information.

This list is by no means comprehensive, nor exclusive. Check the credentials, programmes and advice of one organisation against another. If going on a commercial trek or climb, before signing on any trip remember the addage 'you only get what you pay for', applies equally to this type of holiday experience as it does to any other service.

Australia

Ausventure Holidays, Suite 1, Strand Passage, 870–872 Military Rd, Mosman, NSW 2088.

Himalayan Odyssey, 189 Park St, South Melbourne, VIC 3250.

Kulu Expeditions, 111A William Street, Norwood, SA 5067.

Peregrine Adventures, 258 Lonsdale St, Melbourne, VIC 3000.

The Adventure Club Viva! Holidays, 10th Floor, 141 Walker St, North Sydney, NSW 2060.

Wilderness Expeditions, 8th Floor, 37 York St, Sydney, NSW 2000.

World Expeditions, 3rd Floor, 377 Sussex St, Sydney, NSW 2000.

Bhutan

The Bhutan Tourism Corporation, Box 159, Thimpu, Bhutan.

Canada

Worldwide Adventures, Suite 747, 920 Yonge St, M4W-3C7, Toronto, Ontario.

China

China International Sports Service, 9 Tiyuquan Rd, Beijing.

The Chinese Mountaineering Association, 9 Tiyuquan Rd, Beijing.

The rugged Goodwin-Austen Glacier joins the Baltoro Glacier at Concordia, in a most spectacular mountain setting.

Europe

Artou, 8 rue de Rive, CH -1204, Geneve, Switzerland.

Explorator, 16 Place de la Madeline, 75008, Paris, France.

Hauser Exkursionen, Neuhauser Strasse 1, 8000 Muenchen 2, West Germany.

Tiger Tops Mountain Travel International SA, Rebgasse 21A, 4058 Basel, Switzerland.

World Expeditions, Laederstraede 11B St, 1201 Copenhagen K, Denmark.

India

Delhi Climbers & Explorers Club, Jawahal Nehru Stadium, Gate 28, Room 0157, New Delhi.

Directorate of Tourism, Jammu and Kashmir Government, Srinagar, Kashmir.

Highland Expeditions, PO Box 241, Srinagar, Jammu and Kashmir.

Himalayan Mountaineering Institute, Darjeeling.

Mercury Travels, Jeevan Tara Building Parliament St, New Delhi.

Nehru Institute of Mountaineering, Uttarkashi, Uttar Pradesh.

Sita Travel, F12, Connaught Place, New Delhi 110001.

The Himalayan Club, PO Box 1905, Bombay 400001.

The Indian Mountaineering Foundation, Benito Juarez Rd, New Delhi 110021.

Tiger Tops Mountain Travel India Pvt Ltd, 1/1 Rani Jhansi Road, New Delhi 110005.

Western Himalayan Institute of Mountaineering, Skiing and Allied Sports, Manali, Himachal Pradesh.

World Expeditions (India) Pvt Ltd B 412, Som Datt Chambers-1, 5 Bhikaiji Cama Place, New Delhi 110066.

New Zealand

Venturetreks, 164 Parnell Road, Parnell, Auckland.

Nepal

Ama Dablam Trekking, Lazimpat, PO Box 3055, Kathmandu.

Annapurna Mountaineering & Trekking Durbar Marg, PO Box 795, Kathmandu.

Chitwan Jungle Lodge, Durbar Marg, PO Box 1281, Kathmandu.

CIWEC (Medical) Clinic, PO Box 1340, Kathmandu.

Gaida Wildlife Camp Durbar Marg, PO Box 2056, Kathmandu.

Himalayan Journeys Kantipath, PO Box 989, Kathmandu.

Himalayan River Exploration, PO Box 170, Kathmandu.

In Wilderness Trekking, PO Box 3043, Kathmandu.

King Mahendra Trust for Nature Conservation, National Parks Building, Babar Mahal, PO Box 3712, Kathmandu.

Machan Wildlife Resort Durbar Marg, PO Box 3140, Kathmandu.

Mountain Travel Nepal, PO Box 170, Kathmandu.

Nepal Himal, PO Box 4528, Kathmandu.

Nepal Mountaineering Association (NMA), 16/53 Ran Shah Path, PO Box 1435, Kathmandu.

Sherpa Co-operative Trekking Durbar Marg, PO Box 1338, Kathmandu.

Tenzing Trekking & Mountaineering Thamel, PO Box 1542, Kathmandu.

The Himalayan Rescue Association, GPO Box 495, Kathmandu.

Tiger Tops Jungle Lodge, PO Box 242, Kathmandu.

Pakistan

Adventure Pakistan (Waljis), P0 Box 1088, Islamabad.

Alpine Club of Pakistan, 228 Peshawar Road, Rawalpindi.

Chogori Adventures Ltd, Box 1345, Islamabad.

Government of Pakistan, Tourism Division, College Road, F-7/2 Sector, Islamabad.

Hunza Treks, 253, Street 23 E-7, Islamabad.

Indus Guides, 7 -E, Egerton Rd, Lahore.

Mountain World, PO Box 1421, Islamabad.

Pakistan Tourism Development Corporation, H2, Street 61, F-7/4, Islamabad.

Sitara Travel Consultants, Box 63, 25–26 Shalimar Plaza, Rawalpindi.

United States

Above the Clouds Trekking, PO Box 398E, Worcester, MA 01602.

Adventure Center, 5540 College Avenue, Oakland, CA 94618.

American Alpine Institute Ltd (AAI), 1212/24th C-5, Bellingham, WA 98225.

Bhutan Travel Service, 1133 East 56th Street, New York, NY 10022.

Himalayan Travel Inc., Box 481-0, Greenwich, CT 06836.

Himalaya, 1802 Cedar St, Berkeley, CA 94703.

Inner Asia, 2627 Lombard Street, San Francisco, CA 94123.

Lute Jerstad Adventures, PO Box 19537, Department O, Portland, OR 97219.

Mountain Travel, 6420 Fairmont Ave, El Cerrito, CA 94530.

Overseas Adventure Travel, 349 Broadway, Cambridge, MA 02139.

Sobek Expeditions, PO Box 1089, Angels Camp, CA 95222.

The American Himalayan Foundation, 473 Jackson Street, San Francisco, CA 94111.

Wilderness Travel, 11760 Solano Ave, Berkeley, CA 94707.

United Kingdom

Bufo Ventures Ltd, 3 Elim Grove, Bowness-on-Windermere, Cumbria LA232JN.

Encounter Overland, 267 Brompton Road, London SW5.

Exodus Expeditions, Dept WM, All Saints Passage, 100 Wandsworth High Street, London SW18 4LE.

Explorasia Ltd, Blenheim House, Burnsall Street, London SW3.

Explore Worldwide, 7 High Street, Aldershot, Hants GU11 1BH.

Himalayan Kingdoms Ltd, 20 The Mall, Clifton, Bristol BS8 4DR.

Sherpa, 131A Heston Road, Hounslow, Middlesex.

The Karakoram Experience, The Trekkers Lodge, 32 Lake Road, Keswick, Cumbria CA12 5DQ.

West Himalayan Holidays, 10 Barley Mow Passage, London W4 4PH.

Woodcock Travel Ltd, 25–31 Wicker St, Sheffield S3 8HW.

TREKKING PEAKS IN NEPAL

Group A

Peak fee US $ 300

Hiunchuli	6441 m/ 21,126 ft	Annapurna Himal
Fluted Peak	6501 m/ 21,323 ft	Annapurna Himal
Chulu East (Gundang)	6584 m/ 21,595 ft	Manang Himal
Chulu West	6419 m/ 21,054 ft	Manang Himal
Pisang	6091 m/ 19,984 ft	Manang Himal
Kusum Kangru	6367 m/ 20,890 ft	Khumbu Himal
Kwangde	6011 m/ 19,716 ft	Khumbu Himal
Island Peak	6160 m/ 20,204 ft	Khumbu Himal
Lobuje East	6119 m/ 20,075 ft	Khumbu Himal
Ramdung	5925 m/ 19,434 ft	Rolwaling Himal
Pharchamo	6187 m/ 20,293 ft	Rolwaling Himal

Group B

Peak fee US $150

Tent Peak	5663 m/ 18,575 ft	Annapurna Himal
Mardi Himal	5587 m/ 18,325 ft	Annapurna Himal
Mera Peak	5849 m/ 19,185 ft	Khumbu Himal
Pokhalde	5806 m/ 19,043 ft	Khumbu Himal
Ganja La Chuli	5844 m/ 19,168 ft	Langtang Himal
Mehra Peak	5820 m/ 19,090 ft	Khumbu Himal
Paldor	5896 m/ 19,339 ft	Ganesh Himal

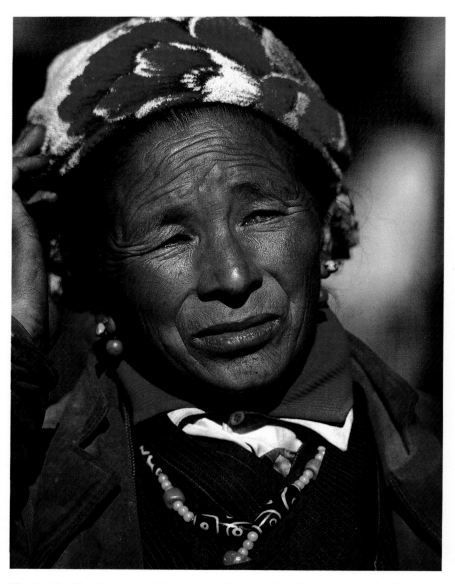

Meeting the Himalayan people is as rewarding as seeing the spectacular landscapes.

GLOSSARY

The glossary has been compiled from common terms found in the various languages used in the Himalaya.

A

AMS	Acute Mountain Sickness.
Annapurna	the goddess of abundance.
Ashoka	Indian emperor who did much to spread Buddhism 2500 years ago.
ashram	place where people live together for spiritual development through yoga and meditation.

B

baku, boku	traditional male dress in Bhutan.
betel	mixture of araca nut and lime wrapped in a betel leaf and chewed for stimulation.
bhat	cooked rice.
bhot, bot	Tibet.
bhotis	Nepali name for people of Tibetan origin.
Bon	the animist pre-Buddhist religion of Tibet.
Brahmins	the priestly caste of Hindus.
burqqa	woman's garment concealing whole body.

C

chadar	woman's veil.
cham	religious dance of Bhutan.
chang	beer from fermented millet.
chang-la	northern step or pass.
chang-tse	northern mountain.
chappati	flat cake of barley flour, cooked on an iron plate.
charpoy	bedstead.
chautara	a wall with two steps which porters use for resting the loads on.
Chetris	prince and warrior caste of Hindus. The present king and all the Ranas were chetris.
chi, chiya	Nepalese tea brewed with milk and spices.
Chomolongma	Tibetan name for Everest, mother goddess of the world.
chorten	a small wayside Buddhist shrine usually in the mountains.
curd	yoghurt, a speciality of Bhaktapur Nepal.

D

dal, dhal	lentil soup, a major part of the Nepali diet.
daju	elder brother
Dalai Lama	the great master, powerful like the sea of wisdom.
dawa	born on Monday.
devangari	Nepali script, identical to Hindi and Sanskrit.
Dharma	Buddhist doctrine, literally 'the path'.
dhoti	loose loin cloth/skirt worn by Hindu men.
didi	sister.
doko	cane basket with a head strap used to carry loads on porters backs.
dorje	'thunderbolt', symbol of Buddhist power.
Druk Yul	'dragon lady', Bhutan.
Dudh Kosi	river of milk
dun	valleys of the inner Terai.
dupatta	woman's scarf.
Duserrha	a Nepalese festival celebrated in September.
dzong	fortress.

F

ferun	woollen smock worn by Kashmiri shepherds.

G

Gadjus, Gujars	shepherds and herdsmen native to Kashmir Hills.
Ganesh	elephant-headed son of Shiva and Parvati, the god of good luck.
ganja	hashish.
Garuda	a mythical eagle, half-human.
Gelukpa	Yellow Hat Buddhist sect, most powerful in Tibet.
ghat	riverside platform for bathing and cremation.
ghee	clarified butter.
gompa	Tibetan Buddhist monastery.
gurkha	derived from the name of the region of Ghorka, it came to be used for soldiers recruited from Nepal for the British army.
guru rimpoche	precious master.

H

HACE	High Altitude Cerebral Oedema (edema).
hanuman	monkey god.
HAPE	High Altitude Pulmonary Oedema (edema).
hashish	dried resin from the marijuana plant.
himal	chain of mountains.
Himalaya	abode of the snow.
hooka, huqqa,	pipe for smoking tobacco or hashish through water.

I

impeyan	Nepal's national bird, a species of pheasant.

J

ju llay	greeting meaning hello, goodbye, how are you?

K

ka-ta, Ka-gta	white silk or muslin ceremonial scarf. In Tibet and among the Sherpas it is offered to important personalities and exchanged with other scarves.
kafir	infidel.
Kali	one of the wives of Shiva, symbol of creative energy.
kang-ri	mountain of snow.
kangri	clay pot filled with hot coals and suspended from a wicker cradle.
Kantipur	the ancient name of present-day Kathmandu.
karma	sum of ones good and bad actions.
khola	small river, the extended meaning — a valley.
khukri	traditional hooked knife, weapon of the gurkha soldiers.
kira	traditional female dress in Bhutan.
kosi	big river.
Krishna	the eighth incarnation of Vishnu.
Kumari	more peaceful incarnation of Kali. The Nepali name for the living goddess in Kathmandu is also Kumari.
kurta	man's skirt with long tails.

L

lakh	unit of counting equivalent to 100,000.
laliguras	national flowers of Nepal, the rhododendron.
Lama	monk, the master, Tibetan Buddhist priest.
Lamaism	Tibetan Buddhism.
lang	Tibetan for 'Yak'.
lassi	iced curd (yoghurt) drink.
lathi	wooden staff.
Laxmi	goddess of wealth, consort of Vishnu.
lhakpa	born on Wednesday.
Lhasa	the land of the gods.
lho	south.
lho-la	southern step or pass.
lho-tse	southern mountain.
lingam	symbol of the fecundity of Shiva.
lobsang	good, intelligent.

M

Maitreya	the future Buddha.
malik	village headman.
Malla	dynasty which ruled the Kathmandu Valley from the 13th to the 18th century and created some of the finest art and architecture .
mandala	geometrical and astrological world representation .
Mani Rimdu	a festival of ritual dances.
mani stone	stone carved with the Buddhist chant 'Om mani pad me hum' — 'Oh you jewel in the lotus'.
mani wall	wall built of mani stones in the hill country. Always walk by one with the wall on your right.
mantra	a string of papers, containing invocations and prayers enclosed in prayer wheels.
mausim	Arabic for 'season'.
mela	festival.
memsahib	honorific title used by Nepalis for foreign females.
migma	red eye, born on Friday.
mir	feudal landlord.
monsoon	rainy period from mid-June to late-September when there is rainfall virtually every day; there is also a very short winter monsoon of a day or two usually in late January.
mullah	holyman.

N

nak	female yak.
nala	snow-fed stream.
namaste, namaskar	traditional greeting which translates 'I recognise all the divine qualities in you'.
nanga parvata	Sanskrit term for 'naked mountain'.
Newars	original people of the Kathmandu Valley who were responsible for the architectural style of the valley.
niki	the spokesman for a team of porters.
nup	west.
nup-la	western fork.
nup-tse	western mountain.

P

pagoda	multistoried Nepalese temple. This style originated in Nepal and was later taken up in China and Japan.

panchayat	village democracy, non-party government of Nepal.
Parvati	the partner of Shiva.
pasang	born on Friday.
penba	born on Saturday.
perak	headdress decorated with turquoise and coral beads.
pipal	a large, long-living fig tree.
pir	saint/hŏlyman.
pokol	beret worn along the frontier at Chitral.
polo	'ball' in the Balti language.
puja	religious ritual or observance.
purdah	curtain or veil used to screen muslim women from public view.

R

raksi	alcoholic drink of distilled spirit.
Ramadan	Muslim month of fasting between dawn and dusk.
Rana	the series of hereditary Prime Ministers who ruled Nepal 1841 to 1951.
rhododendrons	in Nepal rhododendrons are huge, brilliantly-coloured trees which bloom in March and April above 2000 m.
roti	bread.

S

saddu, sadhu	holyman, sage or ascetic.
Sagamatha	Nepalese name for Mount Everest.
sahib	honorific title used by Nepalis for foreign males.
sanyasin	religious ascetic who has renounced his ties with society.
serow	wild Himalayan antelope.
shakti	the female consort of a god, dynamic element in the male female relationship.
shalawar	pantaloons.
shameez	female version of kurta; more shapely.
Sherpa, Shar-pa	people of the east.
Sherpani	Sherpa woman.
shikar	hunting for sport.
Shikara	a gondola type water taxi on the lakes in Kashmir.
Shiva	one of the two main Hindu gods also revered by Buddhists.
sirdar, sardar	head porter or head of the caravan.
Solu Khumbu	Everest region of eastern Nepal where the majority of the Sherpas live.
stupa	hemispherical Buddhist shrine.

T

tal	lake.
tang	Tibetan meaning 'to follow'.
tantra	symbolic and metaphysical religious philosophy evolved in the 10th to 15th century that binds Hindu and Buddhist people in Nepal.
tatopani	hot waters, thermal springs.
Terai	low land, the foothills of Nepal.
Thakalis	people of western Nepal around Jomsong who specialise in running hotels.
thanka, thangka, tanka	rectangular, sacred painting on canvas framed with brocade.
tika	red sandalwood paste spot on the male forehead as a religious mark and on women as an indication of marriage.
tikka	small pieces of meat.
tonga	horse drawn carriage.
topi	the formal traditional Nepali hat.
trek	Africaans word meaning 'a long migration by ox-cart'.
trekken	Middle dutch meaning 'to travel'.
trisul	trident weapon of Shiva.
tsampa, tsumpa	roasted barley flour, a staple food in Tibet.
tump line	the strap porters use for carrying loads on their forehead

V

Vishnu	the preserver, has many incarnations in Nepal.

Y

yak	main beast of burden and form of cattle in the high country above 3000 m.
yatra	pilgrimage.
yatris	pilgrims.
yeti	the mythical anthropoid of the high Himalaya, known in the west as the abominable snowman.
yoga	exercises to produce mental concentration.
yoni	a hole in a stone, a symbol of feminity in Hindu temples.

Z

zopkiok, zopiko	a hybrid bull, the cross between a yak and a cow.
zum, zhum	a hybrid cow , the cross between a yak and a cow.

SUGGESTED READING LIST

General

Eu, G. *South Asia*. Insight Guide. APA Productions (HK), Hong Kong, 1988.

Gerner, M., and Ahluwalia, Major W. P. S. *Himalaya — A Practical Guide*. Himalayan Books, New Delhi, India, 1985.

Nicolson, N. *The Himalayas*. Time-Life Books B. V., Amsterdam, Holland, 1981.

Rowell, G. *Many People Come Looking, Looking*. George Allen & Unwin, London, UK, 1980.

The Royal Geographical Society. *The Mountains of Central Asia*. Macmillan, London, UK, 1987.

Trekking

Cleare, J. *Trekking, Great Walks of the World*. Unwin Hyman Ltd, London, UK, 1988.

Iozawa, T. *Trekking in the Himalayas*. Springfield Books Limited, West Yorkshire, UK, 1984.

Kohli, M. S. *The Himalayas, Playground of the Gods*. Vikas Publishing House Pvt Limited, New Delhi, India, 1983.

Swift, H. *The Trekker's Guide to the Himalaya and Karakoram*. Sierra Club Books, San Francisco, USA, 1982.

Climbing

Barry, J. and Mear, R. *Climbing School*. Simon & Schuster, Sydney, Australia, 1988.

Baume, L. C. *Sivalaya*. The Mountaineers, Seattle, Washington, USA, 1978.

Boardman, P. *Sacred Summits*. Hodder & Stoughton, London, UK, 1982.

Boardman, P. *The Shining Mountain*. Arrow Books, London, UK, 1980.

Child, G. *Thin Air*. Patrick Stephens , London, UK, 1988.

Cleare, J. *The World Guide to Mountains and Mountaineering*. Mayflower Books, New York, USA, 1979.

Faux, R. *Everest, Goddess of the Wind*. The Jacaranda Press, Sydney, Australia, 1978.

Hall, L. *White Limbo*. Weldons Pty Limited, Sydney, Australia, 1985.

Herzog, M. *Annapurna*. Reprint Society Limited, London, UK, 1954.

Hillary, E. *Nothing Venture, Nothing Win*. Hodder & Stoughton, London, UK, 1975.

Rowell, G. *In the Throne Room of the Mountain Gods*. Sierra Club Books, San Francisco, USA, 1977.

Medical

Bezruchka, S. *The Pocket Doctor*. The Mountaineers, Seattle, Washington, USA, 1988.

Dawood, R. *Travellers' Health*. Oxford University Press, Oxford, UK, 1986.

Grimwade, J. *Travel Well*. APC, Sydney, Australia, 1988.

Hackett, P. H. *Mountain Sickness*. The American Alpine Club, Inc., New York, USA, 1987.

Mitchell, D. *Mountaineers First Aid and Accident Response*, The Mountaineers, Seattle, Washington, USA, 1978.

Turner Dr, A. C. *The Traveller's Health Guide*. Roger Lascelles, Middlesex, UK, 1985.

Wilkerson, J.A. *Medicine for Mountaineering*. 2nd ed, The Mountaineers, Seattle, Washington, USA, 1978.

History

Allen, C. *A Mountain in Tibet*. Futura Publications, London, UK, 1986.

Allen, C. *Plain Tales From the Raj*. Futura Publications, London, UK, 1987.

Braham, T. *Himalayan Odyssey*. George Allen & Unwin, London, UK, 1974.

Cameron, I. *Mountains of the Gods*. Century Hutchinson , London, UK, 1984.

Hunt, J. *The Ascent of Everest*. Hodder & Stoughton, London, UK, 1953.

Keay, J. *When Men and Mountains Meet*. Century Hutchinson, London, UK, 1983.

Mason, K. *Abode of the Snow*. Diadem Books, London, UK, 1987.

Newby, E. *A Short Walk in the Hindu Kush*. Secker & Warburg, London, UK, 1958.

Terray, L. *Conquistadors of the Useless*. Victor Gollancz, London, UK, 1963.

Natural History

Asrael, S. and Sinclair, T. *Indian Wildlife — Sri Lanka and Nepal*. Insight Guide. APA Productions (HK) Limited, Hong Kong, 1987.

Cronin Jr, E. W. *The Arun*. Houghton Mifflin, Boston, USA, 1979.

Fleming, R. L. and Bangdel, L. S. *Birds of Nepal*. Vakil & Sons, Bombay, India, 1979.

Schaller, G. B. *Stones of Silence: Journeys in the Himalaya*. André Deutsch Limited, London, UK, 1980.

Schaller, G. B. *Mountain Monarchs: Wild Sheep & Goats of the Himalaya*. University of Chicago Press, Chicago, USA, 1977.

Woodcock, M. *Collins Handguide to the Birds of the Indian Sub-Continent*. William Collins Sons & Co Ltd, London, UK, 1987.

Photography

Calder, J. and Garret, J. *The Travelling Photographers Handbook*. Pan Books Ltd, London, UK, 1985.

Milner, D. *The Photoguide to Mountains*. Focal Press Limited, London, UK, 1977.

Bhutan

Berry, S. K. *The Thunder Dragon Kingdom — A Mountaineering Expedition to Bhutan*. The Crowood Press, UK, 1988.

Gibbons, B. and Ashford, B. *The Himalayan Kingdoms*. The Camelot Press Ltd, Southampton, UK, 1983.

India

Chabloz, Ph. and Cremieu, N. *Hiking In Zanskar & Ladakh*. Artou Guide, Editions Olizane, Geneva, Switzerland, 1985.

Dewan, P. *Hindi/Urdu Phrasebook*. Lonely Planet, South Yarra, Victoria, Australia, 1988.

Genoud, C. *Ladakh Zanskar*, Artou Guide, Editions Olizane, Geneva, Switzerland, 1984.

Israel, S. and Grewal, B. *India — Insight Guide*, APA Productions (HK), Hong Kong, 1987.

Meyer, P. and Rausch, B. *India, Nepal & Sri Lanka, The Traveller's Guide*. Springfield Books Limited, West Yorkshire, UK, 1987.

Naipaul, V. S. *An Area of Darkness*. Penguin Books, London, UK, 1987.

Schettler, M. and R. *Kashmir, Ladakh & Zanskar*. Lonely Planet, Melbourne, Australia, 1985.

Weare, G. *Trekking in the Indian Himalaya*. Lonely Planet, Melbourne, Australia, 1986.

Pakistan

Amin, M., Willetts, D., and Hancock, G. *Journey through Pakistan*. Camerapix Publishers International, Nairobi, Kenya, 1983.

Keay, J. *The Gilgit Game*. Archon Books, Hamden, UK, 1979.

Santiago, J. R. *Pakistan*. Lonely Planet, Melbourne, Australia, 1984.

Nepal

Anderson, J. G. *Nepal*. Insight Guide. APA Productions (HK), Hong Kong, 1987.

Armington, S. *Trekking in the Nepal Himalaya*. Lonely Planet Melbourne, Australia, 1985.

Bezruchka, S. *A Guide to Trekking in Nepal*. Cordee, Leicester, UK, 1985.

Goodman, J. *Kathmandu*. Time Books International, New Delhi, India, 1988.

Hayes, J. L. *Trekking North of Pokhara*. Roger Lascelles, Middlesex, UK, 1987.

Jefferies, M. *The Story of Mount Everest National Park*. Cobb/Horwood Publications, Auckland, New Zealand, 1985.

Martin, S. *Kathmandu & the Everest Trek*. Roger Lascelles, Middlesex, UK, 1987.

Matthiessen, P. *The Snow Leopard*. Pan Books, London, UK, 1980.

Meinhold, M. and Raj, P. A. *Nepal Phrasebook*. Lonely Planet, Melbourne, Australia, 1984.

Nakano, T. *Trekking in Nepal*. Allied Publishers Private Limited, New Delhi, India, 1985.

Tibet

Booz, E. B. *A Guide to Tibet*. William Collins Sons & Co. Limited, London, UK, 1986.

Buckley, M. and Strauss, R. *Tibet — a Travel Survival Kit*. Lonely Planet, Melbourne, Australia, 1986.

Goldstein, M. C. *Tibet Phrasebook*. Lonely Planet, Melbourne, Australia, 1987.

Rowell, G. *Mountains of the Middle Kingdom*. Sierra Club Books, San Francisco, USA, 1983.

Wilby, S. *Tibet: A Woman's Lone Trek Across a Mysterious Land*. Macmillan, Melbourne, Australia, 1988.

Maps

Research Scheme Nepal Himalaya (also known as Erwin Schneider maps) by Kartographische Anstalt Freytag-Berndt und Artaria. The 1: 50,000 series covers parts of Nepal.

U.S. Army Map Service, 1 : 250,000 series U502 covers the entire Himalaya (completed prior to 1960 so little up-to-date road information). Available from Library of Congress, Geography and Map Division, Washington D.C. 20540 USA.

Himalaya Trekking Folio, by Manmohan Singh Bawa, Air-India, Air-India Bldg., Nariman Pt, Bombay, India.

India 1 North. 1 : 1,500,000, APA Maps, APA Press, Singapore.

Indian Subcontinent (India, Pakistan, Bangladesh, Sri Lanka). 1 : 1,000,000, Bartholomew World Travel Map, John Bartholomew & Son Ltd., Edinburgh, Scotland.

Nepal. 1 : 500,000, APA Maps, APA Press, Singapore.

Pakistan. 1 : 1,500,000, APA Maps, APA Press, Singapore.

South-Central Tibet – Kathmandu – Lhasa Route Map. 1 : 1,000,000, Stanfords International Maps, London, 1987.

PHOTO CREDITS

All images by the author except for the following:

Bob Ashford, pages 196,198, 200.
Chris Curry/Hedgehog House N. Z. Polar & Mountain Picture Library, page 33.
Noreen Giles, pages 204, 205, 206–7.
Lincoln Hall, pages 47, 162, 183, 202, 208, 209, 210, 213.
Scott Russell/Hedgehog House N. Z. Polar & Mountain Picture Library pages 32, 78.
Doug Scott Collection pages 36, 37.
James Van Gelder, pages 97, 164.
David Wagland, pages 112, 125, 133, 211.
Garry Weare, page 197.

ACKNOWLEDGMENTS

Many thanks to the editorial team at Simon & Schuster Australia, especially publisher, Kirsty Melville; managing editor, Julia Cain; editor, Gillian Gillett; editorial assistant, Megan Johnston and Janine Duelle for secretarial assistance. The book's visual appeal is the work of designer, Maree Cunnington and Alistair Barnard, who designed and drafted the maps and illustrations.

I would especially like to thank the essay contributors: Mick Chapman of Peregrine Expeditions; Garry Weare and Christine Gee of World Expeditions; Bob Ashford of The Adventure Club; Warwick Deacock, of Ausventure, Sorrel Wilby; Greg Child; Lincoln Hall; and Doug Scott, and for his Foreword, Tim Macartney-Snape of Wilderness Expeditions.

For their assistance and advice in the field and for helpful discussion about the manuscript, my thanks also go to: Nick Deacock; Warwick Deacock; the Badyari Family, Wangchuck Shamshu; Shanker Dahl, The Indian Government Tourist Office, Meraj Din, Garry Weare and Christine Gee, Libby Nugent, Dr James Van Gelder, Dave Wagland, Dr. Mary Hu, Mary Thompson and Terry Ryan.

For the use of photographs of places I am yet to visit and historical photos, I am indebted to: Bob Ashford, Lincoln Hall, Chris Curry, James Van Gelder, Noreen Giles, Colin Monteath, Doug Scott, Garry Weare, and Dave Wagland.

Photographic assistance was also received from: Rudolph Gunz; Hugo the Foto Surgeon; Kodak (Australasia); Maxwell Optical Industries (Nikon); L & P Photographic Supplies; Vision Graphics Processing and Wildlight Photo Agency.

PERMISSIONS

The following individuals and associations gave their permission for reproduction of copyright material:

Sierra Club Books: *The Trekker's Guide to the Himalaya and Karakoram* by Hugh Swift (p.12, and *The Throne Room of the Mountain Gods* by Galen Rowell (p. 96); Chatto & Windus: *The Snow Leopard* by Peter Matthiessen (p. 15); Lonely Planet Publications: *Trekking in the Indian Himalaya* by Garry Weare (p. 16); Century Hutchinson Limited: *When Men and Mountains Meet* by John Keay (pp. 17, 111); *India in Luxury* by Louise Nicholson (p. 158), and *The Shining Mountain* by Peter Boardman (p. 161), Martin Secker & Warburg Limited: *A Short Walk in the Hindu Kush* by Eric Newby (p. 22); Col. Jimmy Roberts: *How It all Began* (p. 26); Jonathan Cape Ltd: *Annapurna* by Maurice Herzog (p. 32); Unwin Hyman Limited: *Himalayan Odyssey* by Trevor Braham (p. 39); Allied Publishers Pvt Ltd: *Tiger for Breakfast* by Michael Peissel (p. 43); Diadem Books: *Upon that Mountain* by Eric Shipton (p. 66), and *Blank on the Map* by Eric Shipton (p. 118); The American Alpine Club Inc: *Mountain Sickness* by Peter Hackett (p. 67); from *The Arun* by Edward W. Cronin Jr, copyright © 1979 by Edward W. Cronin, Jr. Reprinted by permission of Houghton Mifflin Company. (pp. 86, 99); Thames & Hudson: *Monsoon* by Steve McCurry © Thames & Hudson (p. 93); Time Life Books Ltd: *The World's Wild Places, The Himalayas* by Nigel Nicolson © Time Life Books Inc, 1975 (p. 95); Granada Publishing Limited: *Seven Years in Tibet* by Heinrich Harrer (p. 103); Sphere Books Ltd Abacus: *From Heaven Lake* by Vikram Seth (p. 108); Hodder & Stoughton Ltd: *Sacred Summits* by Peter Boardman (pp. 116, 166); Andre Deutsch Ltd: *An Area of Darkness* by V.S. Naipaul (pp. 136, 140); The New South Wales University Press, PO Box 1, Kensington, NSW Australia 2033: *Never Truly Lost* by Paddy Pallin (p. 186); Doug Scott: *A Summary of Climbing and the Anglo-Indian Ascent of Jitchu Drake* (p. 194).

While every care has been taken to trace and acknowledge copyright, the publishers tender their apologies for any accidental infringement. They would be pleased to hear from anyone who has not been duly acknowledged.

Index

223